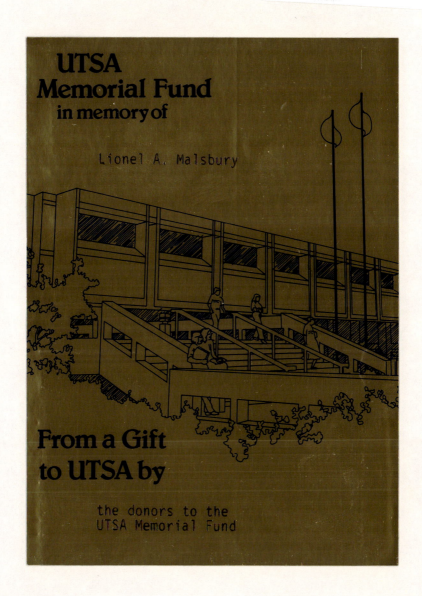

UTSA
Memorial Fund
in memory of

Lionel A. Malsbury

From a Gift
to UTSA by

the donors to the
UTSA Memorial Fund

Inside the US Treasury Market

Peter Wann *PaineWebber, London*

Inside the
US Treasury Market

Q

QUORUM BOOKS
New York · Westport, Connecticut

Published in the United States and Canada by
Quorum Books, Westport, Connecticut

English language edition, except the United States and Canada,
published by Woodhead-Faulkner (Publishers) Ltd.

First published 1989

Library of Congress Cataloging in Publication Data
Wann, Peter
  Inside the U.S. Treasury market/Peter Wann.
      p.   cm.
  Includes index.
  ISBN o089930-492-3 (lib. bdg. : alk. paper)
  1. Government securities—United States—Mathematical models.
2. Money market funds—United States—Mathematical models.
3. Investments—United States—Mathematical models.   4. United
States.   Dept. of the Treasury.   I. Title.
HG4936.W36   1989
332.63'232—dc19   89-3632
                                                                        CIP

Library of Congress Catalog Card Number:
ISBN: 0-89930-492-3
Printed in Great Britain

Contents

Preface

This book is designed as an introduction to the workings of the US Treasury market and the mathematical and investment approaches underlying the market's operations. Many chapters (e.g. on futures, options and investment techniques) are intended simply to illustrate the relevance of these concepts to the US Treasury market and are far from comprehensive. Detailed enlightenment must be sought in specialist works.

My employers, PaineWebber International, have been generous with encouragement. However, all views expressed are my own and not necessarily those of PaineWebber.

The publishers have exuded enthusiasm throughout and, with inveterate optimism, submitted a draft contract reserving the movie rights!

Peter Wann

January 1989

Acknowledgements

Thanks are due to colleagues at PaineWebber, clients, other friends and not a few competitors. My debt to Patrick Phillips of BZW will be clear to any reader of his book *Inside the gilt-edged market* (Woodhead-Faulkner, 1987). He has kindly allowed me to adapt his mathematical proofs and many other valuable thoughts for which I am most grateful. Ken Cholerton of Lombard Odier provided many thoughts on investment theory and strategy and allowed me to draw on his forthcoming *Lectures on risk management and bond investment*. Francis Glenister of Salomon Brothers International gave invaluable advice on the theory of duration and convexity and other esoterica. Others who provided helpful comments include: Scott Dorf of Salomons (market practice), Tom Rostron of Whittingdale (investment strategy) and many public servants in the US, particularly in the Congressional Budget Office, the Treasury and the Federal Reserve. Many have been generous in allowing reproduction or adaptation of copyright material. Particular thanks are due to the Bank Credit Analyst (3463 Peel Street, Montreal, Canada), Ibbotson Associates and Salomon Brothers.

Many PaineWebber London colleagues have helped, including: Muhammad Elhag (futures and options), Roy Robinson (settlements), and Sue Robinson (library and research assistance). Particular thanks are due to my accomplices in the Economics Department: William Dinning for general advice and particular expertise on fiscal policy; Said Desaque for detailed economic and bond market research; Sumedha Edirisuriya for extensive mathematical work and computer programming; Raana Zia for secretarial and research assistance; Nicola Stevens, William Chalmers and Thomas Chetwood for proof-reading and graphical assistance. Gerry Zuchowski of PaineWebber, New York provided valuable insights into monetary policy.

Also a word of appreciation to Ronald Reagan, without whom the US Government bond market might be only half its present size.

Part One

The market and how it operates

1   History and development

Origin

The US Treasury market originated in 1789 when the Federal Government assumed the war debts (totalling $77 m.) incurred by the original 13 states during the War of Independence. Alexander Hamilton, the first US Treasury Secretary, argued that 'A national debt, if it be not excessive, will be a national blessing' because the debt holders would have a vested interest in ensuring the permanence of the Federal union.

Early nineteenth century

The initial debt of $77 m. probably represented about 100% of GNP. However, the American economy grew rapidly and the debt fell steadily as a proportion of GNP, until the surge during the Civil War of 1861–5.

Late nineteenth century

The principles of public finance were very simple. Governments raised money from customs duties and spent it on defence. The US as a protectionist country with light defence commitments normally had a budget surplus and the national debt declined rapidly. By contrast, the UK (a free-trade country with worldwide defence commitments) saw its debt erode only slowly (see Fig. 1.1).

The twentieth century

The debt rose sharply in both world wars but, until 1975, normally fell (as a percentage of GNP) during peacetime.

Although peacetime budget deficits became normal after 1960, the debt-to-GNP ratio initially continued to decline because the debt was eroded by rising inflation.

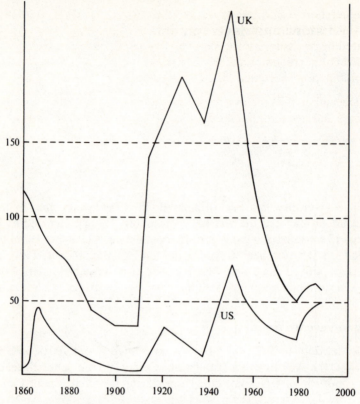

Fig. 1.1 National debt as percentage of GNP.

Average maturity of Treasury securities

World War II issues were mainly long-term. However, after 1945 the average maturity declined rapidly for the following reasons:

1. Long-term investors were deterred because until 1951 Treasury bond interest rates were held artificially low by the peg (see page 6).
2. The Treasury deliberately left long maturities free for business financing, since business overdependence on short-term financing could increase business failures in economic downturns.
3. After about 1958 market yields rose above 4·25% (the statutory maximum coupon rate for long Treasury bonds). New issues were then limited to Treasury notes which then had a maximum maturity of five years.
4. The Kennedy 'twist' (1960–3) tried to combine lower long-term interest rates to stimulate industrial investment in America with

higher short-term interest rates to attract foreign money into the dollar (which was starting to show signs of weakness). This 'twist' necessitated heavy issues of Treasury bills (to push short yields up) partly offset by net redemptions of long bonds to hold long yields down. This combination shortened the average maturity of Treasury debt.

By December 1975 the average maturity of the debt had fallen to only two years and five months (see Fig. 1.2).

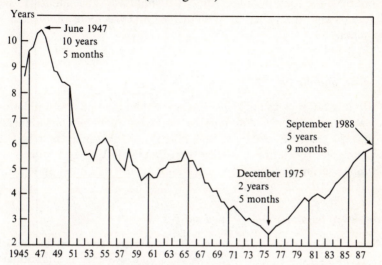

Fig. 1.2 Average length of the marketable debt, privately held. Source: *US Treasury Bulletin*.

The low average maturity alarmed:

(a) The Central Bank of the US (the 'Fed'), which feared loss of control of monetary policy, since a huge volume of debt would on maturity be converted into cash unless immediately refinanced, and
(b) the Treasury, whose plans to sell additional debt (to finance rising budget deficits) were threatened by market congestion from other issues to refinance old debt.

However, after 1975 average maturity rose again, assisted by:

(a) legislative relaxations on the coupon ceiling (see below), and
(b) a change in Treasury financing policy. When monster budget deficits became normal after 1980, the Treasury had no choice but to ease bond sales by spreading new issues over all possible maturities. The long maturity area could no longer be left free for corporate financing.

Legislative relaxations on coupon ceiling

Congress raised the maximum maturity for Treasury notes from five years to seven in 1967 and to ten in 1976. Since notes (unlike bonds) were not subject to the statutory 4·25% interest rate ceiling, the Treasury could then sell a higher proportion of longer maturities.

In 1971 Congress allowed the Treasury to issue $10 bn of long bonds exempt from the coupon ceiling (the $10 bn limit was subsequently raised at intervals until it reached $270 bn in 1987 and was finally abolished in November 1988).

Presidents and the Fed

An administration is usually less concerned than the Fed about inflation risks, and more concerned about recession risks. Only two presidents in the past 50 years (Eisenhower and Ford) have genuinely upheld Fed independence. By contrast, at least two (Truman in 1951 and Johnson in 1968) have seriously considered legislating to curb Fed independence.

Examples of administration v. Fed clashes

1948–51: President Truman wanted the Fed to peg the interest rate on long Treasury bonds below 2·375%. This peg was clearly inflationary since it could only be maintained by the Fed buying up huge quantities of Treasury securities and inflating the money supply. The peg was finally abandoned in 1951 after two Fed Chairmen (Eccles and McCabe) had been sacked for opposing it.

1960–71: The Council of Economic Advisors sent 46 memos to presidents advising that Fed policy was too tight. In the same period only 41 memos advised that Fed policy was correct and not one said Fed policy was too loose, although inflation accelerated from 1% to 4% during the period! (Kettl, *Leadership at the Fed,* Yale University Press, 1986.)

1965: President Johnson refused to raise taxes to finance the Vietnam war and bitterly denounced the Fed for (correctly) raising the discount rate in December 1965 to counter the resultant inflationary pressures.

1972: President Nixon incessantly pressured the Fed for easier money in election year: 'We'll take inflation if necessary but we can't take unemployment.' All independent commentators (with the advantage of hindsight) now agree that Fed policy in 1972, far from being too tight, was already violently inflationary.

1981–8: Reaganites persistently complained that the Fed was sabotaging

Reagan's 'supply-side revolution' by keeping money too tight so that economic growth was unnecessarily slow.

Volckernomics

Paul Volcker was appointed Fed Chairman by President Carter in August 1979. Carter, initially an easy-money enthusiast, had finally become alarmed by an inflationary explosion in 1978–9 and by Fed Chairman Miller's apparent inability to stop it. This was possibly the only time in history when an administration genuinely pressurised the Fed for tighter money.

The Volcker Fed switched from controlling the Fed funds interest rate, to making its immediate policy target the achievement of a specified growth rate in the money supply M-1 (see Glossary for definitions of money-supply measures). The Fed then supplied *only* the limited addition to bank reserves consistent with this M-1 target and let interest rates find their own level.

Prime rate leaped from 10% to 20% in four months, while long Treasury bond yields rose from 10% to 13%. This interrupted the inflationary acceleration, but at the cost of a four-month recession (short but deep) in spring 1980.

Reaganomics

Reagan's initial budgetary policy included tax cuts and a defence build-up, supposedly offset by bigger cuts in non-defence spending. The aim was a balanced budget by 1983. However, the tax cuts were *not* conditional on spending cuts, and budget deficits became astronomic. Revenue growth slumped to only 1.5% p.a. real in 1980–5. At the same time federal government spending continued to grow at 4% p.a. real in 1980–5, exactly the same rate as in 1954–80.

In consequence government debt in the balanced-budget target year of 1983 actually jumped over 20%, a peacetime record. Reagan then abandoned all budget discipline rather than curtail either defence build-up or tax cuts, thus reorganising the Treasury bond market on Ponzi principles.

Fig. 1.3 shows the Federal budget deficit as a percentage of GNP for the years 1960–87.

'Supply-side' fallacies

Many Reaganites initially claimed that bit tax cuts ('supply-side economics') would actually reduce the budget deficit by stimulating the

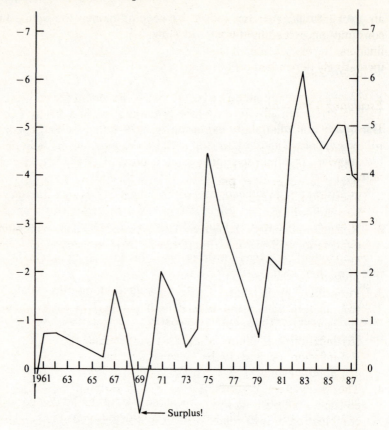

Fig. 1.3 Federal budget deficit as percentage of GNP (NIA basis – calendar years s.a.).

economy. George Bush once called this 'Voodoo economics'. Senator Hollings said it was the sort of thing that gave voodoo a bad name.

Of course the economy can be expanded via supply incentives as well as (or better than) by stimulating extra demand. However, Reaganomic budget deficits actually did much to sabotage the supply side. Massive government borrowing in financial markets crowded out private-sector borrowers, and made it harder to finance housing or business investment (unless also subsidised by deficit-increasing tax incentives).

Budget deficits and trade deficits

Since domestic savings were inadequate to finance the budget deficits the government had to borrow foreign savings. In physical terms, this meant an ever-increasing trade deficit (domestic savings shortfall means consumption exceeding domestic production, i.e. a rise in imports). In financial terms, it meant that the Treasury bond market became increasingly dependent on foreign (especially Japanese) buying.

Escalating interest rates

The causes of ultra-high interest rates in 1981 were as follows:

1. Rising inflationary expectations (major inflation peaks in 1974 and 1980). In fact the 1980 inflation peak was really lower than the 1974 peak; however the public had thought of 1974 as a one-off aberration, but regarded 1980 as confirmation that high inflation had become normal.
2. Reaganomic budget deficits had a disastrous impact on inflationary expectations. The only fiscal result of a conservative election landslide was a trebling of the budget deficit and administration pressure on the Fed to print the money to finance it.
3. Public perception lagged inflationary reality, both when:
   (a) inflation was rising before 1980 (so that investors accepted negative real interest rates for long periods from 1969–79); and
   (b) inflation was falling after 1981 (the public did not trust the inflation decline to be permanent, and so demanded high nominal yields).
4. The tax system deterred saving and subsidised borrowing. All consumer interest was tax deductible until 1988. Moreover, the combination of investment tax credit with accelerated depreciation after 1981 meant that corporations could earn historically high returns on new fixed investment and were prepared to pay correspondingly high interest rates to finance it.
5. Reaganomic budget deficits produced an oversupply of bonds.
6. The increased volatility in bond prices probably raised the interest-rate risk premium that investors demanded to compensate for the additional risk in bond buying.

Tension between Reagan and Volcker

Presidential candidate Reagan had blamed the Fed both for inflationary escalation before 1980 and for inducing the 1980 recession. Once in office Reaganites initially talked of tight money as if it was a form of painless black magic which could cut inflationary expectations by psychological impact alone without any need for economic slowdown and higher unemployment.

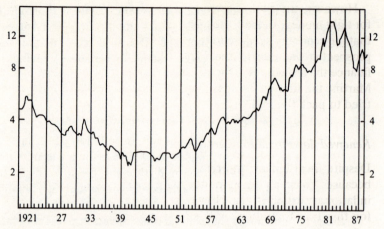

Fig. 1.4 US long Treasury bond yield, 1918–88.
Source: *Pring Market Review*.

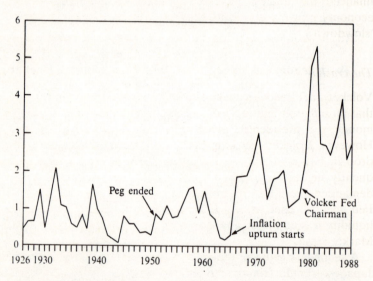

Fig. 1.5 Price volatility of long Treasury bonds. The figure shows
average magnitude (regardless of sign) of month end to month end
percentage price changes for each year. Data is based on Ibbotson
index. The monthly figure for 1987 looks surprisingly low because most
of the volatility occurred within a single month. The 20-year Treasury
bond jumped 11% in five trading days in mid-October but rose only 7%
from 30 September to 31 October (the measure of change incorporated
in the chart). See Appendix 12 for a volatility comparison based on daily
data.

However, the 1981–2 recession destroyed administration enthusiasm for tight money. Indeed, Reaganites now became obsessed with the idea that the economy's failure to grow in line with their optimistic supply-side prospectus was due to the Fed's failure to print sufficient money to finance the growth. Fed Vice-Chairman Schultz was replaced by Preston Martin, the first of the 'easy-money' men with whom Reaganites now tried to pack the Fed.

Renewed downtrend in interest rates

Despite fiscal lunacy, interest rates generally trended down after 1981 because Volcker's tight money policies gradually reduced long-term inflationary expectations. However, Reaganites gave Volcker little credit for this transformation. Volcker was reappointed in 1983 only after intense Wall Street lobbying, and was subjected to perpetual Treasury nagging for easier money (although the Volcker Fed in 1982–7 actually financed the longest peacetime expansion since 1961–9, with the economy growing above its long-term trend even during the 1984–6 'slowdown').

The crash of 1987

Volcker was effectively sacked in 1987 because the administration feared that an inflation-fighting Volcker might give them a third dose of tight money in a presidential election year (as he had in 1980 and 1984). However, Volcker's sacking proved counterproductive. It produced a drop in Fed credibility, a rise in inflationary expectations and consequently higher long-term interest rates. Financial markets effectively demanded overkill in interest rates before they would believe that the Fed was still committed to lower inflation. The resultant squeeze on liquidity was an important short-term cause of the October 1987 Stock Market crash.

A secondary cause of the crash was administration insistence that the Japanese should stimulate their own economy (i.e. cut the Japanese savings rate) to boost US export prospects. The Japanese duly obliged, thus cutting the flow of foreign savings into the US on which the US Treasury bond market had become dependent and forcing up American interest rates.

The budget of 1988

The crash produced an initial political consensus for 'doing something'

about the budget deficit. However, the eventual 'deficit-cutting compromise' was quite phoney. Indeed scheduled Gramm–Rudman spending
cuts of $22 bn were actually halved to $11 bn, while the bond market was
supposedly 'compensated' by the promise of $10 bn asset sales and $9 bn
corporate tax increases (neither of which do anything to reduce
borrowing pressure on financial markets).

Outlook

After the compromise, the deficit actually *rose* from $150 bn in 1987 to
$155 bn in 1988, while Reagan's farewell budget message forecast a deficit
exceeding $160 bn in 1989.

   The Treasury bond market is unlikely to suffer from any supply
shortage for years to come.

2 Principal characteristics of the US Treasury market

Size

The US national debt in early 1989 totalled $2,700 bn, including $1,400 bn of marketable notes and bonds, making it the largest government debt market in the world (see Tables 2.1–2.5).

Table 2.1. US Treasury securities in issue ($bn), end-1988

Bills	410
Notes	1,080
Bonds	310
Non-marketable	860
Total	**2,660**

Table 2.2. Origin of US federal government debt ($bn)

1789–1980	900[a]
1981–1988	1,760[b]
Total	**2,660[c]**

a Combined debt legacy of all 39 US presidents from George Washington to Jimmy Carter inclusive.
b Ronald Reagan solo.
c Effective debt is 'only' 2,200 because end-1988 total of 2,700 (to which statutory debt limit applies) includes 500 owed by US government to itself, mainly as trustee for social security, medicare and other trust funds.

Table 2.3. Total public-sector debt as % GNP

	1975	1986 Q3
Japan	39	91
Canada	53	84
UK	63	58
US	39	54
Germany	25	41

Source: Bank of International Settlements FRB Flow of Funds.
NB UK the only major economy without significant deterioration over the decade.
See discussion in T. Congdon, *The Debt Threat* (Basil Blackwell, 1988).

Table 2.4. Principal government bond markets, end-1987

	Size ($US bn)[a]	Size as % GNP	Central govt and govt agency issues as % total bonds in issue
USA	1,350	30	55
Japan	1,250	44	66
Italy	400	48	57
UK	250	33	77
Germany	200	16	28
France	100	10	77
Canada	80	19	40

Source: Salomon Brothers.
a   Nominal value of outstanding marketable bonds converted at end-1987 exchange rates. Total national debts are larger because these figures exclude Treasury bills and non-marketable securities, as well as agency securities. Figures also exclude local government debt issues.

Table 2.5. Main types of marketable US Treasuries

Security	Initial maturity	Minimum unit ($)
Treasury Bills[a]	3, 6 or 12 months	10,000
Notes[b]	10 years or under	1,000 or 5,000[c]
Bonds	Over 10 years (usually 30)	1,000

a   Bills are sold on a discount basis.
b   Notes and bonds pay coupons half-yearly.
c $5,000 if initial maturity is 3 years or under.

Maturity structure

Average maturity has risen from two years five months in December 1975 to five years nine months in mid-1988 (see Table 2.6 and Fig. 2.1). The amount of outstanding securities with a maturity of under one year (including Treasury bills) has been virtually unchanged since 1985.

Table 2.6. Maturity structure of private holdings of marketable
Treasury securities (%)

	1977	1988
Under 1 year	50	33
1–10 years	45	51
Over 10 years	5	16
	100	100

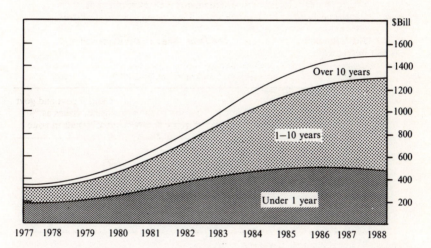

Fig. 2.1 Private holdings of Treasury marketable debt by maturity.

Fed book entry, new issues, investors

Treasury securities issued since July 1986 exist only as book entries on the
Fed computer. The Fed is also converting older securities to book entry as
fast as bondholders agree. Under 10% of all US Treasury securities are
now represented by physical certificates and this proportion is steadily
shrinking.

Banks, thrifts, investing institutions, foreigners and individuals may
open book-entry accounts at the Fed. Brokers and dealers must use a
commercial bank as custodian.

New issues are auctioned on a regular schedule.

Table 2.7 lists the principal private investors in marketable treasuries.

Principal dealers, trading volume, settlement

The Fed recognises 44 primary marketmakers. Trading volume is very high. It averaged \$36 bn daily (about 3% of all notes and bonds) in 1987 (see Table 2.8).

Regular settlement is made on the business day following trade day. Normally settlement is by transfer of computer entries at the Fed against transfer of federal funds (commercial banks' deposits at the Fed).

Table 2.7. Principal private investors in marketable Treasuries (%)

Banks and thrifts	37
Other US financial institutions	40
Households	5
Foreigners	18
Total	100

Table 2.8. Daily trading volume in Treasury coupon securities, 1987

Maturity	\$bn	Outstanding securities (%)
Up to 10 years	28	2.4
Over 10 years	8	4.7
Total	36	2.8

Coupon payments, yield convention

Coupons are paid twice a year. For example, Treasury 12% of 15 May 2005 actually pays a coupon of 6% on 15 May and another 6% on 15 November each year. Annual yields are conventionally quoted as twice the true yield for a half-year. A quoted Treasury yield of 10% p.a. (meaning 5% per half-year) is actually equivalent to a true annual yield of 10·25% (see page 111).

Management of the market and Fed open-market operations

The Treasury has the last word on the size and timing of new issues (which primarily depend upon the US budget deficit).

The New York Fed (under the overall guidance of the Federal Reserve's Open Market Committee) exercises day-to-day management. The Fed also frequently intervenes in the money markets to provide (or drain) liquidity, usually by dealing in Treasury securities (open-market operations). The Fed may buy or sell outright or conduct repos (a sale with simultaneous agreement to subsequently repurchase, see page 79).

Taxation

US residents pay tax on both coupons and capital gains at normal income tax rates. There is no withholding tax for either residents or (on bonds issued since July 1984) for non-residents who have filed a simple declaration of non-residency with their custodian.

Call protection

Some long bonds may be called for redemption at par within five years of final maturity. For example Treasury 14% of 2006–11 matures on 15 November 2011, but the Treasury may redeem at par (on giving four months' notice) at any time after 15 November 2006. The Treasury will probably exercise this option if market interest rates fall significantly below 14% during the call period, so that new borrowing becomes cheaper than paying 14% p.a. interest on the old bond. Many bonds and all notes are non-callable.

Stripped treasuries

All new issues with an original maturity of ten years or longer may be officially 'stripped', i.e. each coupon and the final capital redemption payment at maturity can be separately traded as independent zero coupon bonds on the Fed's book-entry system. About $60 bn of 'strips' are currently held on Fed book-entry.

Other Treasury securities have been stripped unofficially, allowing separate trading of receipts (issued by a bank or investment house) representing future coupons or capital repayment.

Debt limit

The statutory debt limit is $2,800 bn (frequently raised!). The statutory debt limit is a peculiarly American institution. Congressmen can spend 51 weeks of the year voting for spending increases and/or tax cuts. In the 52nd week they can vote against raising the debt limit in order to persuade their constituents that they are opposed to big budget deficits.

Of course, freezing the debt limit does not abolish the budget deficit. It simply makes it more difficult to finance. Inefficient juggling of government bills and a search for accounting gimmicks proceeds ever more frenetically as the theoretical deadline approaches. Meanwhile interest rates on Treasury securities carry a risk premium in case the debt limit is not raised in time and the US government goes into technical default.

3   US and UK Treasury markets compared

Market comparison

Size and volume

The US Treasury market's capitalisation is six times larger than the UK. Moreover, it trades more actively, so the volume of US cash trading is ten times larger and futures trading 13 times larger than in the UK.

Bond price volatility

In 1988, 20-year US Treasury bond prices moved more than 1% on 8% of trading days (UK comparison: on only 1% of trading days). In 1987 both markets moved more than 1% on 15% of trading days.

Similarities in long-term returns

Real returns on long Treasury bonds since 1926 have averaged +1·2% p.a. in the US and +0·3% p.a. in the UK (see Appendix 1).

Factors helping longer-term stability in the UK

Average maturity

Average maturity is 11 years in the UK and six years in the US.

Budget deficit

The US has gone from low deficits to embedded high deficits. By contrast the UK, a high-deficit country in the 1970s, has moved into Budget surplus, giving structural support (supply shortage) to the UK Treasury market.

Table 3.1. US and UK Treasury markets compared

	US	UK
Total debt		
Size	$2,200 bn (= 44% GNP)	£195 bn (= 50% GNP)
Average maturity	6 years	11 years
Debt limit	2,800 (frequently raised)	None
1988 budget	$160 bn deficit	£5 bn surplus
(before asset sales)	170 (= 4% GNP)	3 (= 1% GNP)
Trading volume (US : UK ratio)		
Capitalisation	6	
Cash trading	10	
Futures trading	13	
New issues		
Normal method	Auction (regular schedule)	Fixed-price sale (irregular schedule) and tap stock
Form	Computer-entry only for new issues	Physical certificates
Trading		
Primary marketmakers	44	22
Committed capital	N.A.	£600 m.
Daily volume (as % debt)		
Cash	3	2
Futures	2	1
Minimum unit	$1,000: 4 yrs and longer	£100 in practice
	$5,000: 2 and 3 yrs	1p in theory
Zero coupons	Stripped Treasuries tradeable on Fed computer-entry system	No
Index-linked	No	Available
Settlement		
Normal settlement	Transfer of computer	Town clearing cheque
(day after trade)	entries at Fed against	against physical delivery.
	settlement in Fed funds	Institutional settlement
	(commercial bank deposits	now being converted to
	at Fed)	book entry through Central Gilts Office
Official operations		
Central bank	Federal Reserve (nominally independent)	Bank of England (under direct government control)
Open-market operations	Outright buy and sell. Repos (sale with simultaneous agreement to subsequently repurchase)	Outright buy and sell. Also liquidity influenced via discount houses. No repos.
Withholding tax		
Residents	None	25%
Non-residents	Normally free on application	Normally free on application

National debt to GNP ratios

The ratios in the two countries are now similar *for the first time ever. Historically the UK always had a much higher ratio than the US.*

Summary tables and figures

Tables 3.1 to 3.6 give comparisons of various aspects of the US and UK treasury markets. Figure 3.1 contrasts US and UK inflation and bond yields differentials and Fig. 3.2 shows the budget deficits of the US and UK as a percentage of GNP.

Table 3.2. Comparisons of Treasury bond trading volume

Total trading in Treasury bonds (1987)

	US ($ m.)	UK (£ m.)
Cash	9,100	600
Futures: Chicago	7,200	—
LIFFE	160	350
Total bonds outstanding	1,300	140

Daily trading volume as percentage of outstanding securities (1987)

	Futures	Cash
US Bonds over 10 years	15.0	4.7
Other	0.2	2.4
US Total	2.2	2.8
UK Total	1.0	1.7

Daily trading volume

	1986		1987	
	Futures	Cash	Futures	Cash
US: Up to 10 years	2	23	2	28
Over 10 years	22	7	26	8
US: Total ($ bn)	24	30	28	36
UK: Total (£ bn)	0.5	1.8	1.4	2.3

Table 3.3. Volatility of security prices: percentage of trading days when prices moved more than 1%

	US bonds	UK bonds	US equities	UK equities
1987 H1	14	10	30	31
H2	14	20	48	48
1988 H1	10	2	34	28
H2	6	0	25	13

Bonds: US 9.375% of 2006 (see also Appendix 12)
          UK 11.75% of 2007
Equities: SP100 and FTSE 100

Table 3.4. Cumulative maturity distribution of marketable securities (%) mid-1988

Years	US	UK
Under 1	33	13
Under 5	69	31
Under 10	84	54

NB Only 16% of US debt has a maturity of over 10 years, compared with 46% in UK.

Table 3.5. Ownership of marketable Treasury securities (%), private holders, mid-1988

	US	UK
Commercial banks	14	8
Thrifts/building societies	3	6
Foreign	22	14
Mutual funds	8	1
Persons	33	21
Pension funds	12	22
Insurance companies	8	28
	100	100

Banks, foreigners and individuals more important in US. Insurance companies and pension funds more important in UK.

Table 3.6. Principal debt claims as % GNP, late-1988

Obligations of	US	UK
Central government	44	50
Local government	12	15
Non-financial corporations:		
Bonds	20	2
Bank borrowing	13	26
Other loans	7	2
Commercial paper	2	3
Persons:		
House mortgages	40	54
Consumer credit	15	16
	153	168

Notes
1. Relative unimportance of corporate bonds in UK.
2. High house mortgage borrowing in UK.
3. By early-1989 central govt debt as % GNP was almost equal as UK budget surplus enabled debt repayment, bringing UK ratio down to US level.
4. Corporate equities outstanding in mid-1988 equalled about 65% GNP in US and 90% in UK.

Sources: US FRB Flow of Funds.
        UK Financial Statistics June 1988, Table S6.
        PaineWebber estimates.

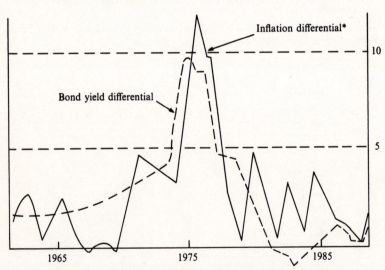

* Based on % change in consumer prices over previous 12 months.

Fig. 3.1 Inflation and bond yield comparison (UK rates minus US).

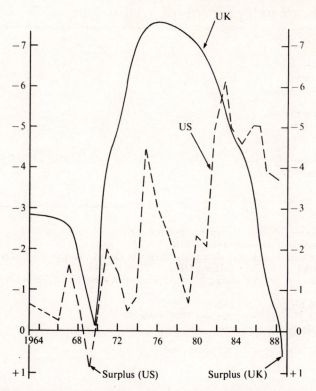

Fig. 3.2 Budget deficits as a percentage of GNP. (US: NIA Basis Calendar Years, UK: Public Sector Borrowing Requirement before asset sales.)

4   Basic determinants of Treasury bond interest rates

The principal factors determining the level of US Treasury bond interest rates are as follows:

1. The economic cycle.
2. Inflation.
3. Budget deficits.
4. Fed policy.
5. Foreign interest rates and the dollar exchange rate.

The economic cycle

Interest rates normally move closely with the economic cycle, rising in booms and falling in recessions (see Fig. 4.1).

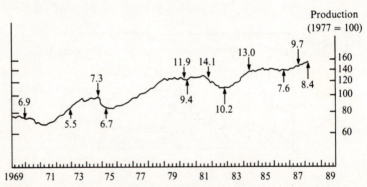

Fig. 4.1 Industrial production and long Treasury bond yield. Arrows show major turning points in interest rates.

As an economy moves into full boom, consumers become more confident of their ability to repay increased borrowings. At the same time corporations borrow to finance capacity expansion to meet booming demand. If this increase in private-sector borrowing demand is not offset by a drop in government borrowing demand, there will normally be upward pressure on interest rates.

The most intense surge in credit demand usually comes very late in the economic cycle when businesses borrow wholesale to rebuild escalating inventories. Inventory building is initially voluntary as corporations overorder in an attempt to meet booming demand. Later, when demand softens, businesses end up with large (involuntary) inventories which also have to be financed by borrowing in the interval before production cutbacks and inventory liquidation can be arranged.

Once demand weakens (either reacting to official policy, e.g. tax increases or tight money, or because consumers have got scared of overborrowing) a fall in interest rates will eventually follow. Consumer borrowing becomes more cautious. Businesses cut back capital investment plans and finally embark on massive inventory liquidation. At this stage, credit demand collapses and interest rates tumble.

Overall credit demand is normally weak in recession because this drop in private-sector borrowing (see Fig. 4.2) is usually much greater than the rise in government borrowing (caused when recession cuts tax revenues and increases the budget deficit).

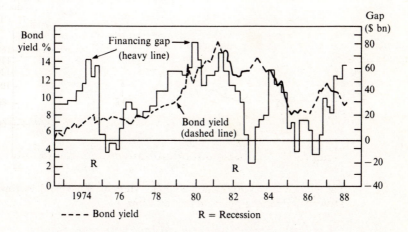

Fig. 4.2 Corporate financing gap and Treasury bond yields.
Note: Financing gap is often replaced by a temporary financing surplus in late recession or early economic recovery (e.g. 1975, 1982). If gap does not turn into a surplus, a bond bull market may prove temporary (e.g. spring 1980, early 1988). Source: Salomon Brothers.

Inflation

Bond buyers normally seek a real return, i.e. an after-tax yield higher than the *future* inflation rate. Accordingly, rising inflation demoralises the bond market. Rising inflationary expectations may be:

(a) cyclical and temporary, related to capacity strains and shortages emerging during an economic upswing (inflation tends to slightly lag the economic cycle);

(b) permanent, related to structural changes in the economy, or long-term shifts in political attitudes (e.g. during 1961–74 US politicians were generally reluctant to support firm anti-inflationary policies; by contrast in 1953–60 and 1979–86 American politicians were relatively amenable to anti-inflationary policies); or

(c) psychological, often related to budget deficit escalation.

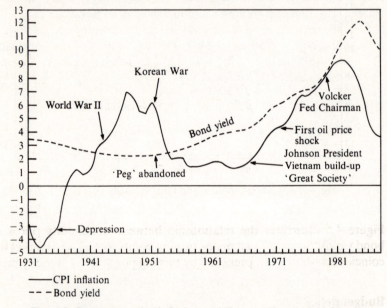

Fig. 4.3 Consumer price inflation and Treasury bond yield (six-year moving averages).

Figure 4.3 illustrates the longer-term link between consumer price inflation and bond yields. This is clearest since 1960. Previously bond yields had been relatively stable, reflecting:

(a) widespread belief that long-term inflation would return to near zero (the historically normal peacetime rate before 1939) and that both the negative inflation of the Great Depression and the high inflation of World War II were temporary aberrations; and

(b) government intervention to hold down long bond yields (via the peg) from 1941 to 1951.

Figure 4.4 illustrates the recent relationship between wages (a more stable measure of inflation pressure than prices) and bond yields. There is a clear cyclical link (e.g. bond yield cyclical peaks in 1970 and 1974, cyclical troughs in 1972, 1976, 1982 and 1986) and also a strong long-term relationship (wages and bond yields were both in long-term uptrend in 1965–81 and in downtrend since 1981).

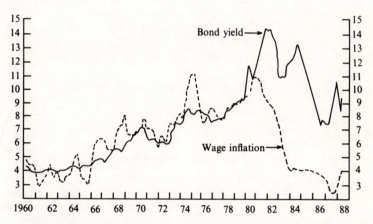

Fig. 4.4 US wage inflation and long Treasury bond yield.

Figure 4.5 illustrates the relationship between commodity prices and bond yields. Since 1977 all major turning points in the bond market have coincided with or been preceded by turning points in commodity prices.

Budget deficits

High budget deficits can normally be financed without strain during a recession when personal saving is high and corporate borrowing is low. High budget deficits at other times tend to push up interest rates:

(a) directly by high government borrowing,
(b) secondarily by overstimulating the economy, or
(c) by raising fears that the deficits will eventually be financed by inflationary money printing.

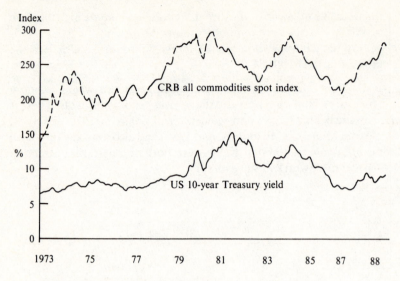

Fig. 4.5 Commodity prices and bond yields: 1973–88.

Fed policy

An anti-inflationary Fed will assist a long-term downtrend in interest rates, although tight money often means *temporarily* higher short-term interest rates. Conversely, Fed attempts to hold short-term interest rates too low can demoralise the long bond market by raising inflationary expectations.

Foreign interest rates and the dollar exchange rate

The globalisation of world financial markets (due to wholesale dismantling of exchange controls and broader horizons of fund managers) means that investments are now judged in an international context.

US institutions are starting to consider the merits of foreign securities as an alternative to US investments for a small but increasing proportion of their funds. Meanwhile, US private-sector saving is inadequate to finance Reaganomic budget deficits, so the US bond market has become increasingly dependent on foreign purchasers. Consequently the scope for US interest rate falls is limited if:

(a)   interest rate differentials with foreign bond markets are unfavourable (see Fig. 4.6), or

(b)   the dollar exchange rate is suspect.

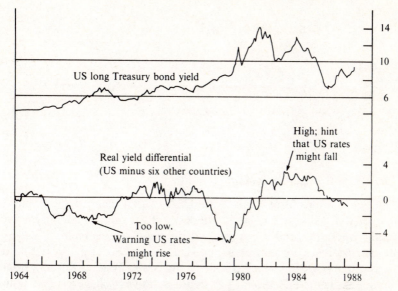

Fig. 4.6 International real yield differential (US real yield minus weighted average for Germany, France, the UK, Italy, Canada and Japan). Real yield = GRY minus CPI inflation rate. Chart adapted by courtesy of Bank Credit Analyst.

US real rates fell 2% below rest-of-the-world real rates in 1968–70 and 1978–80, a warning that US rates might have to rise. US real rates were 2% higher than rest-of-the-world real rates in 1982–85, an indication of potential scope for US rates to fall.

5   Fed management of the market

The Federal Reserve System

The Fed is the Central Bank of the USA, with a role broadly similar to that of the Bank of England. There are 12 regional Federal Reserve Banks operating under the general direction of the Federal Reserve Board. Monetary policy is supervised by the Federal Open Market Committee (FOMC) which consists of the seven Federal Reserve Board members plus five Regional Fed representatives. The President nominates the members of the Federal Reserve Board but (in contrast to the UK system) cannot give it legally binding instructions.

The Fed's legal position

The Fed was established by law in 1913 under Article I of the US Constitution which empowers Congress 'to coin money and regulate the value thereof'. The Fed is legally independent of the administration, but not of the legislature. Congress *could* legislate to alter the Fed's composition or powers or curb its independence.

Practical limits to Fed independence

If Fed policy provokes extreme political discontent (as in the 1982 recession) the Fed must eventually bend to avoid the danger of an exasperated Congress legislating to curb Fed independence, or enforce an easing of policy. Moreover, in practice the Fed can resist a policy change consistently forced on them by a determined administration for not more than six months at the outside.

Nevertheless, even this limited time is useful because it enables the Fed to tighten policy *ahead of* developing inflation. By contrast, politicians normally accept the need for tightening only *after* an inflationary acceleration.

Thus Fed independence is meaningful and significant within narrow limits. It is no accident that the only major economies which have consistently maintained inflation rates lower than that of the US (Japan, Germany and Switzerland) all have independent central banks.

Membership of the Federal Reserve Board

There are seven members each appointed by the President (subject to formal confirmation by the Senate) for a 14-year term and irremovable within that term. The Chairman has a four-year term. Chairman Greenspan's current term expires in July 1991, i.e. 15 months before the 1992 presidential election.

The Federal Open Market Committee (FOMC)

The FOMC, which decides on monetary policy, has the following membership:

1. The seven members of the Federal Reserve Board.
2. The President of the Federal Reserve Bank of New York.
3. Four regional Federal Reserve Bank presidents (these seats rotate among the 11 regional Feds).

Regional Fed influences on the FOMC

The regional Fed presidents tend to be conservatively inclined (their appointment process gives considerable weight to the local business community) and will usually support a firm anti-inflationary monetary policy. However, they are subject to local pressures, e.g. the Chicago and St Louis Feds were foremost in demanding policy easing in the 1982 recession.

FOMC policy making

The FOMC meets about eight times a year to consider the state of the economy and financial market pressures and then issues a policy directive to its operating agent, the Federal Reserve Bank of New York.

Example of an FOMC policy directive (3 November 1987)

For the immediate future the committee seeks to maintain the degree of pressure on reserve positions sought in recent days. Somewhat lesser reserve restraint *would* or slightly greater reserve restraint *might,* be acceptable, depending on the strength of the business expansion, indications of inflationary pressures, and developments in the foreign exchange markets, as well as the behaviour of the monetary aggregates . . . The Chairman may call for committee consultations if . . . reserve conditions are likely to be associated with a fed funds rate persistently outside a range of 4 to 8 percent.

Notes

1. This was the first full FOMC meeting after 'Black Monday' (19 October 1987). Emergency policy easing had been agreed in a telephone conferene on 20 October.
2. The contrast between 'lesser restraint *would*' and 'greater restraint *might*' be appropriate implies a bias towards policy easing.
3. The desired degree of reserve pressure (target for bank borrowings at the discount window) had been $600 m. before Black Monday. It was reduced to $500 m. on 23 October, to $450 m. on 28 October and to $400 m. at this meeting on 3 November. The specific target figure is not disclosed in the minutes and is not published till the following year's spring issue of the New York Fed's *Quarterly Review*.
4. In practice the Fed funds target range appears to be much narrower (perhaps only 50 basis points) than the 400 basis point range stated. The narrower target is not disclosed in the minutes.
5. The minutes of each FOMC meeting are published shortly after the next meeting.

Open-market operations

The New York Fed intervenes in the money markets, pursuant to FOMC directives, either easing or tightening to influence the level of banks' borrowing at the Fed's discount window and the Fed funds interest rate. The main operating tools are Fed purchases (temporary or permanent) or sales of government securities on the open market (see Chapter 12).

6   Dealers and traders

Primary dealers

These are the principal dealers (currently numbering 46) who are rcognised by the Fed. Recognition depends on an applicant satisfying the Fed that it is adequately capitalised and can deal in sufficient size and volume (1% of the market's total turnover is a *minimum*) and provide regular continuous two-way quotations in all active securities.

The privileges of primary dealers include the following:

1. Access to the Fed's trading screen and ability to deal directly with the Fed.
2. Eligibility for inclusion in Fed repo dealing.
3. Ability to borrow bonds from the Fed to settle a trade temporarily frustrated by the failure of a counter-party to deliver. (The Fed will not lend bonds simply to cover a dealer's naked short position.)

Secondary dealers

Numerous other firms, probably accounting for well under 10% of total volume, are classified as secondary dealers. They include the following groups:

1. Firms primarily coping with small retail orders and thus not dependent on ability to obtain the extremely competitive prices in all issues demanded by major institutions.
2. Firms specialising in corporate bonds, who find a minor Treasury bond operation a useful aid to hedging their positions.

Inter-dealer brokers

There are eight firms that act as inter-dealer brokers, seven of whom will quote prices to and trade only with dealers (i.e. they do not trade with investing institutions or the public).

Sources of dealer profits

There are four sources of profits for dealers:

1. Spread on dealing with customers: the difference between dealer's bid and asked price.
2. Positioning: holding bonds which appear cheap against the yield curve while shorting bonds which appear expensive against the yield curve.
3. Betting on future moves in interest rates. It is probable that profits from this source have been greatly exaggerated.
4. Financing positions (see Table 6.1). With a normal positive yield curve, a long bond position yielding 9% can typically be financed at 7% by placing the bond on repo (page 289). The dealer therefore profits from a long position unless interest rates rise and his long bond price falls.

Table 6.1. Primary dealers' average daily positions ($bn)

	1986	1987
Total spot positions		
Treasury securities: under 5 years	26	7
over 5 years	−13	−13
Agency securities	33	32
Sub-total	46	26
Short-term paper		
(CDs, commercial paper, etc.)	23	19
Grand total	69	45
Financing of spot positions		
Repos	244	292
Reverse repos	−207	−273
Other (including capital)	32	26
	69	45
Hedging of spot positions in Treasuries and agencies		
Spot positions	46	26
Futures and forward	−29	−18
Net position		
(Treasuries and agencies only)	17	8

7 Investors

This chapter considers the major investors under the following headings:

1. Federal Reserve Banks.
2. Commercial banks.
3. Thrifts.
4. Households.
5. Private pension funds.
6. State and local pension funds.
7. Non-life insurance companies.
8. Life insurance companies.
9. Money market mutual funds.
10. General mutual funds.
11. Private foreigners.
12. Official foreign assets.
13. State and local government.
14. Non-financial companies.

Tables 7.1 and 7.2 list major institutions' holdings of US Treasuries and other financial assets as at March 1988.

Federal Reserve Banks

Federal Reserve assets are mainly invested in Treasury securities (see Table 7.3). The *size* of Fed security purchases is primarily determined by open-market policy (designed to influence the level of bank reserves and level of interest rates). However, the *maturity distribution* of purchases offers some scope for choice.

The Fed likes to hold high liquidity for operational reasons (coping with seasonal or erratic reductions in currency circulation or bank reserves, and assisting the conduct of monetary policy). Thus over 60% of Fed holdings of Treasury securities mature in less than one year.

Table 7.1. Holdings of US government securities, September 1988

	Treasuries savings bonds and agencies ($bn)	Treasuries ($bn)	% of US Treasury issues	Treasuries as % of sector's financial assets
Federal Reserve Banks	225	218	11	79
Sponsored agencies	20	19	1	5
Foreigners	357	329	16	28
Personal	583	495	25	4
Non-financial corporate business	88	86	4	5
State and local government	258	164	8	30
Commercial banks	367	223	11	8
Thrifts	282	41	2	2
Insurance: Life	133	67	3	6
Other	103	61	3	15
Pension funds: Private	126	68	3	7
State and local	170	112	6	21
Mutual funds: General	134	99	5	21
Money market	45	15	1	4
CMO trusts (a)	105	0	0	0
Total	2996	1996(b)	100	

Notes
(a) Collateralised mortgage obligation trusts.
(b) Compares with corporate bonds outstanding of $800 bn, state and local government bonds outstanding of $500 bn and New York Stock Exchange equity market capitalisation of $2,500 bn.

When purchasing longer-term securities the Fed principally aims to achieve a fair spread of holdings at all maturities. It will not normally make policy-determined purchases designed to influence the shape of the yield curve.

The Fed seeks to maximise return on purchases within each maturity group (competing offers are invited from primary dealers) but it does not trade. Once bought, coupon securities are generally held to maturity as long-term investments. Federal Reserve profits (mainly derived from interest receipts on Fed holdings of Treasury securities) are largely paid into the US Treasury.

Commercial banks

Banks hold Treasury securities primarily as a safe liquid reserve which could be swiftly realised if needed to meet deposit withdrawals or sudden loan demand escalation. Table 7.4 lists the amount of US Treasury holdings held by Commercial and Federal Reserve banks.

Table 7.2. Major institutions' financial assets ($bn), September 1988

	Private pension funds	State and local govt pension funds	Life insurance	Non-life insurance	Commercial banks	Thrifts	Households	Foreigners
US Treasury issues	78	121	63	50	196	19	546	331
US agency issues	53	58	74	28	162	209	174	34
Corporate and foreign bonds	176	163	431	60	86	46	88	171
Municipal bonds		1	11	145	154	1	268	
Mortgages	6	16	227	5	653	745	79	
Corporate equities	500	175	108	79	0		2,230	193
Other financial assets	273	54	182	71	1,599	316	8,371	484
Total financial assets	1,086	587	1,097	435	2,851	1,336	11,755ᵃ	1,214
US Treasuries as % of total financial assets	7.2	20.6	5.7	11.4	6.9	1.4	4.6	30.1

a Household financial assets include equity in unincorporated businesses ($2,500 bn) and interests in life insurance and pension funds ($2,600 bn).

Alternatives are state and local bonds (though their tax advantages have been much reduced for banks by the 1986 Tax Reform Act) and corporate bonds (which are less liquid and more risky, but have a higher return and might help a relationship with banking customers).

Table 7.3. Holdings of US Treasury securities ($bn), end-1988

Maturity (years)	Commercial banks[a]	Federal Reserve Banks
Under 1	20	142
1 to 5	40	55
Over 5	8[b]	39
	68	236

a   Large banks only.
b   Holdings of agency securities have a longer maturity profile.

Table 7.4. Federal Reserve Banks' balance sheet: Nov. 1988

Liabilities		Assets	
Notes in circulation	224	US Treasury securities	233
Commercial bank deposits	40	Agency securities	8
US Treasury deposits	5	Loans to depository institutions	2
Other liabilities and capital	15	Other assets	41
	284		284

Thrifts

Thrifts are non-bank savings institutions. The term includes savings and loan institutions (US institutions roughly equivalent to UK building societies), mutual savings banks and credit unions. They have a more stable deposit base than commercial banks (thrifts are less dependent on volatile money-market deposits) and can therefore hold a higher proportion of their assets in US agency securities (less marketable than Treasuries, but yielding a slightly higher return).

Households

Personal holdings of Treasury securities account for 27% of the US Treasury market but form only 5% of household financial assets. Treasuries face hot competition from tax-exempt municipal bonds. For example, if the investor's tax rate is 28%, a tax-exempt municipal bond yielding 7·2% gives him the same after-tax return as a Treasury yielding 10%.

Private pension funds

Pension funds are long-term investors who can seek the higher returns offered by corporate bonds and equities, and afford the higher risk and sacrifice of liquidity involved. Their Treasury investments are relatively low and are normally held either for short-term liquidity or for trading (where Treasuries' greater liquidity and lower dealing costs give them an edge on corporate bonds).

However, some large pension funds are forced to hold a relatively high proportion of Treasuries because the corporate bond market is insufficiently liquid to absorb buying or selling in their desired size without disproportionate price changes.

State and local pension funds

These hold more Treasuries than private pension funds because their investment ethos is more risk-averse (partly through tradition; partly through constraints imposed by state law).

Non-life insurance companies

Much of the liability structure of non-life insurance is fairly short-term. For example, the interval between receipt of premium and payment of claim is often less than 12 months in the case of household fire or auto insurance. This necessitates a short-term asset structure, often implying high Treasury holdings, since there is a shortage of corporate bonds in short maturities.

Paradoxically, despite their short-term orientation, non-life companies can also maintain high equity holdings, because they are generally well capitalised.

Life insurance companies

The liability structure of life insurance is longer term than for non-life companies. Thus life companies require long-term assets with good return but limited risk, biasing their portfolios towards corporate bonds and mortgages.

Treasury bonds are too low-yielding and are held primarily as a liquid reserve. High equity holdings are too risky because the mutual companies which dominate life insurance are thinly capitalised, and profit-sharing life policies are relatively uncommon.

Money market mutual funds

Such funds must maintain a very short average maturity, be very liquid and have a significant proportion of investments maturing each day to meet any sudden withdrawals. Many funds hold overnight Treasury repos as part of their reserve to meet sudden withdrawals. Holding Treasury bills also increases effective liquidity since Treasury bills can be easily sold in huge size; by contrast, bank negotiable certificates of deposit (CDs) or commercial paper may have to be sold on relatively disadvantageous terms. Some fund prospectuses specify US Treasury holdings only, to appeal to ultra-conservative investors.

Interest rate fluctuations can provoke switching between short-term Treasuries and money market funds. Money market fund yields do not immediately match any change in short-term interest rates, since it may take 30 to 60 days before all of a fund's investments mature and can be reinvested at the new rates. Accordingly if interest rates fall sharply the yield on money market funds will temporarily hold up (until the fund's existing holdings mature). However, the yield on Treasuries will fall immediately. This can provoke switching from short-term Treasuries into money market funds.

Conversely, if interest rates (including Treasury yields) rise sharply, the yield on money market funds will remain temporarily depressed. This can provoke switching from money market funds into Treasury bills and short-term coupon securities.

General mutual funds

Public enthusiasm for bond mutual funds is usually a lagging function of investment fashions. The public tend to buy after market rises and sell after market crashes. For example, after the Stock Market crash in October 1987 there were mass sales of equity mutual funds and heavy purchases of US Treasury funds.

Private foreigners

Private foreign holdings of US assets are split between direct investment, real estate, corporate equities, bonds and short-term money market instruments. US Treasuries currently account for about $80 bn, or 10% of private foreign assets held in the USA and normally appeal most when the dollar exchange rate looks reasonably secure.

Official foreign assets

Central banks maintain foreign currency reserves for various reasons:

1. To support their currency in case of need by foreign exchange intervention.
2. To cover fluctuations in the balance of monthly payments for their exports and imports.
3. As a longer-term investment cushion.

About $200 bn of foreign official reserves are held in US dollars, mainly in US Treasury bills or short-term repos.

However, some foreign governments have begun to invest in longer-term Treasuries realising that their official reserve build-up is to some extent permanent, the counterpart of a long-term deterioration in the US balance of payments.

State and local government

Treasuries are a convenient repository for cash reserves and for liquid funds, including those in trust accounts. By contrast, a bank may pay relatively low interest rates on local government deposits because accepting such deposits may necessitate inconvenient restructuring of the bank's investment portfolio in order to meet the collateral tests for public-sector deposits imposed by state law.

Non-financial companies

Treasury securities (often in the form of repos) are often held as an alternative to short-term bank deposits.

8 New issues

Public auction

The standard method for the sale of new issues is by public auction. The Treasury normally announces the amount and maturity of the securities to be auctioned about ten days in advance, adhering closely to a regular schedule (see Table 8.1).

Table 8.1. US Treasury securities: normal auction schedule

Maturity (months)	Issued	Maturity date
3-month bills	Weekly	Thursday
6-month bills	Weekly	Thursday
12-month bills	4-weekly	Thursday

Maturity (years)	Months issued	Maturity date
2	All	Month-end
4	Late Mar., June, Sep., Dec.	Quarter-end
5	Early Mar., June, Sep., Dec.	15 Feb., May, Aug., Nov.
7	Early Jan., April, July, Oct.	15 Jan., April, July, Oct.
3, 10, 30	Feb., May, Aug., Nov. (main quarterly refunding)	15 Feb., May, Aug., Nov.

Procedure

Investors wishing to participate in the auction file a tender with a Federal Reserve Bank. Tenders may be filed directly but are normally submitted through a commercial bank or primary dealer.

Bids are submitted to the nearest basis point of gross redemption yield (GRY), e.g. an investor might tender for $5 m. of a new issue offering to buy $2 m. at an interest rate of 8·46, $2 m. at 8·47 and $1 m. at 8·48.

Allotment

The Treasury accepts the lowest interest rate tender and then accepts other tenders at progressively higher interest rates until the issue is fully subscribed. At the highest accepted rate, partial allotments will be made to the amount necessary to fill the subscription.

Accepted tenders are converted from an interest rate basis into a price basis expressed to three decimal points. For example, an investor who has successfully tendered for an 8% 10-year bond at 8·02, will be invoiced at a price of 99·864 (the price necessary to produce a GRY of 8·02). On settlement day the investor's bank pays cash to the Fed against a book-entry allotment of the auctioned security.

Non-competitive tenders

Investors may also submit non-competitve tenders (maximum $1 m.). Non-competitive tenders are accepted at the average price of all accepted competitive tenders for that auction. Non-competitive tenders encourage auction participation by small investors, who can thus avoid the risk of making an unrealistic tender due to a late movement in market interest rates immediately before the auction closes.

Table 8.2 gives an example of an auction result.

Table 8.2. Illustration of auction result

Auction: $10 bn of 10-year note

Result: $17 bn of bids: $10 bn accepted ($2 bn non-competitive; $8 bn competitive)
   Average accepted bid: 8.2875% coupon fixed at 8.25%

Rate	Amount tendered	Amount allotted	Price
Non-competitive	2	2 (at 8.29)	99.732
8.27	1	1	99.866
8.28	2	2	99.799
8.29	3	3	99.732
8.30	5	2	99.665
8.31	4	nil	n.a.
	17	10	

$2 bn non-competitive tenders are allotted in full, leaving $8 bn to be allotted on competitive tenders.
Competitive bids at 8.27, 8.28 and 8.29 (totalling $6 bn) are allotted in full.
$2 bn of bids at 8.30 are accepted. Since $5 bn was tendered, tenderers at 8.30 are each allotted 40% of their bid.
Bids at 8.31 are rejected.
The average accepted bid is 8.2875%, so non-competitive tenderers are allotted at 8.29% and coupon is fixed at 8.25%.

Fixing the coupon

At the conclusion of the auction the Treasury selects (to the nearest 0·125%) the highest coupon which will enable non-competitive tenders to be alloted at a price below par.

> *Example*
> Non-competitive tender filled at 8·19%.
> Coupon will be 8·125%, since a coupon of 8·25% would involve an issue price above 100.

Occasionally an auction is a 'reopening' (auction of a new tranche of an existing issue). In reopenings the coupon is already fixed and allotments will be priced above or below par as the range of accepted bids dictates.

Tests of auction success

The following factors can be taken as measures of an auction's success:

1. Amount oversubscribed. This factor is sometimes distorted by large (semi-fictitious) bids at way-out yields.
2. Relation of auction interest rate to immediately preceding market yield for similar maturities.
3. Spread between highest and lowest accepted tenders (the normal test of success). A narrow spread (e.g. 2 basis points on a 30-year Treasury) indicates success. A wide spread (e.g. 6 basis points) indicates failure.

Magnitude of foreign buying

Foreign buying is now highly significant. However, determined-sounding rumours about its size (e.g. the Japanese bought 30% of the auction) are unreliable and the US official figures are of limited value. Foreign tenders submitted through US dealers are not identified, and foreign purchases direct from the Fed are included in 'other purchasers' category which also includes US thrifts.

However, foreigners normally tender through New York while Americans normally tender through their local Fed. Consequently, abnormally high tenders at the New York Fed, e.g. over 90% compared with the usual 88% for long bond auctions, often imply heavy foreign interest (though they sometimes simply indicate aggressive position-taking by US primary dealers) and have been correlated with auction success.

When-issued trading

When an auction is announced, dealers commence trading the new bond immediately even though its coupon and issue price are not yet known. When issued trading is on an interest rate basis (e.g. buy or sell at 8·53%). Yields are converted into prices and settlement made by paying for or delivering the actual bond via Fed book-entry on the day the auction settles.

The new issues of May 1988

Figures 8.1 to 8.4 present details of new issues auctioned in May 1988.

Monday	Tuesday	Wednesday	Thursday	Friday
2	3	4	5 Auction 52 week	6
9	10 Auction 3 year	11 Auction 10 year	12 Auction 30 year Settlement 52 week	13
16 Settlement 3 year 10 year 30 year	17	18 Announce 2 year 5 year	19	20
23	24	25 Auction 2 year	26 Auction 5 year [1]	27 Announce 52 week [2]
30 Holiday	31 Settlement 2 year			

1. For settlement 1 June
2. For auction 2 June and settlement 9 June

Fig. 8.1 Schedule of issues announced and auctioned in May 1988.[1] Issued by US Treasury on 3 May 1988. Schedule omits regular weekly auctions of 3-month and 6-month Treasury bills.

The Treasury will raise about $9,475 million of new cash and refund $16,527 million of securities maturing May 15, 1988, by issuing $8,750 million of 3-year notes, $8,750 million of 10-year notes, and $8,500 million of 30-year bonds. The $16,527 million of maturing securities are those held by the public, including $2,962 million held, as of today, by Federal Reserve Banks as agents for foreign and international monetary authorities.

The three issues totaling $26,000 million are being offered to the public, and any amounts tendered by Federal Reserve Banks as agents for foreign and international monetary authorities will be added to that amount. Tenders for such accounts will be accepted at the average prices of accepted competitive tenders.

In addition to the public holdings, Government accounts and Federal Reserve Banks, for their own accounts, hold $3,563 million of the maturing securities that may be refunded by issuing additional amounts of the new securities at the average prices of accepted competitive tenders.

The 10-year note and 30-year bond being offered today will be eligible for the STRIPS program.

Details about each of the new securities are given in the attached highlights of the offering and in the official offering circulars. The circulars, which include the CUSIP numbers for components of securities with the STRIPS feature, can be obtained by contacting the nearest Federal Reserve Bank or Branch. Financial institutions should consult their local Federal Reserve Bank or Branch for procedures for requesting securities in STRIPS form.

4 May 1988

Fig. 8.2 May 1988 quarterly financing: extract from Treasury announcement. CUSIP is a standardised numbering system used to assist in computerised identification and trading of US securities.

Amount Offered to the Public	$8,500 million

Description of Security:

Term and type of security	30-year bonds
Series and CUSIP designation......................	Bonds of 2018 (CUSIP No. 912810 EA 2)
CUSIP Nos. for STRIPS Components	Listed in Attachment A of offering circular
Issue date	May 16, 1988 (to be dated May 15, 1988)
Maturity date..	May 15, 2018
Interest rate	To be determined based on the average of accepted bids
Investment yield......................................	To be determined at auction
Premium or discount................................	To be determined after auction
Interest payment dates..............................	November 15 and May 15
Minimum denomination available	$1,000
Amount required for STRIPS	To be determined after auction

Terms of Sale:

Method of sale...	Yield auction
Competitive tenders	Must be expressed as an annual yield with two decimals, e.g. 7.10%
Noncompetitive tenders	Accepted in full at the average price up to $1,000,000
Accrued interest payable by investor...................................	One day's accrued interest. Amount to be determined after auction

Payment Terms:

Payment by non-institutional investors...	Full payment to be submitted with tender
Payment through Treasury Tax and Loan (TT&L) Note Accounts................	Acceptable for TT&L Note Option Depositaries
Deposit guarantee by designated institutions	Acceptable

Key Dates:

Receipt of tenders....................................	Thursday, May 12, 1988, prior to 1:00 p.m., EDST
Settlement (final payment due from institutions):	
(a) funds immediately available to the Treasury..........................	Monday, May 16, 1988
(b) readily-collectible check..........................	Thursday, May 12, 1988

Note. These highlights were published by the US Treasury on 4 May 1988. Similar highlights were issued for the offerings of 3-year notes and 10-year notes.

Fig. 8.3 Highlights of Treasury offerings to the public: May 1988 quarterly financing.

The Department of the Treasury has accepted $8,505 million of $21,693 million of tenders received from the public for the 30-year Bonds auctioned today. The bonds will be issued May 16, 1988, and mature May 15, 2018.

The interest rate on the bonds will be 9-1/8%.[1] The range of accepted competitive bids, and the corresponding prices at the 9-1/8% interest rate are as follows:

	Yield	Price[2]
Low	9.16%	99.643
High	9.18%	99.440
Average	9.17%	99.542

Tenders at the high yield were allotted 74%.

1. The minimum par amount required for STRIPS is $1,600,000. Larger amounts must be in multiples of that amount.
2. In addition to the auction price, accrued interest of $0.24796 per $1,000 for May 15, 1988, to May 16, 1988, must be paid.

TENDERS RECEIVED AND ACCEPTED (in thousands)

Location	Received	Accepted
New York	19,837,575	7,947,490
Chicago	1,141,905	480,565
San Francisco	670,571	39,471
Other	43,403	37,373
Totals	$21,693,454	8,504,899

The $8,505 million of accepted tenders includes $462 million of noncompetitive tenders and $8,043 million of competitive tenders from the public.

In addition to the $8,505 million of tenders accepted in the auction process, $200 million of tenders was also accepted at the average price from Government accounts and Federal Reserve Banks for their own account in exchange for maturing securities.

12 May 1988

Fig. 8.4 Treasury announcement of results of auction of 30-year bonds.

9 Settlement

Regular settlement is made the following day by delivery of the Treasury security via Fed book entry against payment into the seller's bank's account at the Fed. Between primary dealers, 'good delivery' means via Fed book entry.

Delivery of physical securities

From the general public, old physical securities will often be accepted which the dealer will then convert into book entry (this may take up to two days at the Fed). Physical delivery will usually be made against a cheque or promise of immediate credit to the seller's bank account.

Accrued interest

Invoices include accrued interest for the days to settlement date, calculated as a percentage of the true number of days (including 29 February where applicable!) covered by the half-year coupon. The number of days per half-year varies between 181 and 184.

> *Example*
> Bond nominal value :$1,000,000
> Bond coupon   :12% p.a.
> Coupon paid   :6% on 15 May and 15 November each year.
> Settlement   :24 June 1988
> Last coupon paid   :15 May 1988
> Days since last coupon payment : 40 days
> Days in half-year   :184 days
> Accrued interest   :$1,000,000 $\times \dfrac{6}{100} \times \dfrac{40}{184}$ = \$13,043.48

Notes

1. The number of days per half-year can vary between 181 and 184.

2. US Treasury publishes official tables for calculation of accrued interest, which can obviate the need for individual calculation on every trade.

Payment of coupons after trade

If a bond is sold for settlement before coupon date the coupon is paid to the buyer. If settlement is on or after coupon date, the coupon is paid to the seller. Thus, there are no complications with ex-dividend dates and no need for subsequent chasing of coupons between buyer and seller (as in the UK gilts market).

Forward deals

Occasionally Treasury securities are sold for delivery at some time after the regular date. Five-business-day settlement (to match settlement terms on equities and corporate bonds) is quite common. Marketmakers frequently deal for other periods (usually with each other) in order to balance their books.

Part Two

The economic background

10 Fundamental analysis: the economic cycle

Interest rates and the economic cycle

Link between the real economy and financial markets

Strains in the real economy will sooner or later be mirrored by strains in financial markets. Thus, capacity shortages, tight labour markets and rising inflation are normally associated with rising interest rates. Conversely, a slowdown in the real economy normally assists falling interest rates because it usually indicates weaker demand and easing capacity strains.

However economic slowdown occasionally reflects not demand weakness but supply disruptions, e.g. strikes, drought, raw material and component shortages, skilled labour shortages. In such cases slowdown is a sympton not of strains easing (good for bonds) but of strains getting worse (bad for bonds).

Normal timing

On average, interest rate peaks and troughs have roughly coincided with economic peaks and troughs (see Tables 10.1 and 10.2). If inflation is not serious, even a deceleration in economic activity without an actual downturn may spark a significant bull market, as happened in early 1966 and 1984–6.

On only three occasions since 1950 have economic turning points and interest rate turning points diverged by more than three months:

1. 1970–2. Remarkable collective blindness: the bond market ignored excess money growth for nearly two years, possibly beguiled by Nixon's initial success in temporarily suppressing inflation by price controls (consumer price inflation remained below 4% until spring 1973).

Table 10.1. Interest rate peaks and the economic cycle

Economic peak	Interest rate peak: Months' lead (−) or lag on economic cycle[a]	
	T-bills	Long bonds
July 1953	−1	−1
Aug. 1957	2	2
Apr. 1960	−1	−3
Dec. 1969	1	1
Nov. 1973 (Sept. 1974)[b]	9 (−1)	9 (−1)
Jan. 1980	2	−1, 2[c]
July 1981	−2	2
Average (excluding 1973–4)	0	0

a e.g. bond yields peaked in June 1953 (1 month before economic peak) and Oct. 1957 (2 months after economic peak).
b timing of economic peak ambiguous.
c bond yields had double top in December 1979 and March 1980.

Table 10.2. Interest rate troughs and the economic cycle

Economic trough	Interest rate trough: Months' lead (−) or lag on economic trough	
	T-bills	Long bonds
May 1954	1	2
Apr. 1958	2	0
Feb. 1961	−2, 5	3
Nov. 1970	4	11, 24
Mar. 1975	3	−1
July 1980	−1	−1
Nov. 1982	−1	0
Average (excluding 1970–2)	1	0

2. 1973–4. The November 1973 economic peak was not due to demand weakness (good for bonds) but to an inflationary supply disruption (the Arab oil embargo) which was bad for bonds. Genuine demand weakness began only in September 1974, closely coinciding with the interest rate peak.

3. 1984–6. Bond bull market (yields fell from 13·0% to 7·6%) occurred *without* a recession (though the economy did decelerate). Similarly the bond mini-bull market from October 1987 to March 1988 occurred without a recession. Could these timing aberrations reflect investor recognition of am emerging long-term inflation downtrend?

There was a precedent in 1929! (Bond yields peaked in January 1929: the economy not till August 1929.)

Figure 10.1 shows the economic indicators and interest rates for the years 1967–88.

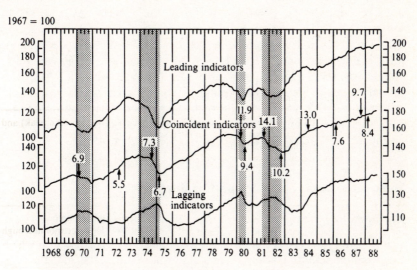

Fig. 10.1 Cyclical economic indicators and interest rates. Shaded areas indicate recession periods; arrows show timing and level of Treasury bond interest rate peaks and troughs. Source: US Commerce Dept.

Cyclical indicators and interest rates

In a normal economic cycle a downturn in the leading indicators index is usually the first sign that a sustainable *future* drop in interest rates is possible. When coincident economic indicators (e.g. industrial production) weaken, bond buying normally becomes relatively safe.

Difficulties in interpretation

Unfortunately economic turning points are easy to pinpoint only with hindsight. In the real world 3% GNP growth generates a mixture of indicators: some suggesting 6% growth, some 3% and some zero. If a zero indicator appears, the investor has to guess whether this is the first sign of the economy moving into recession or simply a statistical aberration.

Economic indicators appear with significant time lags and initial data are subject to major later revisions. Thus the first thing to forecast is the present.

An example of the hazards in interpretation
The leading indicators index has fallen for four consecutive months on nine occasions since 1945. On seven of these occasions a recession followed.

Leading indicators fell 1·7% in October 1987 (after Black Monday), 0·1% in November 1987 and 0·2% in December 1987. Recession enthusiasts then eagerly awaited a fourth consecutive fall from the January index (which was to be published on 3 March). January was duly reported as −0·5. However, December was simultaneously revised up from −0·2 to +0·3 and the anticipated signal of four consecutive declines disappeared. A bond market correction then began.

Some indicators helpful in spotting interest rate trends

Housing starts

The housing starts series measures the number of new houses on which construction activity has commenced in each month. Housing construction tends to move extremely early in the economic cycle. Thus it is virtually impossible for a bond bull market to start until long after housing starts have peaked out, and unusual for a bond bear market to start until after housing starts have begun to recover (see Fig. 10.2).

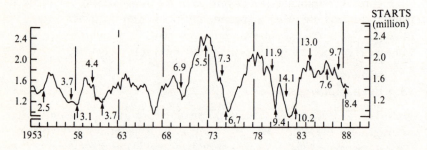

Fig. 10.2 Housing starts and Treasury bond yield. Starts are shown as three-month moving average; arrows indicate major turning points in interest rates.

Consumer expectations index

An extremely valuable (and underpublicised) index, based on a Gallup poll which simply asks respondents whether in six months' time they expect the following to be better or worse:

1. The economy in general.
2. Job prospects.
3. Their own financial position.

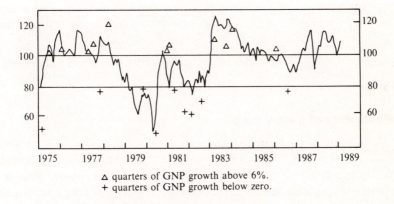

    △ quarters of GNP growth above 6%.
    + quarters of GNP growth below zero.

Fig. 10.3 Consumer expectations index and the economy.
Source: Conference Board.

Figure 10.3 indicates the index's normal range (80 to 100) and its superb forecasting record, as borne out by the following facts:

1. We have never yet had a recession with the index above 85.
2. In 1985–8 the index consistently warned that the economy would remain strong.
3. Even after Black Monday it remained above 90 (the mid-point of its normal long-term range), strong evidence against an early recession.

Purchasing managers' survey

A useful coincident indicator, published on the first Monday of each month is the purchasing managers' composite index (see Fig. 10.4).

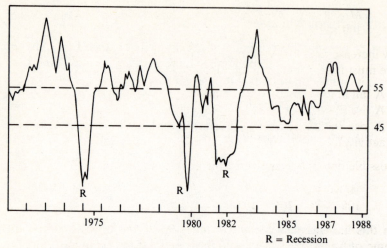

Fig. 10.4 Purchasing managers' composite index. Index at 55 usually implies 3% GNP growth; index below 45 is a recession warning.

Significance of money supply

Money, inflation and the economy

Money supply trends, if *correctly interpreted*, are an extremely powerful tool of economic forecasting. This springs from the identity:

$$MV = PT$$

Money × Velocity = Prices × Transactions
M = The money supply
V = Velocity of circulation (the frequency with which money is spent)
P = Average price level
T = The number of transactions

The equation may be verified as follows:

1. MV (Money × Velocity) = the total amount spent.
2. PT (Price level × Number of transactions) = the total cost of the goods purchased.

These two (the amount spent and the amount bought) are obviously equal.

Consider the following illustration:

Suppose all four figures are initially 100:

$$M \times V = P \times T$$
$$100 \times 100 = 100 \times 100$$

Now increase the money supply to 105. To keep the equation balanced, there must follow some combination of the following changes:

1. A fall in the velocity of circulation.
2. A rise in the price level.
3. A rise in the number of transactions (i.e. the level of economic activity).

A possible outcome is shown by the equation:

$$M \times V = P \times T$$

M	V	P	T
105	99	101	103

In this illustration velocity has fallen while the price level and the volume of transactions have both increased. (If the economy is already operating close to its capacity limit, there will be little scope for increasing the level of transactions, so an increase in money will be more swiftly reflected in increased prices.)

Money supply and the bond market

Either rising inflation or higher economic activity are normally bearish for bonds. Therefore an increase in money supply is normally bearish for bonds. Conversely, a fall in money supply normally means either a drop in future economic activity or lower inflation, either of which is bullish for bonds.

There are two situations when an increase in money supply is not inflationary:

1. If the resulting increase in the number of transactions (the level of demand in the economy) is less than the underlying long-term growth of supply (probably about 3% p.a. in the US economy).
2. If the increase in money supply is offset by a fall in velocity of circulation so that actual spending does not increase proportionately. This occurred in 1982–6 when M-1 velocity fell sharply in contrast to its historic norm of 3% p.a. rise. The reason for this fall were:
   (a) 15% interest rates in 1981 had given people an extraordinary incentive to minimise their holdings of non-interest-bearing demand deposits. Minimising these deposits had artificially depressed the level of M-1 and thus raised M-1 velocity. This incentive to minimise M-1 deposits eroded as interest rates trended down after 1981;

(b) structural changes in the US banking system introduced into M-1 novel interest-bearing checkable deposits some of which were long-term savings (with a very low velocity of circulation) and not spending money.

Secondary indicators of monetary conditions

Since nominal money supply figures can be distorted, the investor should seek confirmation from secondary indicators of monetary conditions, e.g. stock market prices, the dollar foreign exchange rate and dollar commodity prices. These three all tend to respond sensitively to increases or decreases in the *effective* money supply, even if the published money figures are distorted. The following examples may be cited:

1. Weak stock market and falling commodity prices in early 1982 suggested that money conditions were really tight, even though nominal M-1 growth was apparently excessive.
2. Rising stock market and falling dollar exchange rate in 1985–6 confirmed that monetary conditions were relatively easy.
3. The reported money slowdown in summer 1987 was consistent with the mild recovery in the dollar exchange rate and then spectacularly confirmed by the stock market collapse (which was thus a major bull signal for long bonds).
4. The stock market recovery after December 1987 was a signal that easy money (and future inflation?) conditions were returning and that recession forecasts and bond euphoria were being overdone.

However, the secondary indicators can sometimes give false signals, as the following examples indicate:

1. Mid-1988. The strong dollar exchange rate reflected not tight money in the US but loose money elsewhere, especially in Germany and the UK.
2. 1983–4. The strong dollar reflected not tight money, but a need for extremely high interest rates to offset Reaganomic budget deficits' excessive stimulus to domestic demand. Excess domestic demand had to be offset by weaker net exports (achieved by an overvalued exchange rate) to prevent total demand reaching inflationary levels. In this peculiar situation, the strong dollar did not imply domestic austerity (the real test of tight money) but its reverse! Total money creation still proceeded apace since high interest rates were merely a partial offset to monster budget deficits.

The yield curve as an indicator of monetary conditions

Unusual differentials between short-term interest rates (heavily influenced by the Fed) and long-term interest rates (heavily influenced by investors' inflationary expectations) are sometimes a useful indicator of monetary conditions.

Short rates well below long rates usually indicate easy money. This situation often results if the Fed pumps liquidity into the market to push down short rates, while long rates still reflect high inflationary expectations (which unjustified Fed easing might actually make worse). Conversely, an inverted yield curve indicates a shortage of liquidity (tight money) while long rates below short rates suggest that inflationary expectations are under control. The Fed itself now regards a steep positive yield curve as a possible indication of rising inflationary expectations and possible need for money tightening.

Warning: Spectacular false signals are possible

Two examples may be cited where the yield curve did not serve as a reliable indicator:

1. Summer 1986. The yield curve was flat because the oil price collapse had produced unrealistically low inflationary expectations, although Fed policy was really loose.
2. October 1987. The yield curve was very steep, because of inflationary fears and complete loss of market confidence in American politicians. However, Fed policy was really tight, as soon demonstrated by Black Monday.

Yield curve comparisons distorted over time

Deliberate Treasury policy to extend the average maturity of the national debt has produced a supply shortage of Treasury bills (pushing down short-term interest rates) and heavy issues of long bonds (pushing up long-term interest rates). As a result, a steeply positive yield curve has become more normal (and less conclusive evidence of easy money) than it used to be.

Similarly, the very tight money conditions formerly associated with a steeply inverted yield curve could now be indicated by only mild inversion or even a flat yield curve (see Fig. 10.5).

Inflation

Interest rates are related to long-term inflation trends (hence the secular

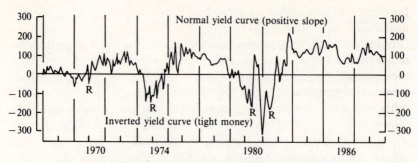

Fig. 10.5 Yield differential: 2½-year Treasury minus 6-month Treasury, 1967–88. Note: All recent major recessions have been preceded by an inverted yield curve (often a symptom of tight money).

uptrend in US interest rates from 1947 to 1981 and short-term cyclical inflation turning points. In both cases the causal relationship is clear, but the timing relationship is variable. Sometimes bond yields react after turning points in inflation; sometimes yields anticipate the turning point. For example, yields rose in early 1983 when most indicators of current inflation were still falling (see Fig. 10.6).

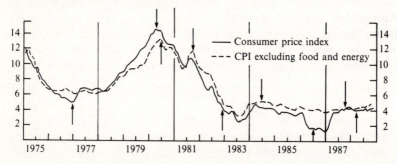

Fig. 10.6 Consumer price inflation (% change on year ago) and long Treasury interest rates. Arrows indicate major turning points in interest rates. Source: Bank Credit Analyst.

The underlying inflation rate

What matters for the bond market is the *underlying* rate of inflation undistorted by erratic fluctuations (often due to food or energy prices). For example, underlying consumer price inflation (CPI) (excluding food and energy) remained remarkably stable around 4% in the period 1985–7. This was a warning that bond bull euphoria in spring 1986, when the oil price collapse produced a temporarily low overall inflation rate, might be unsoundly based. (A similar warning had appeared in autumn 1976.)

Industrial commodity prices (see Fig. 10.7) are a more sensitive indicator of inflation pressures than consumer prices and move earlier in the economic cycle. Unfortunately they are so volatile that false warning signals are common and they should only be used in combination with other indicators.

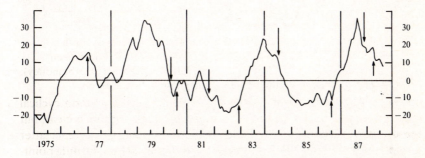

Fig. 10.7 Commodity prices (% change on year ago) and interest rates. Arrows indicate major turning points in interest rates. Source: CRB index of raw industrial material prices.

Agricultural commodity prices are seldom a useful guide to underlying inflation (excess demand) pressures because they are so sensitive to short-term weather distortions.

Useful leading indicators of inflation can include the following:

1. Money supply.
2. Sensitive commodity prices.
3. Excessive economic growth.
4. Tight labour market (very low unemployment).
5. Shortage of plant and equipment (high capacity utilisation).
6. Weakness in US dollar foreign exchange rate.

Forecasting the inflation rate

Normal CPI inflation measures (e.g. percentage change over preceding 12 months) react too slowly to be used as bond market signals. However, a leading inflation indicator may give more timely warnings. For example, the PaineWebber index (see Fig. 10.8) produced the following useful signals:

1. Turned down four months before July 1984 peak in bond yields.
2. Turned up eight months before May 1986 bottom in bond yields.

3. Stabilised four months before October 1987 peak in bond yields.

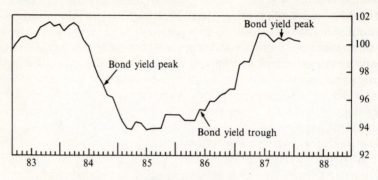

Fig. 10.8 PaineWebber leading index of inflation. Source: Maury Harris, PaineWebber New York.

Composition of inflation-warning indices
The PaineWebber leading indicator consists of three sensitive price indices, three measures of capacity strain and the dollar exchange rate.

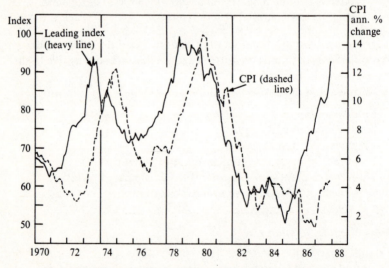

Fig. 10.9 Bank Credit Analyst leading index of inflation.

The Bank Credit Analyst's general inflation-warning indicator is simply the capacity utilisation index divided by the Dallas Fed's index of the trade-weighted dollar exchange rate. The rationale is that the normal inflation dangers of capacity strain are intensified by a falling exchange rate, implying excess money creation plus increasing demand for exports and import substitutes.

The wage-pressure upswing indicator has given four major inflation warnings (shown by arrows on Fig. 10.10) since 1963. Each was followed by sharp consumer price acceleration within two years. The wage-pressure indicator consists simply of the past year's increase in average hourly earnings, divided by the current unemployment rate. Unemployment is used as a divisor because a wage upturn is most likely to accelerate when unemployment is low (e.g. mid-1988) and least likely to accelerate when unemployment is high (e.g. late 1980).

The indicator's past successes illustrate the maxim that the simplest indicators are often the most useful. (A logical and consistent relationship between three inflationary variables is a safer bet for the bond investor than any number of 15-equation econometric models.)

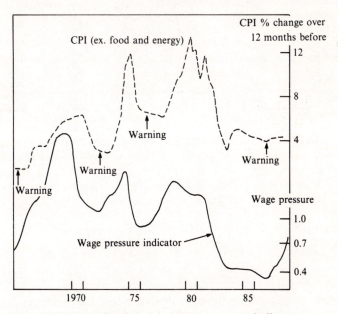

Fig. 10.10 Bank Credit Analyst wage-pressure indicator.

Capacity utilisation and inflation

Capacity utilisation above 82% tends to be associated with accelerating inflation and bond market weakness. Similar but less consistent relationships apply with other measures of capacity shortage (e.g.

delivery delays, low unemployment, abnormally high imports) (see Fig. 10.11).

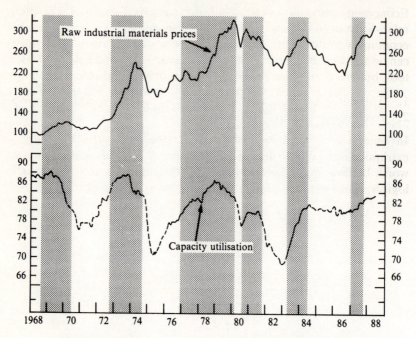

Fig. 10.11 Capacity utilisation, inflation pressures and interest rates. Shaded areas show periods of rising interest rates; dashed line on capacity utilisation shows periods of decelerating consumer price inflation. Note: Peaks and troughs in raw material prices usually lead changes in both CPI and interest rates.

Warning: Inflation pressures seldom disappear overnight

Mild deceleration in GNP growth (as in late 1979) will not prevent inflationary acceleration (and bond market weakness) *until* capacity utilisation drops below the critical point.

Suppose capacity utilisation is currently 82%, and capacity is growing around its long-term average of 3% p.a. In this case GNP growth below 3% will soon result in capacity utilisation falling below 82%, implying decelerating inflation and falling interest rates. However if capacity utilisation is 84%, it could take nine months of zero GNP growth or two years of 2% GNP growth before capacity utilisation falls below 82% and inflationary pressures clearly decelerate.

If capacity utilisation is very high, beware of premature bond buying on the first hint of economic deceleration.

Econometric modelling

Econometric modelling is a specialised branch of mathematics in which relationships between one indicator (e.g. interest rates) and other economic variables (e.g. industrial production, inflation, budget deficit) can be analysed on a best-fit basis. It has proved to be a superb historical tool, but it is a dubious forecasting tool for the following reasons:

1. The mathematical relationships are not necessarily cause-and-effect.
2. Even causal relationships do *not* stay constant in economics.

In general it pays to be suspicious of the precision 'forecasts' (i.e. extrapolations of past experience) produced by such models. It is rarely worth betting a bond portfolio on an equation unless the equation is logical, consistent and simple.

Introduction

US economic statistics are released on a regular pre-published schedule. To illustrate, we give release dates (with some New York release times) for major indicators referring to February 1988 and for quarterly indicators referring to 1988 Q1 (i.e. the first quarter of 1988). Release dates may vary slightly from year to year.

Caution

US indicators are published very early by international standards (e.g. industrial production normally appears only 15 days after the end of the month to which it refers) and partly for that reason are subject to major later revisions.

Appearance and significance of economic indicators for February 1988

1 Feb.   *Exchange rate, stock market indices and commodity prices (for same day).* Prices are the only economic indicators that are actually up to date, i.e. published as they occur and not a week or month later. Exchange rates, stock market and commodity prices are all valuable secondary indicators of monetary conditions. Commodity price *acceleration or deceleration* is also a useful primary leading indicator of general inflation. (Commodity price *levels* tend to be a slightly *lagging* indicator.)

11 Feb.   *Money supply (for week ending 1 February).* Money (16.15)   supply appears every Thursday referring to the week (NY time) ending ten days earlier.

15 Feb.   *Domestic-make auto sales for first ten days of February*. The earliest indicator of consumer demand, but volatile over ten-day periods and often distorted by manufacturers' sales promotions.

18 Feb.   *Initial claims for state unemployment benefits (for*
(14.00)   *week of 4 February*. Released every Thursday 14 days in arrears. These give the earliest indicator of labour market conditions. It is a valuable leading indicator, but weekly figures are erratic so the investor has to use a smoothed measure (e.g. a four-week moving average) to assess the underlying trend.

23 Feb.   *Consumer expectations survey (Conference Board*. A valuable indicator of consumer optimism and future spending.

3 March   *Monthly auto sales*. Includes both domestic makes and imports.

4 March   *Employment data*. Unemployment rate, total employ-
(08.30)   ment, number of workers on non-farm payrolls, average hours worked. These provide the first major indicator of the general state of the economy. The signals sometimes appear inconsistent, e.g. a weak reported figure for employment (estimated from a Gallup-poll type survey of the whole population) may be contradicted by a strong payroll figure (estimated from returns by companies accounting for about 60% of total employment). The analyst must then guess which is the true underlying trend and which is the aberration.

4 March   *Hourly earnings*. These are the first indicator of wage
(08.30)   inflation but usually reported misleadingly low (frequently revised up later to take account of backdated settlements) and exclude fringe benefits.

7 March   *National Purchasing Managers' Survey*. The survey is based on about 250 purchasing managers at major companies. It provides a composite index plus series for delivery delays, price rises, orders, employment and inventories. The Chicago Purchasing Managers' (separate) survey of delivery delays is a component of the leading indicators index.

11 March   *Retail sales*. These are the first general indicator of
(08.30)   consumer spending, but erratic and subject to major revisions. Watch the underlying trend in *non-auto*

sales (auto sales are extremely volatile and can distort the total retail sales figure).

11 March *Producer prices.* Watch the underlying inflation trend
(08.30)   in the sub-index for 'all finished goods excluding food and energy'. Food and energy prices are very volatile and often distort the trend. A surge in raw material and intermediate prices is a warning of probable future acceleration in finished goods prices. Non-food producer finished prices normally move about two to six months ahead of consumer prices. The lead time for food prices is often only one month or even less.

16 March *Housing starts and building permits.* These are an
(08.30)   extremely useful leading indicator, but often distorted by the weather, and occasionally by tax changes.

16 March *Industrial production.* Perhaps the most significant
(09.15)   overall indicator of economic activity. It is subject to moderate revisions. Production significance can be distorted by exchange-rate changes. For example, industrial production understated the strength of the economy in 1984–6 when services were booming, although manufacturing was weak in response to the overvalued dollar exchange rate.

17 March *Capacity utilisation.* This is a useful indicator of
(09.15)   potential inflationary pressures but subject to major measurement errors.

21 March *Federal budget deficit.* An indicator of government
(14.30)   borrowing demands; however monthly data are very erratic. (N.B. unexpectedly high tax receipts may indicate that the economy is growing faster than forecast.)

22 March *Durable goods orders.* The first orders report includes
(10.00)   defence (extremely volatile), autos (very volatile), other consumer durables, and capital goods orders (very useful but sometimes erratic).

23 March *Consumer prices.* Watch the underlying trend ('all
(08.30)   items except food and energy'). Monthly changes can be erratic, so a minimum of four months is normally necessary to be sure of a change in trend.

24 March *Personal income.* An indicator of potential consumer
(10.00)   buying power. Watch non-farm income (monthly

farm income is horribly distorted by fluctuations in government subsidies). Personal income from wages and salaries is a useful check on the industrial production figures.

24 March   *Personal consumption.* This provides a useful check on retail sales. (The consumption series is broader and includes spending on services.)

24 March   *Personal savings ratio.* Very low saving (e.g. 2·8% in 1987 Q3) implies that the consumer is getting overstretched and may have to restrain his spending in the near future.

29 March   *New home sales.* An indicator of potential future housing activity.

29 March   *Leading indicators.* A composite index, composed of
(08.30)   11 component sub-series, which gives an indication of future economic trends.

29 March   *Coincident indicators.* A useful check on industrial
(08.30)   production.

30 March   *Factory orders.* These are a revision of 22 March data
(10.00)   for durable orders, and provide a first estimate for non-durable orders.

1 April   *Construction spending.* This includes housing, factory
(10.00)   building and public-sector construction.

14 April   *Inventory-to-sales ratio.* An inventory build-up im-
(10.00)   plies production running ahead of demand indicating possible future weakness in the economy if production is cut back to match demand. However, possible inventory excesses must be checked against both historically normal inventory levels and survey data showing whether businessmen actually think their current inventories are high or low.

17 April   *Trade deficit.* This indicator can have a big impact on
(08.30)   the bond market. However, this impact is slightly illogical since the trade deficit is a *lagging* indicator of the economy, e.g. the 17 April trade release includes February imports, probably based on December shipments responding to the strength of US consumer demand in October and November.

Major quarterly indicators referring to 1988 Q1

26 April   *Gross national product.* This is the most comprehen-
(08.30)   sive survey of economic activity, but is subject to big revisions (starting on 26 May and 23 June).

26 April   *Compensation and productivity (revised on 6 June).*
(10.00)   Compensation includes fringe benefits (e.g. pensions
                and medical insurance) as well as basic earnings.
                Weak productivity growth late in the economic cycle
                is often a warning sign of emerging capacity short-
                ages.

26 May   *Corporate profits.* Watch the national income series
(08.30)   for profits after deducting inventory profits and
                replacement cost depreciation ('profits with inven-
                tory valuation adjustment and capital consumption
                adjustment'). This is the best guide to underlying
                profit trends without inflation distortions. A peaking-
                out of corporate profits late in the economic cycle
                (when inventory building and fixed investment
                financing needs are still strong) is often a warning of
                heavy corporate borrowing in the financial markets.

9 June   *Plant and equipment survey.* This lists businessses'
(10.00)   capital spending plans for 1988.

28 June   *Balance-of-payments current account.* This includes
(10.00)   estimates for services (e.g. insurance, shipping,
                tourism) and investment income, as well as merchan-
                dise trade.

12   Fed open-market operations

Fed operating targets

Fed intervention in the money markets often has the immediate aim of influencing the federal funds interest rate (the interest rate for overnight unsecured interbank lending of surplus funds in banks' accounts at the Fed). The main operating target is the level of borrowing at the Fed's discount window.

Reserve requirements

Each depository institution (including all commercial banks and thrifts) must maintain reserves equal to specified percentages of its deposits (see Table 12.1).

Table 12.1. Depository institutions' reserve requirements

	Reserves as % of liabilities
Demand and other checkable deposits (included in M-1)	
First $40 m. per bank	3
Other	12
Eurocurrency liabilities	3
Non-personal time deposits (with original maturity less than 18 months)	3

Required reserve fluctuations thus principally reflect changes in the demand and other checkable deposits included in M-1.
Reserves may be held as either:
(a) cash in a bank's vault;
(b) non-interest-bearing deposits in a bank's account at the Fed.

Reserve maintenance periods

Reserve maintenance periods cover two-week periods ending on alternate Wednesdays. Required reserves relating to M-1 deposits are calculated from a bank's average deposits during the overlapping two-week period ending on the preceding Monday, e.g. required reserves for 9–22 February 1989 were based on average deposit levels for 7–20 February. The smaller amount of required reserves relating to euro-currency and non-personal time deposits are based on average deposits in the prior two-week period (in this case 24 January to 6 February).

Reserve maintenance: an illustration

If the reserve requirement is 12% and a bank has average relevant deposits of $200 m. during the two weeks ending Monday 15 February 1988, it must maintain *average* reserves of $24 m. in the two-week period ending Wednesday 17 February. However, the bank need not hold $24 m. on each day of the two-week period. It can meet an average $24 m. required reserve by holding $24 m. for each of the 14 days, or it can hold zero reserves for 13 days and then hold $336 m. (= 24 × 14) on the last day. In each case the maintained reserve will *average* $24 m. over the whole period and so satisfy the Fed's requirements.

There is also a further margin of flexibility in that the Fed allows a bank to have a reserve shortfall or excess of 3% in any statement period which may be carried forward to be offset in the subsequent period without penalty.

Excess reserves

Because of unpredictable deposit flows, banks often fail to judge their reserve requirement precisely and banks in aggregate (particularly smaller banks with ultra-cautious management) usually hold slightly more reserves than required. These surpluses are called excess reserves.

Borrowed reserves (discount window borrowing)

A bank may obtain reserves by borrowing cash at the Fed's discount window if it has suitable collateral (usually Treasury bills). The discount window interest rate is not penal (unlike Bank of England last-resort facilities) but over-frequent use is discouraged by zealous arm-twisting.

Non-borrowed reserves

'Non-borrowed reserves' is a catch-all term covering all sources of reserves, other than discount window borowing. The main factors producing changes in non-borrowed reserves are the following:

1. Fed open-market operations.
2. Treasury balance at the Fed.
3. Currency in circulation.
4. Float.

Fed open-market operations

The Fed frequently buys or sells government securities, usually under repo agreements (temporary purchases or sales which automatically reverse within a few days; see page 79). When the Fed buys securities it pays by crediting the seller's bank's account at the Fed. This inflates bank reserves either temporarily (if the purchase was on repo) or permanently if the purchase was outright. Conversely, if the Fed sells securities, this drains reserves by depleting the buyer's bank's account at the Fed.

Open-market operations are the principal means by which the Fed influences the level of interest rates and the main long-term influence on the level of non-borrowed bank reserves.

Treasury balance at the Fed

Treasury cash balances are held at:

(a) Commercial banks (in so-called 'tax and loan accounts'). In this case Treasury cash (e.g. from clearing a taxpayer's cheque) remains within the commercial banking system and continues to form part of banks' reserves.
(b) The Fed (the account from which Government bills are paid). If cash is moved to the Treasury's account at the Fed (e.g. by transfer from a tax-and-loan account, or by direct clearing of a cheque payable to the government and drawn on a commercial bank) the cash leaves the commercial banking system and no longer forms part of bank reserves.

A rising Treasury balance at the Fed reduces bank reserves as can be seen in the following examples:

1. If the money comes directly by transfer from a tax-and-loan account, the Treasury's balance at the Fed will rise and the commercial bank's balance at the Fed falls (depleting reserves).
2. If a cheque, representing payment for a newly auctioned Treasury bond, is paid directly into the Treasury's account at the Fed, then the bondbuyer's bank's balance at the Fed will fall when the cheque clears.

Management of Treasury balances

Commercial banks must pay interest on Treasury deposits at 25 basis points below Fed funds rate *and* collateralise the deposits with holdings of government securities. These conditions imply some limit (recently about $32 bn) to the Treasury deposits that commercial banks wish to accept.

The Treasury normally aims to keep its cash balance at the Fed around $3 bn (see Fig. 12.1). However, Treasury deposits in tax-and-loan accounts may tend to rise well above the $32 bn practical limit, especially at peaks in the tax-gathering season. The Treasury then has to transfer the excess deposits into its account at the Fed (thus draining bank reserves). This unwanted reserve draining will need to be offset by vigorous reserve-adding open-market operations.

Conversely, Congressional delays in raising the debt ceiling occasionally cause the Treasury balance at the Fed to fall close to zero. This inflates bank reserves and will need to be offset by Fed draining.

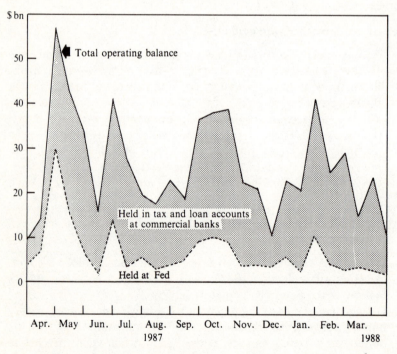

Fig. 12.1 Treasury cash balance.

Currency in circulation

If the public deposits cash in banks, the banks' holdings of vault cash (which form part of bank reserves) will rise. Conversely, if the public withdraws cash from banks, the banks' vault cash is depleted. Cash in banks' vaults counts as reserves; cash circulating outside banks does not. Thus a rise in currency in circulation represents a contraction in bank reserves.

Float

When a bank presents a cheque for clearing via the Fed's clearing system, the presenting bank must be credited with the value of the cheque within two days. However, it sometimes takes the Fed more than two days to collect from the paying bank. In this interim period *both* banks are able to use the value of the cheque as part of their reserves. This double usage is referred to as float. Thus a rise in float inflates bank reserves.

Fog-bound aircraft are sometimes alleged to be a cause of delayed cheque clearing and consequent unplanned increases in float and bank reserves.

Illustration of factors influencing movements in reserves

Tables 12.2 and 12.3 detail reserve movements in early November 1987.

In this period reserves were inflated by a big fall in Treasury balances at the Fed and a small rise in float. However, these reserve-adding factors

Table 12.2. Level of bank reserves ($m.), November 1987

	4 November	18 November	Change
Banks' deposits at Fed	38,353	37,525	−828
Banks' vault cash	23,464	23,622	158
Total	61,817	61,147	−670
Required reserves	60,256	60,665	409
Excess reserves	1,561	482	−1,079
Total	61,817	61,147	−670
Discount-window borrowings	677	561	−116
Non-borrowed reserves	61,140	60,586	−554
Total	61,817	61,147	−670

Table 12.3. Factors causing a change in bank reserves ($m.) (statement fortnight ending 18 November 1987)

	Change[a]	Impact on reserves
Fed holdings of securities	−4,440	−4,440
Treasury balances at Fed	−6,698	+6,698
Currency circulation	+3,282	−3,282
Float	+670	+670
Other		−316[b]
Total change in reserves		−670
Change in borrowed reserves from (discount window)		−116
Change in non-borrowed reserves		−554
		−670

a   Data represent averages of daily figures for the two-week period ending 18 November, compared with averages for the previous two-week period ending 4 November.
b   Includes *inter alia:*
   (i)   foreign official balances at the Fed; an increase represents dollars removed from the commercial banking system and thus reduces reserves;
   (ii) Fed foreign exchange intervention. If the Fed sells dollars in intervention they enter the commercial banking system and inflate reserves. If the Fed buys dollars, they are removed from the commercial banking system, thus draining reserves. (The dollar seller may acquire Deutschmarks in exchange, but these cannot be used to meet Fed reserve requirements which must be held in US dollars.)

were more than offset by a jump in currency circulation and heavy Fed sales of Treasury securities (mainly temporary sales on reverse repo).

The net result was a $554 m. drop in non-borrowed reserves in a period when the reserves required (reflecting deposit levels shortly before) actually rose by $409 m. However, banks were able both to meet this $963 m. shortfall and to repay $116 m. borrowing from the discount window, simply by reducing the great excess of reserves held in the prior period.

Reserve adding

There may be a need for temporary reserve adding to offset seasonal or erratic fluctuations. Permanent reserve adding is needed to underwrite sufficient long-term monetary expansion to support real economic growth. Even with zero inflation, M-1 might need to grow around 3% p.a. to finance real economic growth. This implies a need to add permanent reserves at a minimum $2 bn per annum.

The principal means of adding reserves via open-market operations are the following:

1.   System repos.
2.   Customer repos.
3.   Outright purchases ('passes').

A *repo agreement* is an agreement to sell a security with simultaneous agreement to repurchase at a specified price and date.

System repos

The Fed purchases a security from a government security dealer, the dealer simultaneously agreeing to repurchase either on the following day (overnight repo) or in a few days' time (term repo) at a predetermined price. The effect is temporarily to increase reserves in the banking system when the Fed pays for the security by crediting the dealer's bank account. This addition to reserves automatically reverses when repurchase day arrives. The dealer then buys back the security and pays by transferring a deposit from his own bank account to the Fed.

The dealer has effectively obtained a short-term loan from the Fed, using a government security as collateral.

Customer Repos

Foreign monetary authorities (Fed customers) often invest in repos. If they either hold deposits at the Fed or buy repos direct from the Fed, this implies foreign monetary authorities have removed money from US commercial banks, thus draining bank reserves.

However, the Fed often arranges for a foreign central bank to buy repos from a US primary dealer (instead of from the Fed). This puts the foreigners' cash back into the US commercial banking system when the foreigners pay for the repo. (Cash going into a US bank account forms part of a bank's reserves. A foreign deposit at the Fed does not.)

Customer repos tend to be smaller than system repos. Typical size is between $700 m. and $3 bn. There is a practical minimum since a $700 m. overnight repo adds only $50 m. of reserves averaged over a 14-day reserve period ($700 \div 14 = 50$). Table 12.4 gives the average size of customer and system repo agreements (1986).

Outright purchases ('passes')

Repos are purely temporary additions to reserves. The deal automatically

Table 12.4. Average size of repo agreements ($bn), 1986

Customer :	overnight[a]	1.6
System :	overnight	4.4
:	term[b]	2.5

a   Fed has not conducted a term customer repo since January 1986.
b   Term system repos up to seven days are fairly common.

reverses and the cash soon returns to the Fed when repurchase day arrives. However, when the Fed buys securities outright ('conducts a pass') reserves are added permanently.

The Fed purchases outright when a reserve add-need is large (e.g. $3 bn) and extends for more than one reserve period. Outright purchases have a seasonal pattern with large extended add-needs usually occurring in April, June, August–September and November–December. Table 12.5 gives the average size of outright Fed purchases in 1986 and 1987–8.

Table 12.5. Average size of outright Fed purchases

	1986	1987–1988 H1
Treasury bills	2.0	[a]
Coupon securities	1.3	3.0

a   Bill purchases temporarily suspended due to supply shortage. US Treasury was reducing the stock of outstanding Treasury bills as a policy move to extend the average maturity of the national debt.

Outright purchases may be either external purchases in the open market or internal purchases from foreign official accounts.

Internal purchases (Fed buying from foreign official accounts)

The Fed frequently makes small (e.g. $100 m. to $500 m.) internal purchases, buying Treasury securities from foreign official accounts. The selling foreigner normally intends to put the cash proceeds back into the commercial banking system, e.g. a central bank intervening to support its currency by selling dollars on the foreign exchange market, or the World Bank dispensing a loan via payment into the recipient's commercial bank account. Thus internal purchases normally result in inflating US bank reserves.

Internal purchases in a particular Thursday to Wednesday period are shown only in the Fed statistics released on the following Thursday evening. By contrast external purchases (larger but less frequent) are announced as they occur.

Choice of reserve-adding methods

Customer repos are normally used for temporary add-needs below $1·5 bn and system repos (possibly mixed with customer repos) above $1·5 bn. Term repos will probably be included if add-needs exceed $3 bn. Outright purchases will be used if the Fed anticipates a need to add reserves permanently (or at a minimum to meet a large add-need extending over more than one statement-fortnight).

Reserve draining

The Fed can drain reserves by one of the following methods:

1. Matched sale (reverse system repo). The Fed sells securities to a dealer, simultaneously agreeing to buy them back overnight or in a few days' time at an agreed price.
2. Outright Treasury bill sale. (The Fed does not sell notes or bonds outright because it never needs to drain permanently. A Treasury bill sale is not really a permanent drain because liquidity returns to the commercial banking system in a relatively short time when the Treasury bill matures.)
3. Selling Treasury bills to foreign customer account.
4. Rolling off a proportion of Fed holdings of Treasury bills as each issue matures.

Matched sales

The Fed sells securities to a dealer on repo, simultaneously agreeing to repurchase at a specified price and date. Reserves are temporarily drained when the dealer pays for the securities by transferring cash from his bank deposit to the Fed. Reserves are automatically replenished when repurchase day arrives; the Fed gets the security back and pays by crediting the dealer's bank's account.

Rolling off Treasury bill holding

The Fed holds a portion of each existing Treasury bill issue. An issue matures every Thursday. For example, if the Fed holds $3 bn of the maturing issue but invests only $2 bn in the new issue, then Fed holdings of Treasury securities fall $1 bn, draining reserves by $1 bn.

Fed open-market operations in 1986–7

Fed open-market operations added $30 bn to bank reserves in 1986 and
$10 bn in 1987. As usual, lasting reserve additions came mainly from
outright purchases but the vast majority of Fed transactions were
temporary and self-reversing transactions (repos and matched sales) (see
Tables 12.6–12.8).

Table 12.6. Fed open-market activity ($bn), 1986–7

	1986		1987	
Volume of transactions (1986)	Gross	Net[a]	Gross	Net[a]
Outright	28	20	53	21
Repos	393	11	801	−11
Matched sales	1,855	−1	1,902	0
Net impact on reserves	n.a.	30	n.a.	10

a   Equals net impact on reserves (see Table 12.7).

Table 12.7. Fed open-market operations: net purchase of securities ($bn)

	1986	1987
Outright purchases : Bills	23	19
: Notes and bonds	1	18
Outright sales : (Bills only)	−3	−7
Redemption of securities held by Fed	−1	−9
Repos	11[a]	−11
Matched sales	−1[b]	0
	30	10
a Gross purchases by Fed	202	395[c]
Repurchases by seller	−191	−406
	11	−11
b Gross matched sales by Fed	−928	951
Repurchases by Fed	927	951
	−1	0

c   In addition Fed arranged $155 bn gross of customer (official foreign) repos.

Table 12.8. Monthly change in Fed holdings of US Treasury and agency securities ($bn), 1987

Jan.	−10
Feb.	−9
Mar.	2
Apr.	25
May	−14
June	5
July	−4
Aug.	−1
Sept.	4
Oct.	8
Nov.	1
Dec.	3
Total	10

NB   Strong seasonal influences, e.g. massive Fed purchases in April to relieve liquidity shortage caused by heavy tax payments around 15 April personal income tax payment deadline.

13 Fed watching

Introduction

Significance of Fed watching

In the old days Fed watching was extremely significant, because the bond market invariably reacted in the 'right' direction to any Fed policy change. Fed easing produced lower short-term interest rates and lower long-term interest rates and a rise in bond prices. Conversely, Fed tightening produced a fall in bond prices.

These days investors are more sophisticated. If a Fed easing appears unjustified, it can swiftly raise inflationary expectations and demoralise the bond market. For example, long bond yields actually rose from 7·15% and 7·65% and long bond prices fell 5% in three days after the April 1986 discount rate cut. Thus economic analysis has become relatively more important, and Fed policy nuance-chasing less important.

What Fed watchers watch

There are three areas that signal Fed policy:

1. Fed open-market operations (often the first clue to a policy shift).
2. The federal funds interest rate.
3. Fed policy statements (e.g. governors' speeches; Chairman's Congressional testimony).

Significance of open-market operations

Fed policy shift: increasing the borrowing target

Suppose the US dollar is weak, the economy robust and inflation accelerating. The Fed tightens by squeezing the supply of non-borrowed reserves and increasing the proportion of reserves which are only supplied at the discount window ('increasing the borrowing target').

Impact of squeeze on non-borrowed reserves

If total non-borrowed reserves in the system are inadequate to meet banks' total reserve requirements, some banks will eventually be forced to the discount window. However, banks are reluctant to use the discount window too frequently. Thus they will initially react to a reserve shortfall by trying to borrow off each other in the Fed funds market. This raises the Fed funds interest rate.

Perspective for judging the significance of Fed operations

The following aspects should be taken into consideration:

1. Type of operation. A tightening Fed may do a matched sale when no intervention appeared necessary, or do a customer repo instead of a (larger) system repo. An easing Fed may do nothing when draining is expected, or add reserves when no intervention is expected.
2. Size of operation. For example, $5 bn repos when $3 bn had appeared sufficient can indicate easing.
3. Fed funds interest rate. With stable Fed policy, Fed funds will usually establish a 'normal' trading range. The Fed will normally drain when Fed funds are near the bottom of the range and supply when Fed funds are at the top. The Fed may then signal a policy change by intervening at a different level. For example, if the trading range has been 6·5% to 7%, the Fed might:
   (a) signal policy easing by not draining till Fed funds fell to 6·25%;
   (b) signal tightening by draining with Fed Funds still at 6·75%.
4. Timing of operation. The Fed sometimes deliberately mistimes its intervention to signal a policy change. For example, if an add-need is concentrated in the period Monday to Wednesday, the Fed may signal a policy easing by doing the necessary repos on the prior Thursday or Friday. Deliberate mistiming can influence market sentiment and assist the Fed in pushing interest rates in the desired direction.

Spotting a policy change

Suppose the Fed raises its borrowed reserve target by $2 bn when there is a $3 bn add-need. The Fed now sees an open-market add-need of only $1 bn (since the other $2 bn will be supplied from the discount window). However, market estimates still show the Fed needing to supply $3 bn.

If the add-need is evenly distributed throughout a reserve period (starting on the Thursday) the market will expect 3 bn system repos on the Thursday and Friday. However, the Fed now wishes to add only $1 bn on average. It may therefore add nothing on the Thursday and add only $2 bn on the Friday.

The market must now guess if the Fed is supplying fewer non-borrowed reserves because it has raised its borrowing target, or if the basic add-need is in fact smaller than the market had estimated.

Difficulties in diagnosing Fed intervention

There are large errors even in the Fed's own reserve forecasts. In 1987 the Fed's own estimate of changes in reserve factors erred by $100 m. even on the last day of each statement fortnight, and by $1,200 m. on the first day. $1,200 m. equals the reserve impact of five average overnight system repos.

Market estimates of reserve-adding (or draining) need are normally much more inaccurate than the Fed's estimates. Thus unexpected activity may reflect market forecasting error rather than Fed policy change.

The Fed typically changes its borrowing target in small stages. It is not easy to determine, in the context of large forecasting errors, if a $2 bn customer repo (instead of the expected $1 bn) might reflect a $50 m. drop in the borrowing target. A single overnight repo of $1 bn raises reserves by a daily average of only $71 m. (1,000 ÷ 14) in a 14-day reserve maintenance period.

Hazards in interpreting the Thursday data on discount window borrowing

The following factors may make it difficult to interpret discount window borrowing figures:

1. Banks can go to the discount window voluntarily and not solely in response to Fed policy changes. Thus a change in borrowings may indicate a change in fund management policy in the banking system rather than a change in Fed policy.
2. The Fed may have misestimated the movement in other reserve factors. If, in consequence, the Fed has inadvertently undersupplied (or oversupplied) non-borrowed reserves, discount window borrowings will be distorted in the opposite direction.
3. It can be a mistake to deduce too much from a single borrowing number. Indeed the Fed can have problems hitting its borrowing target for a number of consecutive weeks.

4. The Fed's normal target is average borrowings for a full two-week reserve maintenance period. Sometimes borrowing in the first week will be so far off target that it is impracticable to ratchet borrowings sharply in the opposite direction to achieve the desired average for the full two weeks. The Fed may then settle for hitting the target in the second week alone. In this case the two-week average will look very different from the target but the difference will not be a policy indication.

Federal funds watching

In general, deducing Fed policy from discount window borrowing changes is so difficult that better results are often obtained from the (simpler) procedure of watching the Fed funds interest rate, and allowing for erratic movements which can occur:

(a) at times of seasonal pressure (e.g. commercial banks' year-end window dressing);

(b) in the last day or two of the two-week reserve maintenance period (when the scramble to match actual and required reserves becomes most intense); and

(c) at times of market panic over possible bank failures.

What the Fed says

Fed Governors' speeches

Governors' speeches can be used for kite-flying; for example in 1987 they were the first indication that the Fed was looking at commodity prices as a criterion for monetary policy. A more comprehensive list of 'useful' policy criteria was given by Fed Vice-Chairman Manuel Johnson on 25 February 1988: 'Information contained in the term structure of interest rates (the yield curve), the foreign exchange market and certain broad indices of commodity prices.'

Chairman's Congressional testimony

This is usually a collection of platitudes ('we will foster growth but resist inflation'). However, the accompanying monetary targets and economic forecasts sometimes do mean something. For example, Chairman Greenspan's testimony in February 1988 combined:

(a) low economic forecasts for real GNP (+ 2 to 2.5) and inflation (+3 to 4)

(b)   a lowering of 1988 money growth targets (to 4–8% p.a. for M-2 and M-3 from their provisional range of 5–8% p.a.).

This *combination* implied that the Fed would find mild economic deceleration acceptable.

Perspectives for judging Fed policy

Fed operations should not be categorised uncritically

It is common for any Fed-induced rise in interest rates to be described as policy tightening and any Fed-induced fall in interest rates to be described as easing. However, this is not always true, as the following examples demonstrate:

1.   Rising rates and easy money coincided in 1978. A policy of inadequate gentle interest rate rises in 1978 while inflation soared was really policy easing since it allowed continued money acceleration and further inflation build-up. Indeed, Fed Chairman Miller gave the game away by boasting to a Congressional committee that he had tightened monetary policy without reducing housing starts!
2.   In early 1988 the Fed funds rate rose 50 basis points (described as Fed policy tightening) between January and June. However, in January the consensus expectation was sharp economic slowdown (or even recession) and peaking of inflation. By June the economy was still buoyant and commodity prices soaring. To raise interest rates 0·5% while inflationary expectations rise 1% is not tightening but loosening.
3.   The reverse situation occurred in early 1986. Fed interest rate cuts lagged behind the fall in inflationary expectations so that policy was really becoming tighter and produced a nine-month economic slowdown starting in spring 1986.

Fed minutes

The minutes of each FOMC meeting are released about six weeks after the meeting. Thus they are too outdated to give direct indications on current policy. However they can provide useful illumination on the general drift of Fed thinking: has recent Fed discussion been evenly balanced between tightening and loosening? Or was there a bias to ease (as in the example on page 32)? Or to tightening?

The FOMC policy vote reveals the size of the dissenting minority. In addition, the minutes can give clues as to the extent to which Fed members voting for the majority policy may have reservations; a particular viewpoint may be described as having been argued by 'a member', 'a few members' or 'several members'.

Another valuable clue is the order in which the minutes cite the Fed's criteria for policy assessment (see Table 13.1). For example, in early 1988 the Fed gave top priority to not damaging fragile confidence in the financial markets (in the aftermath of Black Monday). In June the Fed promoted inflation to public enemy No. 1. The dollar exchange rate and nominal money supply growth still ranked very low, as influences on Fed policy, in contrast to March 1987 when exchange rate and money supply were cited as the two principal influences.

Table 13.1. Order of FOMC policy criteria 1988

	Jan.–May	June	August
1.	Financial market conditions	Inflation	Inflation
2.	Real economy	Real economy	Real economy
3.	Inflation	Exchange rate	Money supply
4.	Exchange rate	Financial market conditions	Exchange rate

Tests of tight money

The following may be taken as criteria for judging whether monetary policy is tight:

1. Genuinely tight money is never painless. Howls of anguish don't guarantee policy is tight, but an absence of howls usually means policy is easy.
2. Tightening requires interest rates to rise faster than inflationary expectations.
3. Real money tightening is likely to be accompanied by confirmatory signs from the secondary money indicators (see page 60) and will eventually be reflected in a slowdown in the real economy.
4. Once inflationary expectations have become firmly embedded they are seldom shifted by a small temporary rise in interest rates. Reversing a major build-up of inflationary momentum may require a *minimum* of three to six months' economic austerity.

Mild tightening is most likely to be effective if it comes early, if inflationary expectations are subdued, and if private-sector debt ratios are high, so that the economy is abnormally sensitive to a rise in interest rates.

14   Budget watching

Economic significance

Big budget deficits threaten the bond market because they:

(a)   increase the supply of bonds;
(b)   produce an overall shortage of savings in the economy (unless private savings are adequate to finance both the government deficit and private-sector credit demand);
(c)   are likely, sooner or later, to be financed by inflationary money printing; and
(d)   imply a need for future tax increases, which will reduce the after-tax yield from bonds.

Budget deficits and the economic cycle

Budget deficits can normally be financed without difficulty when the economy is in recession and private-sector credit demand is weak. However, if the budget deficit remains high during an economic boom, trouble is virtually inevitable.

A drop in the budget deficit will normally benefit the bond market only if it reflects a genuine tightening in underlying budget discipline. A temporarily lower deficit which simply reflects temporarily surging tax revenues as the economy moves into economic boom will not be much help. Its temporary impact in reducing government borrowing will normally be more than offset by a boomtime explosion in private borrowing.

Figure 14.1 attempts to distinguish between changes in the underlying budget deficit trend and temporary fluctuations which simply reflect short-term swings in the economy. The 'cyclically adjusted deficit' is an estimate of what the deficit would be if the economy grew at a steady rate without violent fluctuations into recession or unsustainable boom. The cyclically adjusted deficit is thus lower than the reported deficit during a recession (1982) but higher at the peak of a boom (1979, 1988).

The cyclically adjusted deficit may rise during an economic boom even though the reported deficit is falling gently, as in 1983–4. This is a danger sign. The reported budget deficit must fall rapidly during economic boom to offset credit strains from escalating private borrowing.

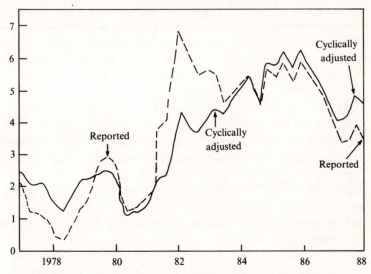

Fig. 14.1 US budget deficit as percentage of GNP (years plotted at Q1). Cyclically adjusted deficit shows estimated deficit if unemployment remained at constant 7.4%. The cyclically adjusted deficit has recently exceeded the reported deficit because the economy is currently (temporarily) above its long-term trend. Cyclically adjusted deficit in early 1988 was higher than before Black Monday, despite all the propaganda about the deficit-cutting budget compromise. Source: St Louis Fed.

The total savings picture

Budget deficits in context

High budget deficit matched by high private-sector savings (the usual situation in a recession) need not produce financial market strains. Conversely, a reduction in the budget deficit which does not increase total savings will do nothing to reduce interest rates. For example, to increase government spending by $20 bn and then raise capital gains tax (largely paid out of savings) by $25 bn might reduce the budget deficit, but could also reduce overall savings and raise interest rates.

The Reagan Tax Reform Act of 1986 is a cautionary tale. Even if it had been 'revenue-neutral', as originally claimed, it could have increased interest rates because it handed out $30 bn p.a. to consumers (low savers) and removed $30 bn p.a. from corporations (high savers).

Savings impact of budget deficit changes

The bond investor should be most encouraged by *genuine* reductions in government spending. Second best is budget deficit reduction by increases in broadly based consumer taxes (excise taxes or the lower rates of income tax) or withdrawal of tax loopholes which subsidise borrowing (mortgage interest deductibility).

By contrast, bond investors should be downright suspicious of deficit reduction to be achieved by taxes that fall mainly on high savers (corporate tax, capital gains tax and high marginal rates of income tax).

US savings trends since 1960

An overall US savings shortage began to develop in the late 1960s (initially reflecting a drop in corporate savings, consequent on the 1965–74 decline in corporate profitability) and became chronic after 1981. Heavy government dissaving after 1981 (reflecting Reaganomic budget deficits) was not offset by higher personal saving. In fact personal saving fell at the same time (see Fig. 14.2).

A shortage of overall savings will result in some combination of higher interest rates, lower investment and more dependence on borrowing from abroad.

The total US savings shortfall for the years 1960–87 is shown in Fig. 14.3.

International comparisons

German and Japanese budget deficits (both typically around 3% of GNP, a similar figure to that of the US) can be financed with less strain because German and Japanese personal savings ratios are much higher than that of the US (see Table 14.1).

UK experience offers an odd contrast. Extreme fiscal rectitude (the budget actually moved into surplus in 1988) was offset by an even sharper contraction of personal saving so that the overall savings shortfall actually worsened (see Table 14.2). Symptoms included surging imports and sharply rising interest rates in mid-1988.

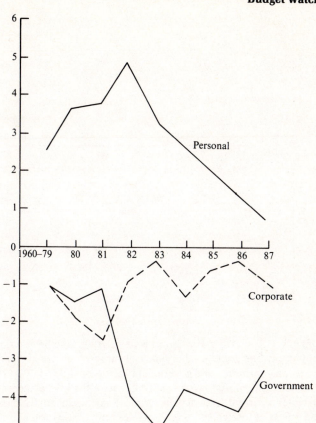

Fig. 14.2 US financial surpluses (gross savings less physical investment).
Source: OECD.

Table 14.1. Savings comparison as % GNP, 1987

	US	Japan	Germany	UK
Government	−3	−1	−2	−2
Personal	3	12	8	4
Combined	0	11	6	2

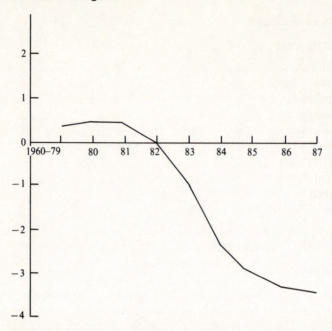

Fig. 14.3 Total US savings surplus or shortfall. The line on the figure represents the grand total of financial surpluses or deficits for US personal, corporate and government sectors as shown in Fig. 14.2. The overall US domestic savings shortfall equals the US balance-of-payments current account deficit, i.e. US savings shortfall is balanced by an inflow of foreign goods and services representing foreign savings.

Table 14.2. Financial surplus as % GNP[a]

	US		UK	
	1980	1987	1980	1987
Personal	4	1	7	0
Government	−1	−3	−4	−2
Corporate	−2	−1	−1	2
Total[b]	1	−3	2	0

Source: OECD.
a   Saving *minus* investment for each sector.
b   Equals (apart from statistical errors) total domestic savings surplus or shortfall = balance-of-payments current-account surplus or deficit.

Budget assessment

Budget forecasts

Official forecasts should be treated with due suspicion since their economic, legislative change and costing assumptions are usually overoptimistic. Congressional Budget Office forecasts are usually more accurate than the administration's.

Press-release glosses can be particularly misleading. The December 1987 'Budget Compromise' (which actually allowed the deficit to increase from $150 bn in 1987 to $160 bn in 1989) was headlined 'Agreement to cut budget deficit by $75 bn in two years'. The 'cuts' were fictitious, being measured not from the 1987 baseline but from spending increases previously legislated for 1988 and 1989.

Moral: Watch the bottom line not the smoke-and-mirrors!

Budget gimmicks

Genuine deficit reduction depends on genuine revenue increases and/or genuine spending cuts. The reported deficit is often massaged down by accounting gimmicks which do nothing to reduce total borrowing. Examples include: selling assets instead of cutting spending, and replacing a specific subsidy (counted in the budget deficit) with a loan guarantee; this increases overall borrowing (by giving the marginally creditworthy priority access to financial markets) but is not counted in the budget deficit till the borrower formally defaults.

The true budget deficit is much higher than reported if one allows for federal agency borrowing and accumulating government guarantees on loans raised by the marginally creditworthy (e.g. Farm Credit Banks, Federal Savings and Loan Insurance Corporation and many private borrowers) as illustrated in Table 14.3.

Table 14.3. US government and government-assisted borrowing ($bn)

	Outstanding end-1987	Change during 1987
Federal govt debt	1,900	+150
Federal govt agencies' debt	600	+100
Private borrowing under express govt guarantee	500	+50
	3,000[a]	+300

Source: US Budget 1989 Special Analyses, Tables F10 and F11.
a   Excludes implied and contingent guarantees (e.g. for farm credit banks, national flood insurance and bank and thrift deposit insurance) and unfunded trust fund obligations, e.g. for social security, benefits and federal employee pensions.

Budget danger signs

The following are useful warning signs for budget watchers:

1. 'Cuts' made by temporarily postponing capital spending (e.g. on roads and sewers) rather than permanently reducing current spending.
2. Slippage in budget timetable.
3. Congressional Appropriations Committees producing total outlay proposals above the supposedly agreed overall target.

15   The US budget process

Budget jargon

Authorisation	Basic law permitting a programme to exist, defining its purpose and usually setting a spending ceiling.
Appropriation	Specific law voting a particular sum of money (future outlays) to be spent on a particular programme over a given time period.
Outlays	Amount actually spent.
Reconciliation	Process of proposing and passing changes in law necessary where current law would lead to spending too high or revenue too low to meet the Congressional Budget Resolution targets.
Gramm–Rudman	Act-of-desperation law passed in 1985 to enforce adherence to budget deficit targets by automatic spending cuts.

Types of spending

Appropriated	There are annual votes on 13 major categories (e.g. defence, energy, agriculture, transportation) which cover about 50% of all spending. Much other spending is permanently funded and not subject to annual votes (e.g. social security benefits, debt interest).
Entitlement	Benefit legally secured to all persons who meet the eligibility requirement, e.g. social security, veterans' benefits.

Relatively uncontrollable Spending that will occur without any new action by Congress, e.g. entitlements, debt interest, permanent appropriations and commitments coming due from budget authority enacted in previous years. Much of this spending is not really uncontrollable. It could be cut given political will and courage.

Congressional budget committees

The following committees are involved in the budget process:

1. The Overall Budget Committee produces overall budget resolution.
2. The House Ways And Means Committee and Senate Finance Committee consider revenue proposals and tax changes. They also supervise spending for social security and medicare (the government programme financing medical care for the old).
3. Authorising Committees (14 in Senate, 18 in House) are the normal Congressional Committees with jurisdiction over particular areas, e.g. defence, education, transportation, etc. They are responsible for proposing changes in law necessary to meet the spending targets in budget resolutions.
4. Appropriations Committees (with 13 appropriations sub-committees) are responsible for proposing legislation to appropriate particular sums of money to be spent on various activities. About 50% of spending proceeds without annual appropriations and is (loosely) supervised by other committees.

Budget vetters

The three official vetters of budget policy are the Congressional Budget Office (CBO), the Office of Management and Budget (OMB) (Administration) and the General Accounting Office (GAO).

Budget timetable for fiscal year 1989

Supposed deadline	Action to be completed
4 January 1988	President sends budget to Congress.
15 February	CBO sends its budget assessment to House and Senate Budget Committees.

25 February	Other Congressional committees send their views on the President's proposals (and their own counterproposals) to the budget committees.
15 April	Congress passes Budget Resolution. This divides permitted outlays between relevant Congressional Authorising Committees and directs them to recommend changes in law sufficient to meet the resolution's outlay targets (thus 'reconciling' current law and the projected budget targets). After passage of Budget Resolution, Congressional Appropriations Committees begin consideration of proposals to appropriate sums of money to fund particular programmes. (House Appropriations Committee starts consideration on 15 May even if a Budget Resolution has not been passed.)
15 June	Congress completes reconciliation legislation (incorporated in a single omnibus Reconcilation Bill).
30 June	House completes annual Appropriations Bills. (House cannot adjourn for more than three days in July, unless the annual appropriations have been passed.)
15 August	CBO sends revised 1989 deficit estimate to President.
25 August	OMB sends deficit estimate to President. If OMB estimates a deficit $10 bn or more above Gramm–Rudman target (allowing *only* for spending programmes or savings *already legislated)* the President must issue preliminary sequester order for automatic spending cuts. Details of cuts must be sent to Congress within 15 days.
September	Congress reviews sequester order, and considers alternative deficit reduction plans.
30 September	Deadline for Senate passage and presidential signature of annual Appropriations Bills.
1 October	1989 fiscal year begins
1 October	If Appropriations Bills have not been passed for any of the 13 appropriations sub-categories, temporary spending authority must be legislated in a continuing resolution (actually a full law

requiring passage by both Houses of Congress and presidential signature). Continuing resolutions specify the permitted expenditure; the specified figure is often based on either the spending level for the prior year or the full Appropriations Bill still under discussion in Congress.

1 October   The President's Gramm–Rudman sequester order nominally takes effect unless Congress has *legislated* an alternative deficit-reduction plan. Sequestered funds are put in escrow, but in practice there is plenty of other money to finance spending this early in the fiscal year.

15 October   OMB sends revised deficit estimate to President. If OMB estimate is still $10 bn over limit, sequester order really takes effect.[a]

15 November   GAO issues compliance report.[b]

Notes

(a) The 15 October sequester order is mandatory under Gramm–Rudman law. Other dates are merely guidelines (mainly from the Congressional Budget Impoundment and Control Act of 1974) and are frequently missed. Reagan sent his 1989 Budget to Congress on 17 February 1988, six weeks after the supposed deadline.

(b) There is now *no* enforcement mechanism for meeting the Gramm–Rudman target ($136 bn for FY 1989) even if GAO reports that sequesters are inadequate.

Tables 15.1 and 15.2 summarise President Reagan's budget proposals for the fiscal year ending 30 September 1990 (submitted to Congress on 10 January 1989).

Table 15.1. Administration proposed budget ($bn) 1989

	1989	1990
Outlays		
Defence	298	303
Social security	232	247
Health	136	147
Debt interest	166	170
Other	316	285
	1,138	1,152

Table 15.1. Continued

	1989	1990
Revenues		
Income tax	425	467
Social insurance contributions	364	392
Corporate tax	107	117
Excise taxes	34	35
Other	46	48
	976	1,059

Table 15.2. Budget deficit summary ($bn)

	1989	1990
On-budget	−218	−161
Off-budget[a]	−56	+68
Total deficit[b]	−162[c]	−93[d]

a Mainly the year's net cash inflow (contributions received less benefits paid out) into certain branches of the social security system.
b The deficit figure to which Gramm–Rudman targets apply.
c Compares with Reagan's February 1988 forecast of $130 bn deficit.
d Most private commentators thought Reagan's 1990 costing was ludicrously optimistic.

Part Three

Analytical methods

16   The mathematics of fixed-interest markets

This chapter outlines compound interest theory and the mathematical basis of bond pricing.

Conventional notation

P = bond price
g = coupon annual rate
y = yield
i = $y \div 200$ (half-yearly interest factor)
v = $1 \div (1 + i)$ (half-yearly discounting factor)
x = $(1 + i)$ (half-yearly compounding factor)
n = number of time periods (normally half-year periods in US Treasury analysis)

PV = present value
FV = future value
$a_{\overline{n}|}$ = discounted present value of a regular stream of equal future payments
S_n = accumulated future value of a regular stream of equal future payments (with these payments reinvested as received and accumulating at compound interest).

The above notation (except for x) is common to many texts.

Compound interest theory

Consider an investment paying a return of 8% per half-year. After the first half-year, an initial investment of 1 will receive interest of 0·08 and will have grown to 1·08.

After the second half-year, further interest equal to 8% of 1·08 is received. The initial investment of 1 has now grown to $1 \times 1·08 \times 1·08 = (1·08)^2 = 1·1664$.

The investment increases by a factor of 1·08 each half-year. After

n half-years, an initial investment of 1 will have increased to $1 \times (1{\cdot}08)^n$. For example, after six half-years, the initial \$1 will have accumulated to $1 \times (1{\cdot}08)^6 = 1{\cdot}587$.

Conversely, the present value (discounted at 8% per half-year) of \$1 receivable in one half-year's time will be $1 \div (1{\cdot}08) = 0{\cdot}926$

Similarly, the discounted PV of \$1 receivable in n half-years will be:

$$PV = 1 \div (1{\cdot}08)^n$$

For example PV of \$1 receivable in 10 half-years is $1 \div (1{\cdot}08)^{10} = 1 \div 2{\cdot}159 = \$0{\cdot}463$.

Algebraic derivations

Compound interest and future value

Consider an investment of 1 receiving interest of $y\%$ per annum, payable half-yearly.

After one half-year the investor receives interest of $y \div 200$ (conventionally denoted as i). The sum invested has increased to $(1 + i)$. Similarly, after n half-years, the sum invested will have increased to $(1 + i)^n$.

Present value

Conversely, the present value of \$1 receivable in one half-year will be $1 \div (1 + i)$. This expression is conventionally denoted by v.

Similarly, the present value of \$1 receivable in n half-years will be:

$$\frac{1}{(1 + i)^n} \quad \text{or} \quad v^n$$

Present value of a regular stream of future payments (annuity certain)

Consider a bond paying a coupon of 1 at regular half-yearly intervals for a period of n half-years.

The present value of the first coupon will be:

$$\frac{1}{(1 + i)} \quad \text{or} \quad v$$

The PV of the second coupon is v^2.

The PV of the nth coupon is v^n.

PV of the total stream of coupons:

$$PV = (v + v^2 + v^3 + \ldots + v^n)$$
$$= v(1 + v + v^2 + \ldots + v^{n-1})$$

$$\therefore \text{PV} = \frac{v\,(1 - v^n)}{(1 - v)}$$

$$= \frac{(1 - v^n)}{(1 + i)\,(1 - v)}$$

$$= \frac{(1 - v^n)}{(1 + i)\,\left(1 - \dfrac{1}{1 + i}\right)}$$

$$= \frac{(1 - v^n)}{(1 + i) - 1}$$

$$\therefore \text{PV} = \frac{(1 - v^n)}{i}$$

Annuity certain

The expression $(v + v^2 + \ldots + v^n)$ is known actuarially as an *annuity certain* and is conventionally denoted a_n:

$$a_n = \frac{(1 - v^n)}{i}$$

Present value (price) of bond

The price (= present value) equals PV of capital redemption at par on maturity, plus PV of future half-yearly coupons

PV (capital) = $100\,(v^n)$, assuming n half-years to maturity.

PV (coupons) = (Annuity certain for n periods) × (half annual coupon)

$$= a_{\overline{n}}\,(g \div 2)$$

$$\therefore \text{Bond price} = P = 100v^n + \frac{g}{2}(a_{\overline{n}})$$

The future value of a regular stream of equal payments (S_n)

Consider a bond paying interest of $1 half-yearly. Each time the investor receives a coupon he reinvests it, and allows the proceeds to accumulate until the original bond matures in n half-years' time (see Table 16.1). The assumed reinvestment rate is known as the *roll-up rate* and the half-yearly compounding factor is designated by x in Table 16.1.

Table 16.1. Future value of coupons at time (n) when bond matures

Number of coupon[a]	Accumulated future value of coupon at end of period n[b]
1	x^{n-1}
2	x^{n-2}
...3	... x^{n-3}
$n-2$	x^2
$n-1$	x
n (at maturity)	1
Grand total	$1 + x + \ldots + x^{n-1}$

a Identified by time period at end of which coupon is paid.
b For example, coupon number 1 accumulates (is multiplied by x) for $(n-1)$ periods until bond matures at end of period n. Similarly, coupon 2 accumulates for $(n-2)$ periods.

Accumulated value of all coupons (S_n)

$$S_n = (1 + x + x^2 + \ldots + x^{n-1})$$
$$= \frac{(x^n - 1)}{(x - 1)}$$

Or, $S_n = \dfrac{(1 + j)^n - 1}{j}$

Where j = assumed roll-up rate $\div$ 200
$x = 1 + j$ = half-yearly compounding factor
For example, if roll-up rate is 12% p.a., $j = 0.06$ and $x = 1.06$.

Future value of bond

$$FV = 100 + \frac{g}{2}(S_n)$$

Or, $FV = 100 + \dfrac{g\left((1 + j)^n - 1\right)}{2j}$

17   Yield and return calculations

Introduction

This chapter outlines definitions, uses and calculation methods for the principal yield and performance measures:

1. Flat yield.
2. Redemption yield.
3. Accumulated return.
4. Performance yield.
5. Net yield.

Flat yield

Flat yield is a simple measure of the income from a bond (without allowing for capital gains) and is defined as

> Flat yield = Bond's nominal annual coupon ÷ Bond price
> *Example*
> Bond coupon rate   12
> Bond price   95
> Flat yield   12·6%   (12 ÷ 95 expressed as a percentage)

Gross redemption yield (GRY)

This is a measure which allows for both the flat yield and the eventual capital gain (or loss) arising if the bond is held to maturity (see next section for a formal definition). If the bond price is below par, implying a capital gain to maturity, redemption yield will exceed flat yield.

US Treasury yield convention

US Treasury bonds pay interest half-yearly. Annual yields are conventionally quoted at twice the yield for a half-year. For example, a quoted yield of 10% per annum on a Treasury bond actually means a true yield of 5% per half-year. The true yield for one year is actually slightly higher since the investor can earn additional interest from reinvesting the mid-year coupon (see Table 17.1).

Table 17.1. Conventional and true annual yield (illustration with bond price 100, bond coupon 10%)

Estimate of true annual yield	
Mid-year coupon	5
Additional interest	0.25[a]
Year-end coupon	5
Estimated true annual yield	10.25

Conventionally quoted annual yield = 10.00
a   Six months' interest from mid-year to year-end from reinvesting the mid-year coupon at an assumed rate of 10% p.a.

A comparative table of conventionally quoted annual Treasury yields and true annual yields is given in Appendix 5. This book follows (under protest) the convention, which is also used in the UK gilts market.

Return difference between annual and semi-annual compounding

Over long periods the difference between annual and semi-annual compounding becomes very significant. For example, consider $1 compounding:

(a) at 10% per annum for 20 years.
     Value after 20 years = $(1 \cdot 10)^{20}$ = $6·73;
(b) at 5% per half-year for 40 half-years.
     Value after 20 years = $(1 \cdot 05)^{40}$ = $7·04.

The difference of $0·31 is over 30% of the original one dollar and almost 5% of the final amount.

Gross redemption yield (GRY)

Formal definition

GRY is the interest rate at which the bond's price equals the discounted present value of all the bond's future payments (income plus capital repayment on maturity) (see Fig. 17.1).

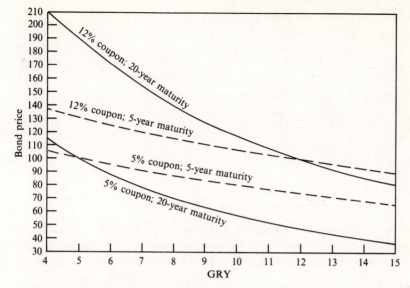

Fig. 17.1 GRY and bond price.

GRY is also the total return to maturity that would be achieved from capital repayment and coupons, *if* all coupons could be reinvested at GRY for the remaining period to maturity.

Note
The redemption yield is *not* a guaranteed return over the lifetime of the bond, since the interest rate at which future coupons can be reinvested is not guaranteed.

Algebraic formula to calculate bond price from GRY

$$P = 100v^n + \frac{g}{2} a_{\overline{n}|}$$

or $$P = 100 v^n + \frac{g(1 - v^n)}{2i}$$

Example of calculation
Coupon: 6%
Maturity: 8 years (= 16 half-years)
GRY: 10%
$g = 6$
$n = 16$
$i = \cdot 05$

$$v = 1 \div 1 \cdot 05 = 0 \cdot 9524$$

$$v^n = v^{16} = 0 \cdot 4581$$

$$P = 100\, v^n + \frac{g\,(1 - v^n)}{2i}$$

$$= 100\,(0 \cdot 4581) + \frac{6(1 - 0 \cdot 4581)}{0 \cdot 10}$$

$$= 45 \cdot 81 + \frac{6\,(0 \cdot 5419)}{0 \cdot 1}$$

$$= 45 \cdot 81 + 32 \cdot 51$$

$$= 78.32$$

Calculating GRY from price

There is no mathematical formula. An accurate GRY can be attained (preferably by computer) only by some iterative process (i.e. trial-and-error involving successive approximations to the true answer).

The rule-of-thumb approximation for estimating GRY from price
GRY $\approx$ Adjusted flat yield (based on a price half-way between the bond's actual price and par) plus annual capital gain.

$$\therefore \text{GRY} \approx \frac{\text{Coupon} \times 200}{(100 + P)} + \frac{(100 - P)}{(\text{Years to Maturity})}$$

The rationale for the approximation is as follows. The income component of GRY approximates to the coupon divided by the *average* price of the bond over its remaining life (which will be roughly half-way between par and its current price). The capital gain approximates to the annual appreciation or depreciation of the bond price towards par.

Example A
Bond price 112·58
Coupon   15%
Maturity   6 years

$$\text{Approx. GRY} = \frac{15 \times 200}{100 + 112 \cdot 58} + \frac{100 - 112 \cdot 58}{6}$$

$$= \frac{3{,}000}{212 \cdot 58} - \frac{12 \cdot 58}{6}$$

$$= 14 \cdot 11 - 2 \cdot 10$$

$$= 12 \cdot 01$$

True GRY $= 12 \cdot 00$

Example B
Bond price 82·8
Coupon   9%
Maturity   10 years

$$\text{Approx. GRY} = \frac{9 \times 200}{(100 + 82·8)} + \frac{100 - 82·8}{10}$$
$$= 9·85 + 1·72$$
$$= 11·57$$

True GRY $= 12·00$

Caution
This approximation becomes increasingly inaccurate the further a bond price is from par, particularly if the bond is priced *well below* par. For example, if a six year bond has a coupon of 10%, the rule-of-thumb approximate GRY will be at least 10 basis points too low if the bond price is outside a range of 95 to 115 (corresponding to a GRY range of 7% to 11·2%). Figure 17.2 illustrates this inaccuracy.

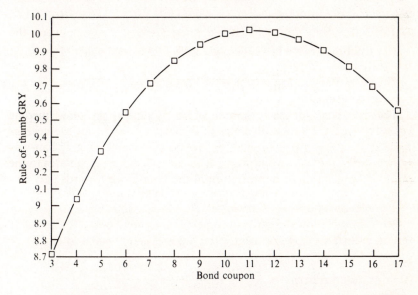

Fig. 17.2 Inaccuracy of rule-of-thumb method: 6-year bond, true GRY 10% with different coupon rates. Example: If coupon is 4% (bond price 73·41) the method gives GRY of 9·04%, 96 basis points below true GRY of 10%. However, in this example, for bond prices between 91 and 120 (equivalent to coupon rates between 8% and 14·5%) the error is less than 15 basis points (rule-of-thumb GRY between 9·85% and 10·02% compared with true GRY of 10%).

Illustration of redemption yield

To assist in illustrating how GRY combines income and capital gain in a measure of total return, Table 17.2 shows the prices of two bonds at different maturities, in each case assuming GRY of 12%.

Table 17.2. Bond prices at GRY of 12%

Years to maturity	Bond A Coupon 4%	Bond B Coupon 16%
10	54·12	122·94
9·5	55·37	122·32
9	56·69	121·66

Consider the total return from holding the 4% bond while its maturity shortens from 10 years to 9·5 years. During this period:

(a)   a half-yearly coupon of 2·0 is received;
(b)   the bond's price (assuming a constant GRY of 12%) rises from 54·12 to 55·37, producing a capital gain of 1·25.

The total return is 3·25 (2·0 income plus 1·25 capital gain). The initial investment was 54·12.

The percentage return = 3·25 ÷ 54·12 = 6% over the half-year = 12% p.a. (conventionally quoted).

Similarly, consider the 16% bond while its maturity shortens from 9.5 years to 9 years. Its total return comes from:

(a)   half-yearly coupon of 8;
(b)   price change from 122·32 to 121·66 (capital loss of 0·66).

Total return = 7·34 (8 income minus 0·66 capital loss).
Percentage return over half-year = 7·34 ÷ 122·32 = 6%.

Both examples illustrate the maxim: if I buy a bond on a GRY of x and sell on a GRY of x, my return for the holding period will also be x.

Accumulated return

Accumulated return is the total compound rate of return (to a bond's maturity) allowing for:

(a)   capital redemption on maturity;
(b)   coupon receipts; and
(c)   estimated income from reinvesting each coupon as received for the time remaining till the bond matures.

The 'roll-up' rate and income from reinvested coupons

The income from reinvested coupons depends on the 'roll-up' rate at which the coupons can be reinvested. Accumulated returns will be higher or lower than GRY, depending on whether the roll-up rate is higher or lower than GRY.

Formula for accumulated returns (future value of bond)

$$FV = 100 + \frac{g}{2} \cdot S_n$$

$$\text{or } FV = 100 + \frac{g\left((1 + j)^n - 1\right)}{2j}$$

Where j = Assumed roll-up rate (% p.a.) $\div$ 200

> *Example: Calculation of accumulated returns*
>
> | | | |
> |---|---|---|
> | Bond coupon: | 10% | $(g = 10; g \div 2 = 5)$ |
> | Bond maturity: | 8 years | $(n = 16)$ |
> | Assumed roll-up rate: | either 6% | $(j = 0\cdot03)\ S_{16} = 20\cdot157$ |
> | | or 10% | $(j = 0\cdot05)\ S_{16} = 23\cdot657$ |
>
> If roll-up rate is 6%:
> $$FV = 100 + 5S_n = 100 + 5(20\cdot157) = 200\cdot8$$
>
> If roll-up rate is 10%:
> $$FV = 100 + 5S_n = 100 + 5(23\cdot657) = 218\cdot3$$

Table 17.3 shows a method of converting accumulated return calculations to an annual rate.

Table 17.3. Expressing accumulated returns at an annual rate

	Case 1	Case 2
Bond maturity (years)	8	8
Bond coupon	10%	10%
Roll-up rate	6%	10%
FV (after 16 half-years)	200·8	218·3
PV (current price)	90[a]	90
Total performance[b]	2·231	2·425
Half-yearly compounding factor[c]	1·0515	1·057
Half-yearly yield	5·15	5·7
Annual yield (conventional)	10·3%	11·4%

a   Current price assumed for purposes of illustration.
b   Performance = future value $\div$ present value.
c nth (16th) root of performance.

Differing roll-up rates can produce big variations in accumulated returns. This variability increases:

(a) the longer the life of the bond. For example, in Fig. 17.3 the accumulated returns for the 5% bond differ by 0·6% p.a. on a bond life of five years and by 2·7% p.a. on a bond life of 20 years;

(b) the higher the coupon on the bond. In Fig. 17.3 at ten-year maturity the annual accumulated returns are 9·1 and 10·4 for the 5% bond, but 8·8 and 10·6 for the 10% bond.

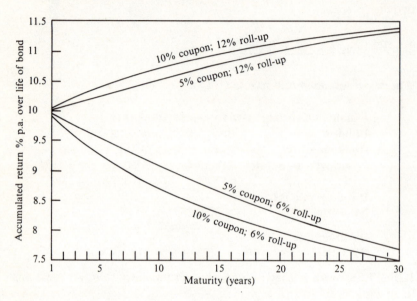

Fig. 17.3 Accumulated returns: initial GRY 10%, differing roll-up rate.
Note: Accumulated return is close to GRY for short maturities, but tends toward roll-up rate for long maturities. Accumulated return varies less for the lower-coupon bond where the guaranteed non-variable capital gain to maturity forms a higher proportion of total accumulated return.

Roll-up rate assumption and portfolio selection

Simply picking the highest GRY from two bonds of the same maturity is no guarantee of the best accumulated return since it may mean buying the higher coupon bond just when interest rates are about to fall. In this case the low coupon bond might outperform since its accumulated return is less sensitive to a reduction in the roll-up rate at which coupons can be reinvested.

Performance yield

Performance yield is a convenient (but not universally used) term to describe the total return (flat yield plus capital gain) from holding a bond over a particular period.

Principle of calculation

Performance yield is calculated similarly to GRY. However, there are two differences:

1. 'Maturity' is the period between purchase and sale (or valuation).
2. 'Redemption value' is the sale or valuation price (instead of par).

> *Example of calculation*
> 10% bond bought at 88·5
> Sold at 97, three years later.
> Performance yield is calculated from the relationship:
> Initial price = Discounted PV of (future bond price + future coupons)
> $$\therefore 88\cdot5 = 97v^6 + 5a_{\overline{6}|}$$
> $97v^6$ is the PV (at purchase date) of the future sales proceeds.
>
> $5a_6$ is the PV of six half-yearly coupon payments, each of 5.
>
> The equation is a variant of the GRY formula and must also be solved iteratively. In this case:
> $$88\cdot5 = 97v^6 + 5a_{\overline{6}|}$$
> $$= 97v^6 + \frac{5(1 - v^n)}{i}$$
> Whence
> $v = 0\cdot9346$
> $1 + i = v^{-1} = 1\cdot07$
> $i = 0\cdot07$ (half-year basis)
> Performance yield = 14% p.a.

This performance yield incorporates both the initial flat yield of 11·3% (10 ÷ 88·5) and allowance for the capital gain from 88·5 to 97 over three years.

Calculating performance yields from conventional GRY yield tables or calculators

Bond price and coupon must be adjusted since such tables assume a redemption price of par.

Example:
10% bond bought at 96
Sold two years later at 103
The results of the calculation are shown in Table 17.4.

Table 17.4. Illustrating adjustment to calculator entries when calculating performance yield

	True situation	Calculator entry
FV	103	100
PV	96	93·2 (96 ÷ 1·03)
Coupon	10	9·71 (10 × 93·2 ÷ 96)

In both cases initial flat yield is 9·71%, and capital gain is 7·29%. In both cases yield to redemption is 13·71%.

Accrued interest and yield calculations

True flat yield
A bond buyer must also pay for accrued interest which is effectively dead money (yielding no return) until it is repaid to him on the next coupon date. Suppose a 12% bond is priced at 95, with two months' accrued interest. The buyer pays 97 (95 capital + 2 accrued interest). His true initial flat yield is thus only 12·4% (12 ÷ 97) and not 12·6% (12 ÷ 95). True flat yield and quoted flat yield equalise on coupon payment date, when the bond trades with zero accrued interest.

Accrued interest impact on GRY
Even a bond trading at par has a GRY slightly lower than coupon rate except on an actual coupon payment date. However, the difference becomes significant only if bond life is very short. Moreover, at very short maturities the accrued interest effect is partly offset by the compound interest opportunities.

For example, the buyer of a 12% bond with two months to maturity (and four months' accrued interest) has a true flat yield of 11·54% (12 ÷ 104) (see Table 17.5). However, the two-month-bond buyer has three opportunities to compound his interest within six months. Allowing for this, his true yield on a six-monthly basis is:

$$\left[\left(\frac{106}{104}\right)^3 - 1\right] \times 200 = \left[1·0588 - 1\right] \times 200 = 11·76\%$$

Other peculiarities may significantly affect true yield at ultra-short maturities. Be wary of buying bonds maturing on a Saturday. You won't get paid till Monday!

Table 17.5. How accrued interest effect lowers GRY (illustration with bond coupon 12%; bond price 100)

Bond maturity (years–months)	GRY	GRY with compounding effect
5–0	12·00	
4–9	11·99	
2–0	12·00	
1–9	11·95	
1–6	12·00	
0–9	11·88	
0–6	12·00	12·00
0–5	11·88	11·94
0–4	11·76	11·88
0–3	11·65	11·82
0–2	11·54	11·76
0–1	11·43	11·70

NET YIELD

Yields are usually quoted gross (i.e. before tax). However, net (after-tax) yields can also be calculated.

Example of net flat yield
Coupon   : 12%
Tax rate   : 28%
Bond price : 95
Gross flat yield = $12 \div 95 = 12·6\%$
Net flat yield   = $(12 \times 0·72) \div 95$
                = $8·64 \div 95 = 9·1\%$

Net redemption yield

This is defined as the interest rate at which the bond price equals the discounted present value of *after-tax receipts* from coupon and capital redemption (allowing for both income tax and capital gains tax liability). The GRY formula is :

$$P = 100v^n + \frac{g(1 - v^n)}{2i}$$

Adapted to allow for tax this becomes:

$$P = 100v^n - v^n (100 - P) c + \frac{g(1 - t) (1 - v^n)}{2i}$$

where $c =$ capital gains tax rate (assumed payable when the bond matures).

t = income tax rate

Both c and t are expressed as decimal fractions of unity, e.g. if income tax rate is 28%, $t = 0.28$. If $c = 0$ and $t = 0$, the net yield formula converts back into the GRY formula.

Example of net redemption yield calculation

Bond with 8% coupon and five years to maturity, priced at 94·25. Income tax rate 28%. Capital gains tax rate 15%.

$P = 94.25$

$g = 8$

$n = 10$ (half-years)

$t = 0.28$ (income tax rate)

$c = 0.15$ (capital gains tax rate)

$$P = 100v^n - v^n(100 - P)c + \frac{g\,(1 - t)\,(1 - v^n)}{2i}$$

$$94.25 = 100v^{10} - 0.8625v^{10} + 2.88\,\frac{(1 - v^{10})}{i}$$

Whence, $v^{10} = 0.709$

$v = 0.9662$

$1 + i = 1.035$

$i = 0.035$

Net redemption yield = 3·5% per half-year

= 7% p.a. (conventionally quoted)

GRY for same bond = 9·46%.

Delayed tax payment

In practice, tax is usually paid some time after the coupons and capital gain are received. If the average lag is nine months (to normal personal tax settlement on 15 April of the following calendar year) the conventionally calculated net yield is enhanced by nine months' after-tax interest on the tax liability.

In this case, the additional interest is approximately 7% p.a. (the after-tax yield) for 0.75 years on the tax due.

Annual tax $\approx$ Gross yield minus net yield

= 9·46 − 7

= 2·46

∴ additional interest $\approx$ 0·07 × 0·75 × 2·46

= 0·0525 × 2·46

= 0·13

Thus, in this case the conventionally quoted net redemption yield of 7% approximates to a true net redemption yield of 7·13%.

Net cash-flow yields

Conventional net yield calculations assume an unchanged future tax rate. However, reality may differ. For example, the maximum rate of US income tax fell from 50% in 1986 to 38% in 1987 and 28% in 1988.

A truly precise calculation of a specific bond's worth to a taxed investor requires each future net coupon (after allowing for its own estimated future tax rate) and net capital gain to be discounted individually, at its own estimated future tax rate. Rates of return so calculated are called *net cash-flow yields*.

Income and capital gains tax rates

Income and capital gains are now nominally taxed at the same rates in both the US and the UK. However, this may not always be the case and there may still be an *effectively* lower capital gains tax rate even under current law. For example:

(a)   in the US, a capital gain may be effectively tax free if it can be offset against a capital loss;

(b)   UK inflation-indexing provisions reduce the effective rate of capital gains tax. (Moreover, UK gilts and some other UK fixed-interest securities are exempt from capital gains tax.)

'Modified duration' (known as 'volatility' in the UK gilts market) is a specific measure of a bond price's sensitivity to a change in interest rates. It is closely related to 'Macaulay duration', a measure of a bond's effective life.

Macaulay duration

Concept: the effective life of a bond

A bond price represents the present value of a stream of future payments (coupons plus capital redemption). All but one of the coupons will be received before maturity. Thus a bond's effective life is really shorter than its quoted maturity, which refers only to the date when its capital value is repaid.

Formal definition

Macaulay duration is the weighted average length of time to receipt of a bond's benefits (coupons and capital redemption payment), the weights being the present values of the benefits involved.

Mathematical description of Macaulay duration

Duration (in half-years) = $(\Sigma\, nv^n\, (\text{benefit})) \div$ bond price
Where n = number of periods
     v = discounting factor per period.
A 'period' is the interval between coupon payments. Bond price includes accrued interest.

Example with US Treasury bond (coupon paid half-yearly)
GRY 12% p.a. or 6% per half-year.
v = half-yearly discounting factor
$= 1 \div (1 + i)$
$= 0 \cdot 9434$
Formula measures Macaulay duration in half-years.

Illustrations of Macaulay duration calculation

	Bond A	Bond B
Maturity (years)	2	2
Coupon	6% (3 per half-year)	14% (7)
GRY	12% (6 per half-year)	12% (6)
v	0·9434 (1 ÷ 1·06)	0·9434
Bond price	89·6	103·5

Macaulay duration of A $= [v(3) + 2v^2(3) + 3v^3(3) + 4v^4(3) + 4v^4(100)] \div 89 \cdot 6$ (in half-years)

$= [(0 \cdot 9434)(3) + 2(0 \cdot 8900)(3) + 3(0 \cdot 8396)(3) + 4(0 \cdot 7921)(103)] \div 89 \cdot 6$

$= (2 \cdot 83 + 5 \cdot 34 + 7 \cdot 56 + 326 \cdot 35) \div 89 \cdot 6$

$= 324 \cdot 08 \div 89 \cdot 6$

$= 3 \cdot 82$ half-years

$= 1 \cdot 91$ years

Macaulay duration of B $= [v(7) + 2v^2(7) + 3v^3(7) + 4v^4(107)] \div 103 \cdot 5$

$= 3 \cdot 63$ half-years

$= 1 \cdot 815$ years

Influences on length of duration

Three factors contribute to short duration:

1. Short maturity.
2. A high coupon rate (a higher proportion of a bond's payments are received earlier).
3. A high GRY (distant payments will be more lightly weighted).

Figure 18.1 illustrates this.

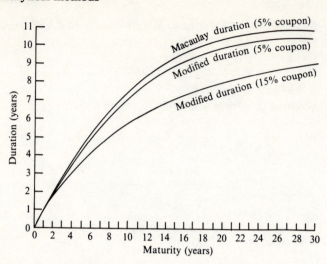

Fig. 18.1 Maturity and duration: illustration with GRY 10%.

Modified duration (volatility)

Definition

Volatility is the proportionate percentage change in bond price caused by a small percentage change in interest rates.

Background

Macaulay proposed his duration formula in 1938. Hicks in 1939 independently developed a formula specifically to relate the percentage price sensitivity (or volatility) of a bond to a change in interest rates (detailed formula on page 130) and found that:

Volatility = v(Macaulay duration)

Where v = discounting factor per period.

Hence volatility in this sense is usually referred to as 'modified duration' in US markets.

Volatility formula for US Treasury bond (two coupons per annum)

$$\begin{aligned} \textit{Modified duration} &= v(\text{Macaulay duration}) \\ &= \text{Macaulay duration} \div (1 + i) \\ &= \text{Macaulay duration} \div 1 + \left(\frac{\text{GRY}}{200}\right) \end{aligned}$$

Since, for a US Treasury bond, i = yield for six months
$$= GRY \div 200$$

Example (bond A on page 123)
GRY = 12% p.a.
$i = 12 \div 200 = 0 \cdot 06$
$1 + i = 1 \cdot 06$

Modified duration = Macaulay duration $\div (1 + i)$
$$= 1 \cdot 91 \div 1 \cdot 06$$
$$= 1.80 \text{ years}$$

Interpretation of example
One would expect a 1% fall in interest rates to raise the bond price by about 1·8%, and a 1% rise in interest rates to lower the bond price by about 1·8%. In fact this is not strictly true since the formula for modified duration (volatility) is based on *infinitesimally small* changes in yield. With a 100 basis points change in interest rates an investor will actually do slightly better than the modified duration implies, *irrespective of whether the interest rate change is up or down* (see 'convexity', page 128).

In the case of bond A (modified duration 1.8 years) a 1% interest rate fall actually raises the bond price by 1·83% (from 89·6 to 91·24) while a 1% interest rate rise lowers the bond price by 'only' 1·77% (from 89·6 to 88·01).

Caution: volatility has two different meanings

The term 'volatility' is used with two different senses:

1. The *specific* sensitivity of a bond price to a change in interest rates (the sense used in this chapter, as measured by 'modified duration').
2. The *general* tendency of bond prices to fluctuate over time (see Appendix 12).

American parlance ('modified duration' rather than 'volatility') reduces confusion between the two senses and is used in this book where ambiguity might arise.

Variability of bond price sensitivity to interest rate changes

Because bonds differ in maturity and coupon rate, the same change in yield can produce widely differing changes in price (see Table 18.1).

Table 18.1. Sensitivity of bond price to changes in interest rates

	Maturity (years)	Bond price with GRY 10%	Bond price with GRY 11%	Price change (%)
5% bond	3	87·31	85·01	−2·6
	10	68·85	64·15	−6·8
	20	57·10	51·86	−9·2
12% bond	3	105·08	102·50	−2·5
	10	112·46	105·98	−5·8
	20	117·16	108·02	−7·8

Influences on modified duration

Three factors tend to increase modified duration:

1. Long maturity (for exceptions see page 230).
2. Low coupon rate.
3. Low GRY.

Figure 18.2 illustrates this.

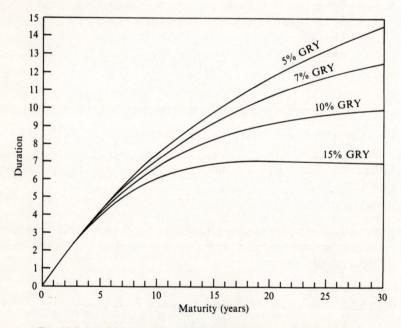

Fig. 18.2 Modified duration and maturity: bond with 7% coupon, varying GRY. Source: Salomon Brothers.

A high coupon bond has a shorter modified duration because more of its return comes from coupons which are paid relatively early. A low coupon bond has a longer modified duration because the eventual capital repayment on maturity forms a higher proportion of its benefits. This is illustrated in Fig. 18.3.

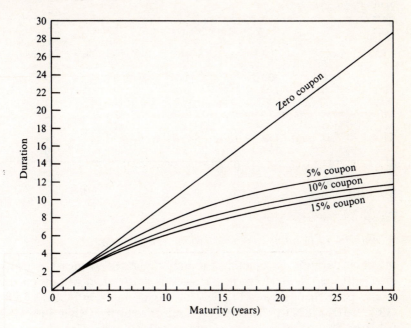

Fig. 18.3 Modified duration and maturity: GRY 7%, varying coupon rates. Source: Salomon Brothers.

Bond prices react more violently to a given interest rate change when GRY is low. This can be seen most clearly in the case of a perpetual bond (see Table 18.2).

Table 18.2. Price of perpetual bond with 4% coupon

Yield %	Price	Bond price change from 1% rise in yield (%)
1	400	−50
2	200	−33
3	133·3	−25
4	100	−20
5	80	−17

The same principle applies to dated bonds. In Table 18.3, if GRY falls by 1% from 10% to 9%, the bond price rises 10·3%; if GRY falls by 1% from 5% to 4%, the bond rises by 15·2%.

Table 18.3. Bond price sensitivity to changes in interest rates (bond with 10% coupon, 30 years to maturity)

GRY	Price	% bond price change from		Modified duration (volatility)	Macaulay duration
		1% fall in GRY	1% rise in GRY		
10	100·00	10·3	−8·7	9·5	9·9
9	110·32	11·1	−9·4	10·2	10·7
8	122·62	12·1	−10·0	11·0	11·4
7	137·42	13·0	−10·8	11·8	12·2
6	155·35	14·1	−11·5	12·7	13·1
5	177·27	15·2	−12·4	13·7	14·0
4	204·28	16·4	−13·2	14·7	15·0

Convexity

Asymmetry of bond price reaction to interest rate change

Modified duration is sometimes loosely described as measuring price reaction to a 1% yield change. However, a 1% yield rise produces a smaller price change than a 1% yield fall. For example, in Table 18.3 a 1% GRY rise from 8% to 9% lowers the bond price by 10% while a 1% GRY fall from 8% to 7% raises the bond price by 12·1%. This discrepancy occurs because the relationship between bond price and GRY is not linear but curved, as can be seen in Fig. 18.4.

The asymmetry increases the sharper the curvature ('convexity') of the graph of bond price against yield, i.e. the more it diverges from a straight line tangent to the bond curve. This effect is particularly marked with a long-maturity zero coupon bond (see Fig. 18.5).

Value of convexity

A range of possible interest rate changes averaging zero, gives a range of possible bond price changes with an average higher than zero (see Table 18.4).

Paying for convexity

With two bonds of equal duration, the bond with higher convexity is the

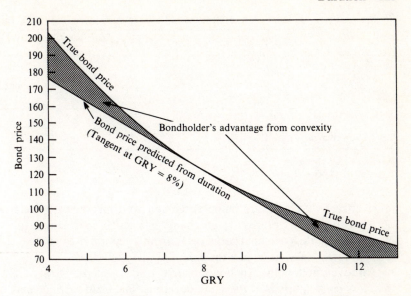

Fig. 18.4 Bond price and convexity: 30-year bond with 10% coupon.

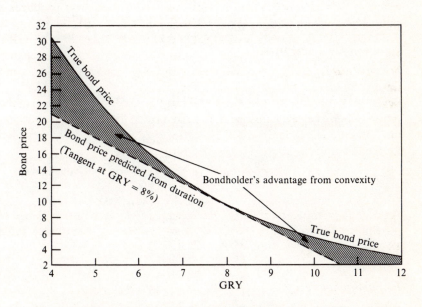

Fig. 18.5 Bond price and convexity: 30-year bond with 0% coupon.

Table 18.4. Sources of bond price performance (10% coupon, 30-year maturity)

	GRY fall from 7% to 6%	GRY rise from 7% to 8%	Average
Modified duration (at GRY 7%)	11·8	−11·8	zero
Convexity	1·2	1·0	1·1
Total price change	13·0	−10·8	1·1
Total GRY change	−1%	+1%	zero

Average GRY change   : zero
Average bond price change : +1·1%

more attractive. However, the potential benefit from convexity (relative outperformance if interest rates change) is small in relation to the possible absolute losses that could result from a general rise in the level of interest rates, or even from a reshaping of the yield curve.

Moreover, high-convexity bonds usually trade on slightly lower GRYs than less convex bonds of the same duration. The yield sacrifice may be worthwhile only in an unstable market. Convexity brings no benefit unless interest rates change (and then stay changed).

Formula for modified duration (volatility)

$$\text{Modified duration} = \frac{v^2}{2P}\left(100nv^{n-1} + \frac{g}{2}\left[\frac{1-v^n}{(1-v)^2} - \frac{nv^n}{(1-v)}\right]\right)$$

(proof in Appendix 9).

Example

11% bond, with 15 years to maturity. Price 93·118. GRY: 12%.

Values in formula:
P = 93·118
n = 30 (half-years)
g = 11 (coupon)
i = 0·06 (yield on half-year basis)
v = $1 \div (1 + i)$
  = $1 \div (1·06)$
  = 0·9434

$1-v$ = 0·0566
$(1-v)^2$ = 0·0032
v^2 = 0·89
v^{29} = 0·1846
v^{30} = 0·1741

$$\text{Modified duration} = \frac{v^2}{2P}\left(100nv^{n-1} + \frac{g}{2}\left[\frac{1-v^n}{(1-v)^2} - \frac{nv^n}{(1-v)}\right]\right)$$

$$= \frac{0\cdot89}{2\times93\cdot118}\left(3000\,(0\cdot1846) + \frac{11}{2}\left[\frac{(1-0\cdot1741)}{0\cdot0032} - \frac{30\,(0\cdot1741)}{0\cdot0566}\right]\right)$$

$$= 0\cdot89\,[553\cdot8 + (5\cdot5)\,(258\cdot09 - 92\cdot28)] \div 186\cdot236$$

$$= 0\cdot89\,(553\cdot8 + 911\cdot96) \div 186\cdot236$$

$$= 1304\cdot526 \div 186\cdot36$$

$$= 7$$

Notes

1. Volatility (bond price sensitivity to a change in interest rates) measured as a percentage has the same numerical value as modified duration (normally quoted in years).
2. This example and the proofs in Appendices 9 and 10 are adapted from Phillips, *Inside the gilt-edged market* (Woodhead-Faulkner, 1986).

19   Introduction to yield curves

Introduction

Definition

A yield curve is simply a curve drawn through a scattergram comparing bonds' yields and maturities (see Fig. 19.1).

Principal reasons why bonds diverge from the yield curve

Bonds may diverge from the yield curve for the following reasons:

1. High coupon bonds trade on high GRYs because many investors still value income less than capital gains.
2. Callable bonds trade on slightly high GRYs because, if they are called, the investor could be deprived of a high yield otherwise receivable during the last five years of the bond's life.
3. Actively traded recent issues trade on slightly low GRYs because they offer exceptional marketability and above-average opportunities for owning institutions to supplement their yield by lending bonds to cover dealers' short positions.
4. Flower bonds (a few old issues which confer tax advantages if the owner dies) trade on very low GRYs.

Abnormal divergences may be exploitable anomalies.

Normal shape

The yield curve is normally positively sloped (long bonds yielding more than short, because long bonds are more risky). Occasionally, when monetary policy is very tight, the yield curve is inverted and short bonds yield more than longs. Figure 19.2 shows the different types of yield curve.

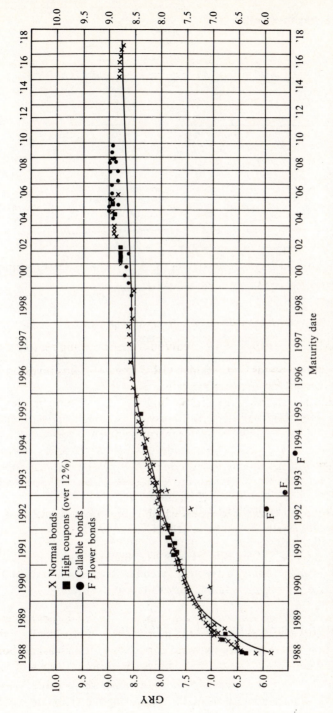

Fig. 19.1 Yields of Treasury securities, 31 March 1988. Yield curve is fitted by eye by US Treasury, based on most actively traded issues. Active (recent) issues tend to trade on GRYs slightly below average, so most seasoned issues have GRYs slightly above a yield curve fitted on this basis. Source: *US Treasury Bulletin*.

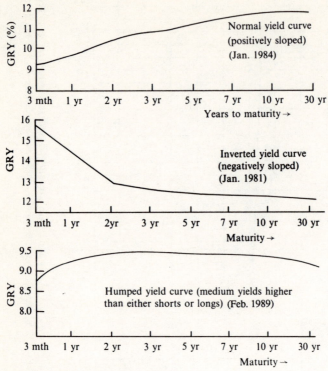

Fig. 19.2 Types of yield curve.

Yield curve jargon

Positively sloped (normal): long rates higher than short.

Inverted: short rates higher than long.

Humped: medium rates higher than both short and long.

Yield curve steepening: increasing spread between short rates and long rates, e.g. long rates rising faster than short (see Fig. 19.3).

Yield curve flattening: narrowing spread between short rates and long rates, e.g. long rates falling faster than short (see Fig. 19.4).

Rationale for slope of the normal yield curve

Risk v. reward

Long bonds must usually yield more than shorts because they are more risky. This can be illustrated by replotting the yield curve as yield

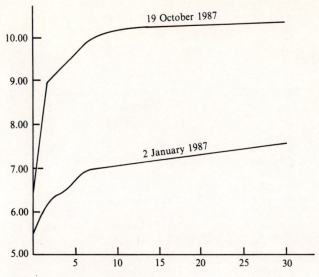

Fig. 19.3 Yield curve steepening.

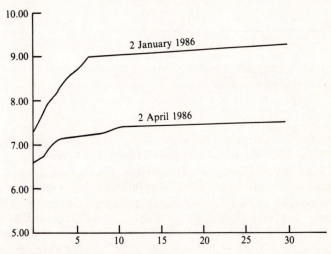

Fig. 19.4 Yield curve flattening.

against duration (as in Fig. 19.5). This shows a smooth, almost linear, progression of yield against risk up to duration of about eight years.

Surprisingly, investors seem prepared to accept increases in duration beyond 8 years without demanding significant additional yield: 30-year bonds (duration 10 years) and even long-dated stripped bonds (with

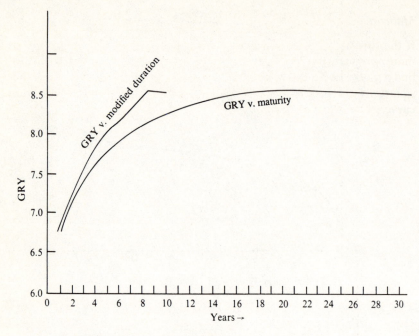

Fig. 19.5 Alternative yield curves.

duration exceeding 20 years) may yield little more than 10-year bonds with a duration of 6 years.

The reasons for investors' tolerance of very long duration include the following:

1. For some investors a guaranteed *long-term* return is more important than reducing the possibility of interim price fluctuations.
2. The disproportionate increase in convexity at long duration offers some compensation for the additional risk.
3. There may be an underlying shortage of long Treasury bonds. In late 1988 only $250 bn of the $1550 bn privately held Treasury bonds had maturities of over 10 years.

Yield curve construction

Manual methods

If the investor simply requires a bird's-eye view of the current (or historic) structure of interest rates, a crude yield curve drawn by eye may suffice.

Mathematical methods

If the investor is using a yield curve to identify switching anomalies, a more consistent mathematical basis is necessary. The normal method is to find a mathematical equation for a curve which minimises the sum of the squares of the vertical distances of individual bonds' positions from the curve (see Fig. 19.6).

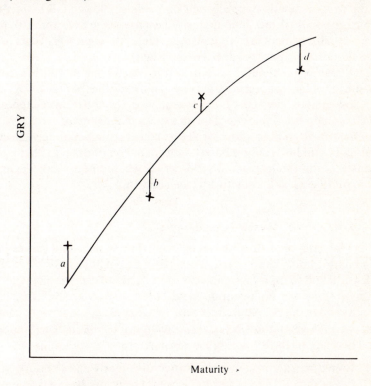

Fig. 19.6 Mathematical fitting of yield curve. An X marks the position of each of four bonds on which the curve is to be based. The fit is the curve which minimises the sum $(a^2 + b^2 + c^2 + d^2)$. The curve may be described by a quadratic (or higher-power) equation, e.g. $GRY = K_1 + K_2 \text{(maturity)} + K_3 \text{(maturity)}^2$.

Many yield curves are based on a quadratic equation which minimises the sum of least squares. (A quadratic equation will give a curve with a single inflection point.) Some yield curves are based on cubic equations and some on equations with higher powers, the sixth power being quite a favourite. However, these subtleties are more popular in the UK than in the US where the standard is usually a simple eye-drawn curve joining on-the-run bonds.

Special yield curves

High-coupon yield curves

Low coupon bonds normally sell on a slightly lower GRY than high-coupon bonds of the same maturity because some investors still prefer capital gains to income (although the preferential capital gains tax rate for US domestic taxpayers has been abolished).

If separate yield curves are drawn for high-coupon and low-coupon bonds, the high-coupon yield curve will normally be (permanently) above the low-coupon yield curve. In consequence, the apparent cheapness of a high-coupon bond might not be an exploitable anomaly.

One can attempt to allow for this by constructing separate yield curves for high- and low-coupon bonds. Alternatively, one can mathematically construct three-dimensional yield curves where bond yields depend on coupon rate as well as maturity (see page 162).

Par yield curves

The high-coupon distortion can be evaded by basing yield curves purely on bonds trading close to par. In this case flat yield and GRY are almost identical and there is no significant capital gain to distort calculations. In August 1988 the high-coupon yield curve was generally 5 to 20 basis points above the par yield curve. Much higher differentials were common before 1986 when the US taxed income more highly than capital gains.

There are hazards in using par yield curves:

1. Sometimes in prolonged bear markets, nearly all bonds are trading below par and a par yield curve cannot be drawn by eye. It can still be constructed mathematically, but it will then relate to purely hypothetical bonds.
2. This is additionally dangerous in practice since par yield curves are often (wrongly) used as indications of average yields from which deviations can be measured.

Par yield curve shifts can be distorted

Suppose the par yield curve at 10 years is 10% (i.e. a 10% coupon bond trades at par). If all market yields now rise by 2%, the 10% bond's GRY rises to 12% (and its price falls to 88·5). However, a bond priced at par will probably need a yield slightly over 12% (e.g. 12·1%) since a high-coupon bond will normally trade on a higher GRY than a 10% bond. In this example every individual bond's GRY has risen by 'only' 2%, but the par yield curve has risen by 2·1%.

20 Further analysis of yield curves

Riding the yield curve

Yield enhancement from maturity shortening

If the yield curve is positively sloped (as normal), an investor's total return over an interim period will exceed the GRY if interest rates remain unchanged. Table 20.1 shows market yields at 11 March 1988. Seven-year bonds yield 8·05%, six-year bonds yield 7·93%.

Table 20.1. Riding the yield curve: projected return assuming interest rates stay unchanged for 12 months

Maturity (years)	GRY (11 March 1988)	Price of notional 8% bond	Capital gain (%)[a]	Total return[b]	Total Return %[c]	Yield enhancement from yield-curve ride (basis points)[d]
1	6·74	101·20	−1·20	6·80	6·74[e]	0
2	7·19	101·48	−0·28	7·72	7·61	42
3	7·40	101·59	−0·11	7·89	7·77	37
4	7·62	101·29	0·30	8·30	8·19	57
5	7·78	100·90	0·39	8·39	8·32	54
6	7·93	100·33	0·57	8·57	8·54	61
7	8·05	99·74	0·59	8·59	8·61	56
8	8·14	99·19	0·55	8·55	8·62	48
9	8·21	98·68	0·51	8·51	8·62	41
10	8·27	98·19	0·49	8·49	8·65	38
17	8·54	95·20	n.a.			
18	8·56	94·90	0·30	8·30	8·75	19
29	8·50	94·64	n.a.			
30	8·50	94·60	0·04	8·04	8·50	0

a Price change of notional 8% bond over following year, e.g. ten-year bond price, initially 98·19; rises to 98·68 over the following year as its maturity shortens to nine years.
b Capital gain plus bond coupon of 8%.
c As % of initial bond price.
d Total return over one-year holding period minus initial GRY.
e The yield curve ride can be further refined. For example, total return rises to 7·23%, if the one-year bond is sold when it has shortened to a six-month bond with GRY of 6·25% and the proceeds are then reinvested in another one-year bond held for the remaining six months.

Suppose an investor buys the seven-year bond (GRY 8·05%) and holds for one year. His seven-year bond will then have turned into a six-year bond and will now have a GRY of 7·93%, if interest rates and the slope of the yield curve have remained unchanged.

He then has a capital gain (the price of his bond rises because six-year bonds yield less than seven-year bonds) which enhances his return from the original GRY of 8·05% to a total return of 8·61%.

Maximum enhancement at intermediate maturities

Riding the yield curve enhances return by over 35 basis points for bonds with maturities between two years and ten years. The maximum enhancement is 61 basis points at a maturity of six years (see Fig. 20.1).

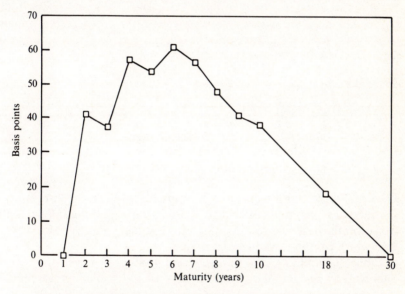

Fig. 20.1 Yield enhancement from riding the yield curve. Plots show the yield-curve ride total return for one year less GRY.

Yield enhancement is greatest for intermediate maturities because in this area a steep yield curve (producing a significant interest rate drop over short holding periods) combines with a duration long enough to produce a meaningful capital gain. At long maturities the yield difference (e.g. between GRY on 29- and 30-year bonds) is normally so small that no significant capital gain results. At very short maturities even large yield changes cannot produce big capital gains.

A different perspective on yield v. risk trade-off

The conventional yield curve in Fig. 20.2 suggests a relatively smooth escalation of risk against yield up to the 18-year maturity.

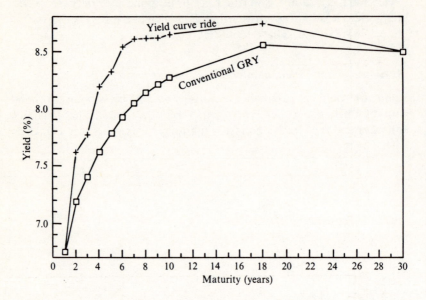

Fig. 20.2 Comparison of GRY and yield-curve ride.

By contrast, plotting prospective yield-curve-ride returns against maturity produces a sharp gradient change at six years, suggesting this maturity may offer the best risk–reward trade-off. A similar picture appears in Fig. 20.3 which compares yield and duration.

Table 20.2 and Fig. 20.4 show possible total returns over one year, if interest rates rise or fall by a maximum of 1%. This analysis also implies an optimum risk–reward trade-off around a maturity of six years.

Implications of projected minimum and maximum returns

If an investor with a one-year time horizon believes that interest rate fluctuation over the next year will not exceed 1%, he should definitely prefer the two-year bond to the one-year bond. His minimum return on the two-year bond is the same, while his maximum return is nearly 2% higher. The trade-off from going longer remains very favourable up to six years. For each year's extension of maturity from two years to six years the minimum return falls by only 0·5%, while the maximum return rises

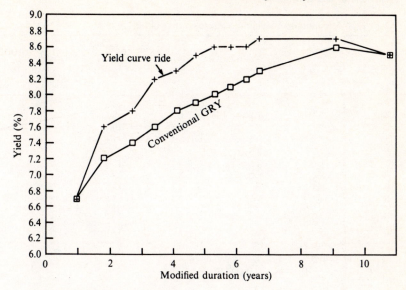

Fig. 20.3 Yield v. duration

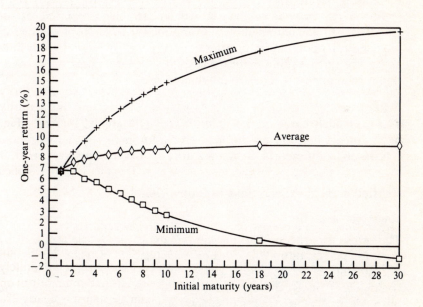

Fig. 20.4 Minimum and maximum return from yield-curve ride.
Note: Projected returns (for one year ahead) assume maximum interest
rate change of plus or minus 1%.

Table 20.2. Minimum and maximum returns from yield-curve ride

| Maturity | GRY | Yield-curve ride | Range of return[a] | | Min.–max. Average |
			Min.	Max.	
1	6·7	6·7	6·7	6·7	6·7
2	7·2	7·6	6·7	8·5	7·6
3	7·4	7·8	6·0	9·5	7·8
4	7·6	8·2	5·7	10·7	8·2
5	7·8	8·3	5·1	11·6	8·3
6	7·9	8·5	4·7	12·5	8·6
7	8·0	8·6	4·1	13·2	8·7
8	8·1	8·6	3·6	13·8	8·7
9	8·2	8·6	3·1	14·3	8·7
10	8·3	8·7	2·7	14·9	8·8
18	8·6	8·7	0·4	17·8	9·1
30	8·5	8·5	−1·2	19·6	9·2

a   Minimum return assumes 1% rise in interest rates.
    Maximum return assumes 1% fall in interest rates.

by 1%. However, for maturities beyond six years the trade-off is nearly even: the minimum return falls by about 0·9% for every 1% increase in the maximum return.

Thus *in this example* an investor with a neutral view on interest rates (small rise or small fall equally likely) and ability to tolerate moderate risk might find his optimum maturity around six years. There is relatively little advantage in extending maturity beyond six years unless the investor thinks rates are more likely to fall than to rise.

Note
This example is based on the yield curve of 11 March 1988. Analysis at other dates will produce a different profile for minimum and maximum returns and a different optimum maturity for risk–reward trade-off.

Implied market expectations of future yields

Breakeven analysis

The present structure of market yields is partly determined by expectations of future yields. For example, an investor would not normally buy a two-year bond yielding 9% (two-year return 18%) if he could buy a one-year bond yielding 8% and expect to reinvest the proceeds at 12% in a year's time (two-year return 20%). Similarly, he would not buy the one-year bond with the expectation of reinvesting at 6% (two-year return 14%) when the two-year bond offered a two-year return of 18%.

However, if he expected to reinvest at 10% (one-year bond yield in one year's time) he might be equally likely to buy either the one-year or the two-year bond at today's yield. Any other figure for future market expectations would be inconsistent with current market yields.

This type of balance-of-term breakeven analysis (detailed explanation on page 156) enables us to take the market's present yield curve and project the market's current anticipations of *future* yield curves.

Implied future interest rates

Figure 20.5 shows the market's implied anticipations of the yield curves for 1990 and 1995, compared with the actual yield curve in 1988. Figure 20.6 shows the market's implied expectations for future yields on five-year and ten-year bonds.

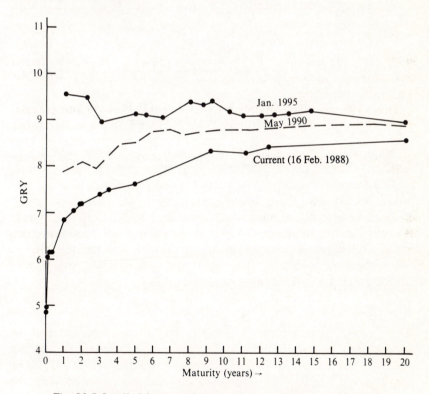

Fig. 20.5 Implied future yield curves as at 16 February 1988. Source: balance-of-term breakeven yields (see page 156). E.g. the breakeven yield between bonds maturing in January 1995 and January 2000 is the implied yield of five-year bonds in January 1995.

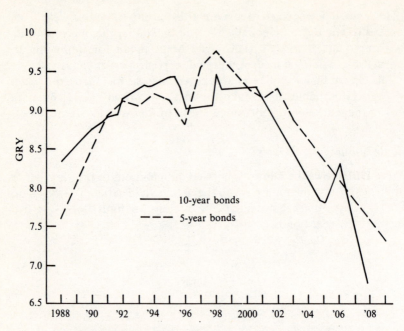

Fig. 20.6 Implied future bond yields as at 16 February 1988.
Source: Balance-of-term yields at 16 February 1988.

Is this a genuine forecast of higher future yields? If the yield curve is positively sloped (as normal) implied anticipated future yields will be higher than current yields. Many investors have portfolio risk constraints which would bias their holdings to shorter maturities even if they expected a better total return from investing longer.

Thus the apparent upward bias in anticipated future yields partly reflects institutional portfolio constraints rather than a genuine forecasting consensus. Such constraints may represent a market imperfection which unconstrained investors can exploit.

Part Four

Bond selection

21 Bond selection methods

The following methods are considered in this chapter:

1. Methods comparing one bond against another:
   (a) yield spreads;
   (b) profit projections on alternative future interest rate scenarios;
   (c) balance-of-term breakeven yields.
2. Methods comparing a bond against the market:
   (a) yield curve analysis;
   (b) price model analysis (three-dimensional yield curves).

Yield spreads

Introduction

Yield differences ('spreads') between two bonds are the most widely used tool for assessing switches. Yield spreads can be:

(a) easily understood (a GRY of 10% is, other things being equal, more attractive than a GRY of 9%);
(b) easily measured (by simple subtraction); and
(c) assessed from a graph (is the current spread sufficiently 'abnormal' to offer a potentially profitable anomaly?).

Figure 21.1 shows a typical yield-spread chart comparing 30-year and ten-year bonds. In this case the average spread (between GRYs) has been seven basis points and the spread has typically fluctuated between +29 and −23. There may therefore be a case for preferring the 30-year bond when the spread exceeds seven basis points and preferring the ten-year bond when the spread is below seven basis points.

Spread-based switching is in principle most effective when comparing bonds of similar coupon and maturity. However, US Treasury spread differences in such cases seldom vary by more than five to ten basis points.

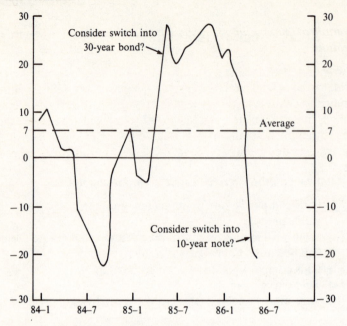

Fig. 21.1 Yield spread 30-year Treasury minus 10-year Treasury, 1984–6.

Thus such switching opportunities are rare, in contrast to the UK gilts market where such spreads may easily vary over a range of 10 to 30 basis points.

Problems with spread-based switching

A number of things can go wrong with switching to exploit abnormal yield spreads:

1. Some new factor might permanently shift the 'normal' yield spread into a new range (e.g. the abolition of the US capital gains tax preferential rate in January 1988 has probably permanently reduced the normal yield spread between high-coupon and low-coupon bonds).
2. The possible profit from a switch may be too low in relation to dealing costs. Superficially attractive switches often fail this test, particularly when they relate to older bonds with poorer marketability.
3. Simple spread differences do not allow for differences in two bonds' durations.

Example of 'successful' yield-spread switch ruined by difference in duration

If two bonds have similar duration, yield spreads are an excellent starting point for comparing relative value. However, where two bonds have significantly different duration and the general level of interest rates changes, it is possible to open a switch to gain yield and reverse the switch later with a further gain in yield but still be a net loser from the switch. The exaggerated example given in Tables 21.1 and 21.2 demonstrates this.

Table 21.1. Yield gains from 'successful' switch

	Bond GRY	Bond price	Modified duration
15 Jan.			
Sell 12% 25-year bond A	15·90	76	6·3
Buy 12% 5-year bond B	16·52	85	3·5
Gain in GRY from opening switch	0·62		
15 July			
Sell 12% 4½-year bond B	12·00	100	3·4
Repurchase 12% 24½-year bond A	12·67	95	7·5
Gain in GRY from reversing switch	0·67		

Table 21.2. Capital loss from 'successful' switch

15 Jan.	
Sell $1,000,000 bond A at 76	Proceeds: $760,000
Buy $894,000 bond B at 85	Cost: $760,000
15 July	
Sell $894,000 bond B at 100	Proceeds: $894,000
Repurchase $941,000 bond A at 95	Cost: $894,000

End result: After two successful switches for yield gain the poor investor ends up with $941,000 of bond A instead of $1,000,000. This occurs because the capital gain from a 323 basis-point fall in yield on bond A (a 25-year bond with initial duration of 6·3 years) is greater than the capital gain from a 452 basis-point fall in yield on bond B (a 5-year bond with duration of only 3·5 years). Source: Patrick Phillips, *Inside the Gilt-Edged Market* (1987) (adapted).

Profit projections

Assessing potential profit from yield-spread changes

An approximate breakeven point (where profit from a correctly anticipated spread change could be lost through an adverse movement in the general level of interest rates) can be directly estimated from two bonds' durations. In the following example, the investor has studied Fig. 21.1 and found the spreads detailed in Table 21.3 and 21.4.

Table 21.3. Yield spread 30-year Treasury minus 10-year Treasury, 1984–6

	Basis points difference	
High	29	
Average	7	
Low	−23	
Current	−22	(15 May 1986)

Table 21.4. Bond price and yield comparison (at 15 May 1988)

Bond		Price	GRY	Modified duration
7·25%	15 May 2016	97·88	7·43	12
7·375%	15 May 1996	98·13	7·65	7
	Difference		−0·22	+5

Potential profit estimate (approximate)

The investor assumes that GRY spread will revert from current −22 to historically normal +7, implying 10-year bond yield falls to 7·36%.

Capital gain on 10-year bond from spread change = 7 × 0·29 (modified duration multiplied by yield change) = 2·03%.

Possible relative underperformance of 10-year bond if overall interest rates fall 41 basis points = 5 × 0·41 (difference in modified duration multiplied by yield change) = 2·05%.

Investment implication

An investor expecting the yield spread to revert to +7 basis points should prefer the 10-year bond, *unless* he also expects 30-year bond GRY to fall to 7·02% or below (i.e. 41 basis points below current level of 7·43%).

This estimation method can also be used in reverse. The investor can project a shift in the overall level of interest rates and then assess what change in spreads would make the 'wrong' bond outperform.

Example

	Case A	Case B
Projected general interest rate change (basis points)	+ 20	− 60
Outperformance by 10-year bond due to shorter duration	+100[a]	−300[c]
Spread change (additional interest rate movement, basis points, in 10-year bond) required to offset this	+ 14[b]	− 43[d]

Notes
a 20 × 5 (difference between the two bonds' durations)
b 100 ÷ 7 (the duration of the 10-year bond)
c 60 × 5
d −300 ÷ 7

In Case A, 10-year bond outperforms unless 10-year GRY rises 14 bp more than 30-year GRY. In Case B, 10-year bond underperforms unless 10-year GRY falls 43 bp more than 30-year GRY.

Sources of inaccuracy
This estimation method suffers from the following sources of inaccuracy:

1. It ignores convexity (see page 128), thus slightly understating the relative attraction of the high duration bond. This source of inaccuracy increases if there is a *big* change in the general level of interest rates.
2. A change in yield spread itself slightly alters the duration difference between two bonds.

Precise methods

Some investors prefer to use exact calculations for a series of possible interest rate and yield spread outcomes. They can then:

(a) see the precise breakeven point;
(b) consider the performance impact of a range of different possible shifts in the level of interest rates (or in the yield spread), assigning a different probability to each and assessing which bond is preferable on a balance of possible scenarios.

Illustration
The investor assumes that the yield spread returns to 'normal', but makes a series of alternative profit projections based on different overall levels of interest rates as in Table 21.5.

Table 21.5. Projected profit possibilities for 15 May 1987 (projected on 15 May 1986)

	7·375% of 1996 (Price on 15 May 1986: 98·13)			7·25% of 2016 (Price on 15 May 1986: 97·88)	
GRY	Projected price on 15 May 1987	Total return since 15 May 1986	GRY	Projected price on 15 May 1987	Total return since 15 May 1986
6	109·46	19·1	6·07	116·01	25·9
7	102·47	11·9	7·07	102·21	11·8
8	96·04	5·4	8·07	90·86	0·2
9	90·12	−0·6	9·07	81·47	−9·4

Notes

1. The investor projects total returns on the 10-year Treasury for one year for a range of possible future yields (in this case between 6% and 9%). For example, assuming yields fall to 7%:

    Capital gain   4·34[a]
    Income   7·38
                                                          ———
                      Total return   11·72[b]
                                                          ———

    a   Projected price of 102·47 (on 15 May 1987) minus current price of 98·13 (on 15 May 1986).
    b   Total Return of 11·72 = 11·9% of current price of 98·13.
2. Comparative total returns are projected for the 30-year Treasury assuming that its yield reverts to the 'normal' 7 basis points above the yield on 10-year Treasuries.

Conclusion

If yield spread returns to normal (7 basis points) the 10-year bond will outperform *unless* the 30-year bond's GRY falls below 7% (i.e. 45 basis below the current level). Tables 21.6 and 21.7 compare the outturn (10-year bond outperformed by 8·4%) with the projected possibilities.

Table 21.6. Actual profit outturn (analysed one year later)

	GRY on 15 May		Price on 15 May		Capital gain	Year's income	Total return since 15 May 1986
Bond	1986	1987	1986	1987			
2016	7·43	8·94	97·9	82·6	−15·3	7·3	−8·0
1996	7·66	8·82	98·1	91·1	− 7·0	7·4	+0·4
Difference	−0·22	+0·12	−0·2	−8·5	−8·3	−0·1	−8·4

Table 21.7. Sources of 10-year bond's outperformance

Higher flat yield	0·1
Normalisation of yield spread[a]	2·0
Additional movement in yield spread[b]	0·1
Yield-curve ride[c]	0·3
Lower duration[d]	7·5
Lower convexity	−1·6
	8·4

a From −22 bp to +7.

b From +7 to +8.

c Nine-year bond yields about 4 bp less than 10-year bond. Holding the 10-year bond for one year while its maturity shortens to 9 years therefore produces a small capital gain, if the general level of interest rates remain unchanged. There is no comparable gain on the long bond because yields on 29-year and 30-year bonds are virtually identical.

d 30-year bond's initial duration was 12 years. 10-year bond's initial duration was only 7 years, giving it superior defensive characteristics in the face of the general interest rate rise of 150 basis points.

Caution: what is normal?

Successful exploitation of yield-spread variations depends on accurate assessment of *future* normality. Future normality will not always equate to past normality (despite the popularity of deducing it from historic graphs) nor is past normality the same in different periods.

For example, if the investor had assessed the 'normal' spread from a longer-run chart (as in Fig. 21.1), he might have abandoned a projected (and profitable) switch from the 30-year into the 10-year bond after noticing the negative spread prevailing in 1977–82 (see Table 21.8).

Table 21.8. Yield spread of 30-year Treasury minus 10-year Treasury, 1977–82

	Basis points difference
High	36
Average	−12
Low	−77
Current	−22 (15 May 1986)

In this case the key to successful switching lay in realising that the large negative spreads common in 1979–82 were 'abnormal' (a consequence of Volckernomics' initial very tight money phase designed to break long-term inflationary expectations) and a bad guide to future normality.

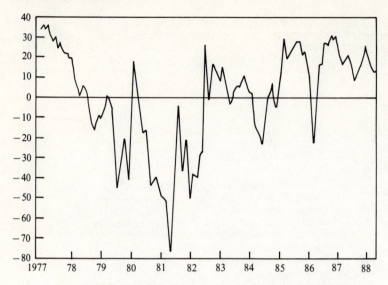

Fig. 21.2 Yield spread 30-year Treasury minus 10-year Treasury, 1977–88.

Warning

A temporarily inverted yield curve is common when tight money is biting just as the economic cycle is about to peak out. Switching short is then inappropriate since these are the very circumstances when the general level of interest rates is likely to fall and longer bonds to outperform.

Balance-of-term breakeven yields (comparing two bonds of different maturities)

The method is to assess whether the more profitable course is to buy the longer bond immediately and hold to maturity, or to buy the shorter bond and (when it matures) reinvest in the longer bond.

> *Example*
> Bond A.   1-year Treasury: GRY 10%.
> Bond B.   2-year Treasury: GRY 11%.
>
> Investment alternatives:
> (a) buy B, and hold for two years;
> (b) buy A, and on maturity reinvest in B.
> Table 21.9 illustrates these alternatives, and Table 21.10 gives another example.

Table 21.9. Assessment of investment alternatives (rough approximation)

1.	Yield on B for 2 years	= 22%
2.	Yield on A for 1 year	= 10%
	Breakeven yield on B for second year	= 12%
	Total yield for 2 years	22%

Buying B immediately guarantees 22% return over 2 years. This will be the better option if B yields less than 12% (the balance-of-term breakeven yield) when A matures in one year's time.

However, if B yields more than 12% in one year's time, buying A now (10% for one year) and then switching into B (over 12% for one year) will produce a total return exceeding 22%.

Table 21.10. Further illustration of assessing investment alternatives (rough approximation)

Bond A: 5-year, GRY 10·0   Bond B: 8-year, GRY 11·5

1.	Yield on B for 8 years	= 92%
2.	Yield on A for 5 years	= 50%
	Breakeven yield on B for last 3 years	= 42% (14% p.a.)
	Total yield for 8 years	= 92%

Implication: Buy B now unless you expect 3-year bonds to yield more than 14% in 5 years' time.

Mathematical analysis of balance-of-term yields

The preceding simplified examples give only rough approximations. Fortunately, a mathematically precise balance-of-term breakeven yield may be calculated from the formula:

$$\text{Breakeven yield} = \frac{Y_B\, a_{\overline{n}|(B)} - Y_A \cdot a_{\overline{n}|(A)}}{a_{\overline{n}|(B)} - a_{\overline{n}|(A)}}$$

(proof in Appendix 11).

Example
Bond A.   GRY 8%, matures in 3 years ($n = $ 6 half-years).
Bond B.   GRY 11%, matures in 10 years ($n = $ 20 half-years).
Assumed roll-up rate : 10% p.a.
$a_{\overline{20}|} = 12·462$ $a_{\overline{6}|} = 5·076$ $Y_A = 4$ (per half-year);
$Y_B = 5·5$ (per half-year).

$$\text{Breakeven yield} = \frac{(5·5)\, a_{\overline{20}|} - 4\, a_{\overline{6}|}}{a_{\overline{20}|} - a_{\overline{6}|}}$$

$$= \frac{5·5\,(12·462) - 4\,(5·076)}{12·462 - 5·076}$$

$$= \frac{68 \cdot 541 - 20 \cdot 304}{7 \cdot 386}$$

$= 6 \cdot 53\%$ per half-year

or $13 \cdot 06$ per year

i.e. 3 years at 8% followed by 7 years at $13 \cdot 06\%$ is equivalent to 10 years at 11%.

Implication

The investor should buy the longer bond immediately *unless* he expects the 7-year bond GRY to exceed $13 \cdot 06\%$ in three years' time.

Rough guideline for using breakeven yields

The higher the breakeven yield, the more likely that buying the longer bond will be the better option. The rationale for this guideline is that buying the shorter bond now will be more profitable *only if* the long bond's GRY exceeds the breakeven yield when the short bond matures. The long bond's future GRY will normally be less likely to exceed a high breakeven yield.

Examples of balance-of-term analysis

Table 21.11 lists 19 Treasury bonds with each bond's balance-of-term breakeven yield (calculated on 15 February 1988) against the next longer bond.

If the breakeven yield is high, the longer bond will normally be the better investment (unless tax considerations suggest otherwise). For example, $7 \cdot 375\%$ of May 1996 appears preferable to $8 \cdot 875\%$ of February 1996 (breakeven yield $10 \cdot 96\%$). Conversely, if the breakeven yield is low the investor should normally prefer the shorter bond. For example, $8 \cdot 5\%$ of May 1997 appears preferable to $8 \cdot 125\%$ of February 1998 (breakeven yield only $7 \cdot 14\%$).

'High' and 'low' are relative terms, comparing with average breakeven yields around that maturity. Thus in Table 21.11 a breakeven yield of $8 \cdot 3\%$ is high for a 1991 bond, but low for the 2006 bond.

Multilateral breakeven yield comparison

Table 21.12 shows a matrix of breakeven yields between different bonds. The highest breakeven yields are:

Table 21.11. Comparison of Treasury bonds at 15 February 1988

Coupon	Maturity	GRY	Balance-of-term breakeven yield[a]	Assessment
8	Feb. 1989	6·78	7·66	
8	May 1989	6·95	7·33	L[b]
7·75	Aug. 1989	7·01	7·53	
6·375	Nov. 1989	7·08	8·00	
7·875	May 1990	7·27	7·75	L
7·375	Feb. 1991	7·38	8·41	
8·125	May 1991	7·45	8·36	H[c]
6·625	Feb. 1992	7·60	8·20	
6·625	May 1992	7·63	7·47	L
7·875	Feb. 1993	7·61	10·19	H
9	Feb. 1994	7·96	8·83	
8·625	Jan. 1995	8·05	9·53	H
8·875	Feb. 1996	8·20	10·96	H
7·375	May 1996	8·26	9·04	H
8·5	May 1997	8·32	7·14	L
8·125	Feb. 1998	8·26	9·15	H
9·375	Feb. 2006	8·51	8·31	L
7·25	May 2016	8·48	8·48	
8·75	May 2017	8·48	n.a.	

a Breakeven yield compared with the following (longer) bond. For example, the breakeven yield between 8% of Feb. 1989 and 8% of May 1989 is 7·66%.
b L = Low. The investor should normally prefer the indicated bond rather than the next longer bond.
c H = High. The investor should normally prefer the next longer bond.

Table 21.12. Balance-of-term breakeven yields between active Treasury bonds at 15 February 1988

7·375	Jan. 90								
7·375	Feb. 91	7·82							
8·25	Dec. 91	8·02	8·31						
8·25	Feb. 93	8·14	8·34	8·36					
9·5	Oct. 94	8·54	8·80	8·97	9·44				
8·25	Feb. 98	8·53	8·68	8·75	8·86	8·51			
8	Aug. 01	8·75	8·90	8·97	9·09	8·97	9·55		
9·375	Feb. 06	8·82	8·94	9·01	9·10	9·02	9·35	9·14	
8·375	Aug. 17	8·66	8·75	8·78	8·83	8·73	8·81	8·48	8·01
Bond maturity		90	F 91	D 91	93	94	98	01	06

Example of interpretation: 8% of Aug. 2001 will yield a better return than 8·25 of Feb. 1998 unless 8% of 2001 (by then a 3½ year bond) yields over 9·55% in Feb. 1998.

(a) 9·44, suggesting that the longer bond (9·5% of October 1994) should be preferred to 8·25% of February 1993;

(b) 9·55, suggesting that 8% of August 2001 should be preferred to 8·25% of February 1998.

Low breakeven yields include:

(a) 8·01, implying that the shorter bond (9·375% of February 2006) should be preferred to 8·375% of August 2017.

(b) 8·14, suggesting that 7·375% of 1990 should be preferred to 8·25% of February 1993.

Caution is necessary where an abnormal balance-of-term yield may simply reflect investors' (permanent?) preference for low-coupon bonds.

Reinvestment coordinates

Multilateral matrices, as in Table 21.12, are cumbersome. Some analysts therefore assess breakeven yield opportunities graphically. Each bond is plotted on a scattergram. Its x coordinate is a_n, i.e. the value of its future coupons, discounted at an estimated roll-up rate. Its y coordinate is a_n multiplied by its gross redemption yield.

The gradient of the line joining any two bonds on the scattergram then represents the balance-of-term breakeven yield between them as calculated from the mathematical formula on page 157. If the gradient is steep, the longer bond is more attractive. If the gradient is shallow, the shorter bond is more attractive. Figure 21.3 shows a scattergram plotting reinvestment coordinates of the 19 bonds in Table 21.11.

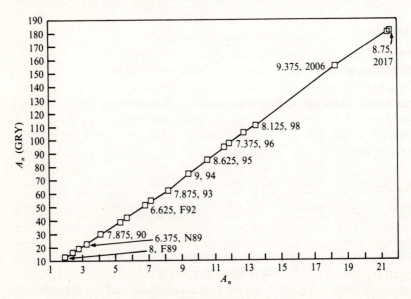

Fig. 21.3 Reinvestment coordinates.

Unfortunately, gradients often appear similar to the naked eye, even when significantly different numerically. However, potentially unusual gradients can often be identified visually and then checked by formula. For example, in Fig. 21.3 the gradient appears steep between 8·625% of 1995 and 7·375% of 1996 (9·78% by formula), so the longer bond may be more attractive. Conversely, the gradient is shallow between 6·625 of February 1992 and 7·875 of 1993 (only 7·66% by formula), so the shorter bond may be more attractive.

When breakeven yield analysis is most useful

Balance-of-term breakeven yields are least risky in identifying discrepancies between bonds of similar coupon and fairly close maturities. If coupons differ, the distortion may turn out to be a semi-permanent feature associated with investors' aversion to high-coupon bonds.

If maturities differ, there is a risk that a correct guess on a yield anomaly might be outweighed by an adverse movement in the general level of interest rates, e.g. a statistically attractive long bond may underperform a shorter bond if the general level of interest rates rises.

Yield curve analysis

This is a method of comparing bonds against the market.

Advantages

The US Treasury market currently has nearly 200 bonds, implying over 19,000 possible different bilateral yield-spread comparisons. However, instead of studying 19,000 bilateral yield spreads, apparently the investor need only study the spread between an individual bond's GRY and the yield curve GRY at that maturity. Switches can then be made from bonds that are expensive against the yield curve into bonds that are cheap against the curve (see Fig. 21.4).

Hazards

Unfortunately, there is no such thing as *the* (unique) yield curve. Rival brokers using different yield-curve-fitting equations can produce differing assessments of a bond's cheapness or dearness against the curve. Furthermore, fund managers are understandably reluctant to abandon bilateral yield spreads (which they can calculate by simple subtraction) in favour of brokers' yield-curve deviation calculations which they have to take on trust.

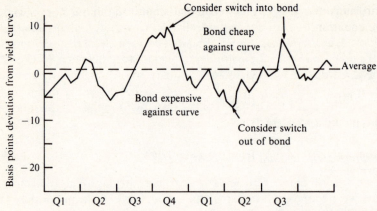

Fig. 21.4 Hypothetical yield curve deviation chart for a single Treasury bond: bond minus yield curve GRY at same maturity.

Use in practice

Deviations from the yield curve are useful for shortlisting *potential* bilateral switches, which should then be checked by other methods:

1. Bilateral spread history (is the current spread an exploitable deviation from normal?).
2. Balance-of-term breakeven yield: is it sufficiently high (if considering switching longer) or low (if considering switching shorter?).
3. Profit projections based on alternative possibilities for future yields.

Price model analysis

Price model analysis is an attempt to refine the yield curve to allow for investor preference for lower coupon bonds. This can be done in one of two ways:

1. Visually, by measuring a bond's deviation from a specially constructed yield curve based purely on bonds of similar coupon to that being considered.
2. By comparing the bond with a three-dimensional yield curve, whose position depends on coupon as well as maturity.

Three-dimensional yield curves

Such yield curves can in principle be constructed physically (extrovert brokers have been known to produce them from bulging attaché cases) but are more conveniently modelled mathematically. In the normal yield curve equation:

$$GRY = K_1 + K_2(\text{bond's maturity})$$

In the three-dimensional yield curve:

$$GRY = K_1 + K_2(\text{bond's maturity}) + K_3(\text{bond's coupon})$$

This model can be used to check whether a particular bond is currently cheap or expensive against the three-dimensional yield curve, and whether a given deviation from the three-dimensional curve is historically abnormal.

Four-dimensional yield curves

There is no need to stop with three dimensions. For example, a fourth term could be added to the equation to capture the impact of convexity on GRY.

Multi-dimensional models open the way to various refined bond selection techniques in which the mathematical framework provides a basis for sophisticated investor judgement. For example, the following questions could be addressed:

1. Is a given bond's divergence from a four- (or five-) dimensional yield curve justified? Is its slightly higher GRY sufficient compensation for below-average convexity?
2. Could the whole four-dimensional yield curve shift position (e.g. if taxes change, or a perceived reduction of interest rate volatility reduces the premium investors might pay for convexity)?

Part Five

Technical methods

22 Technical analysis

Introduction

Technical analysis is a broad term referring to the use of charts (or other methods) to examine past bond market action as a possible guide to future price movements.

The measures examined can include the following:

1. Price patterns.
2. Rate of price change (momentum).
3. Volume of trading.
4. Investor sentiment.

Warning: the whole idea that charts can be used to predict the future is highly contentious!

The key principles of technical analysis are the following:

1. Prices tend to establish underlying trends: up, down or sideways.
2. A trend is presumed to remain in force until it has been clearly broken.

Trendbreaks are a vital key in technical analysis. Trendbeaks may take the form of breaking through a price level, a trendline or a moving average.

Significant chart price patterns

Bearish patterns

These are as follows:

1. Head-and-shoulders top (Fig. 22.1); a breakdown below the neckline is very bearish.

2.   Double top (Fig. 22.2); price advance suddenly runs into resistance and twice fails to break through. This pattern is often followed by price decline.
3.   Topping-out distribution (Fig. 22.3); a more protracted pattern than a double-top, and often followed by price erosion.
4.   Trendbreak below a straight line (as in Fig. 22.4) or moving average (as in Fig. 22.14).

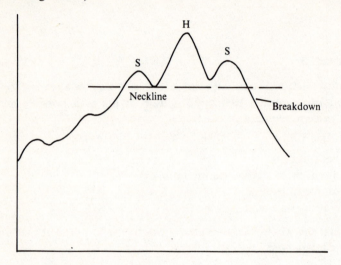

Fig. 22.1 Head-and-shoulders top

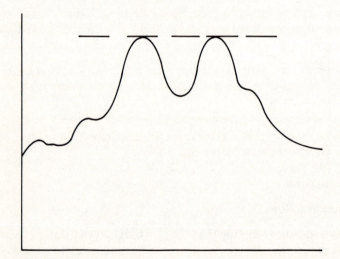

Fig. 22.2 Double top

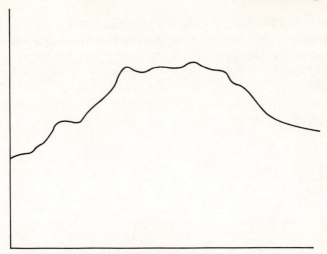

Fig. 22.3 Topping-out distribution

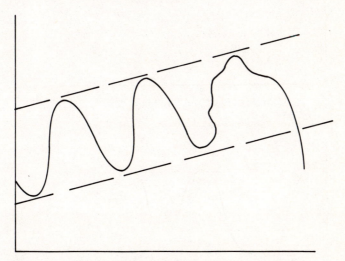

Fig. 22.4 Trendbreak: breakdown through support level

Bullish patterns

These are as follows:

1. Inverted head-and-shoulders (Fig. 22.5); breakout above neckline is bullish.
2. Double bottom (Fig. 22.6).

3. Saucer or bottoming-out distribution (Fig. 22.7).
4. Breakout above a price level or trendline (Fig. 22.8) or moving average; the more frequently the resistance level has been tested (but not broken) in the past, the more significant an ultimate breakout becomes.

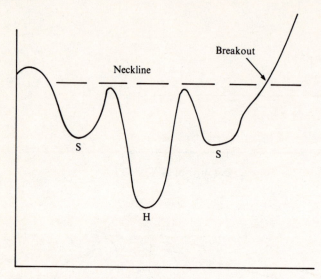

Fig. 22.5 Inverted head and shoulders

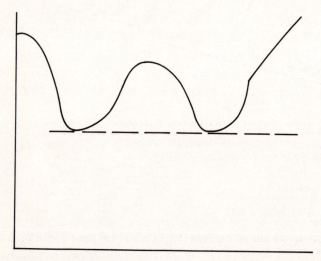

Fig. 22.6 Double bottom

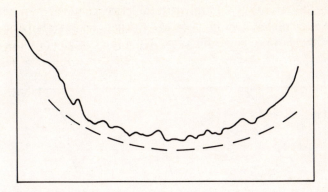

Fig. 22.7 Saucer

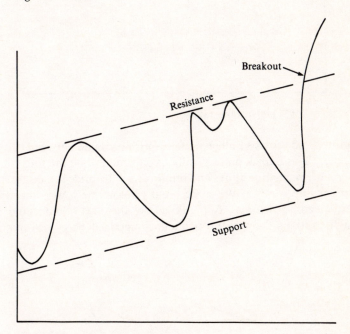

Fig. 22.8 Breakout from resistance

Tramline patterns

A price often appears to be confined between two channelling trendlines (nicknamed a tramline pattern). The existing trend (up, down or sideways) is presumed to remain in force until a breakout (or breakdown) occurs.

Figure 22.9 shows a neutral pattern: price confined between two horizontal trendlines. The direction of the next breakout (above or below the trendlines) often signals the direction of the next major move.

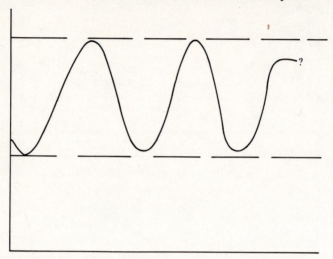

Fig. 22.9 Horizontal tramlines

Figure 22.10 shows a bullish pattern: price confined between two rising trendlines. This bullish pattern will be confirmed while the price remains between the rising trendlines and reinforced if the price breaks out above the upper line. Only if the price breaks below the lower line will the pattern become bearish. A break below the lower line could occur through a sudden drop or through a prolonged sideways movement.

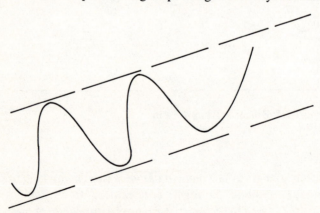

Fig. 22.10 Rising tramlines

Figure 22.11 shows a bearish pattern (price confined between two declining trendlines) which will be reversed only if the price breaks out above the upper line.

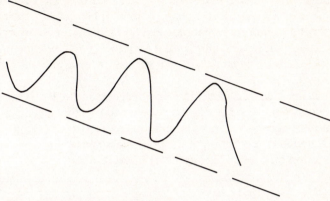

Fig. 22.11 Declining tramlines

Triangle pattern

Figure 22.12 shows a price confined in a triangle pattern between two converging trendlines. This pattern is ambiguous with the direction of the break often signalling the next major move.

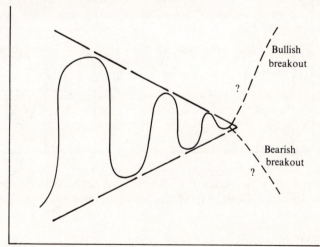

Fig. 22.12 Triangle: direction of break often signals direction of next major move

Momentum and moving averages

Momentum is a measure of the rate at which prices are changing, e.g. percentage price change over the previous 30 days. In a bull market momentum usually decelerates before bond prices actually start falling. However, bull markets sometimes end suddenly after a buying-climax exhaustion spike. Upside momentum extremes, indicating the market is overbought, are a danger sign. Conversely, a downside extreme is a hopeful sign.

What constitutes an extreme must be guessed on the basis of past experience. Figure 22.13 suggests that a rise or fall exceeding 13% in three months normally marks a momentum extreme for the long Treasury bond. A detailed description of the points labelled on Fig. 22.13 is given in the section on pages 176–7 on chart interpretation.

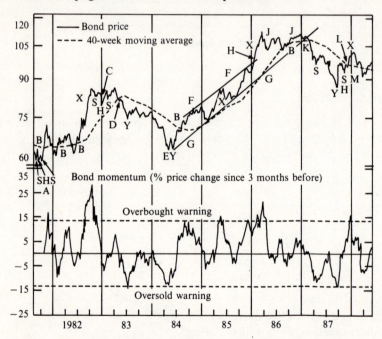

Fig. 22.13 Chart patterns in US Treasury 8·75% of 2008 (see text for explanation). Chart adapted by courtesy of *Pring Market Review*

Moving average

A moving average is a measure formed by averaging prices over a particular past period (e.g. last 30 days, or last six months). The reading will change slightly every day. e.g. a six-month moving average for 31 August will average prices from 1 March to 31 August; the six-month moving average for 1 September will average prices from 2 March to 1 September.

Moving averages can be used as:

(a)   an indicator of long-term trends and changes in trends;
(b)   a support or resistance level;
(c)   a trendline and trendbreak indicator;
(d)   confirmation of a trendbreak by a change in direction; for example, the start of a bond bear market will be signalled by the bond falling below its moving average (trendbreak) subsequently confirmed by the moving average itself turning down, as illustrated in Fig. 22.14.

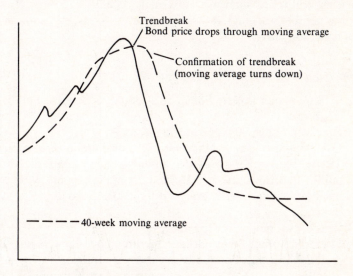

Fig. 22.14 Moving average

Sensitivity of moving averages
Short-term averages change direction and indicate trendbreaks relatively early, but give many false signals. Longer-term moving averages change direction more slowly and give fewer false signals. However, their signals will often be late and miss a significant part of a market move.

Some analysts try to combine the most useful characteristics of short- and long-term moving averages in an exponential moving average, using a relatively long period but weighting recent data more heavily so the average becomes more sensitive to trend changes.

Examples of chart interpretation

A six year chart

Figure 22.13 shows a long Treasury bond with a six-year price history, and a momentum indicator (price change over three months before). Observation suggests that in this case a 13% price movement (either up or down) in three months is a warning sign of momentum extreme.

A market fall exceeding 13% in three months often marks either the end of a bear market (spring 1984 and autumn 1987) or at least its interruption by a prolonged sideways movement (summer 1983). Conversely, a 13% rise in three months is often a warning that the market is becoming overheated and due for a correction (late 1981; mid-1985) or at least a prolonged sideways movement (late 1982; 1986). However, high-momentum warnings at the *start* of bull markets, e.g. autumn 1982, often come too early.

Significant points on six-year chart (Fig. 22.13)

A. SHS marks an inverted head-and-shoulders pattern. Followed by sharp rise.
B. Breakout above 40-week moving average.
X. Overbought warning (market up 15% or more in three months).
C. SHS marks another inverted head-and-shoulders pattern. Normally bullish, but this pattern 'fails' and (as often happens with a failed head-and-shoulders) is followed by a strong move in the 'wrong' direction.
D. Breakdown below moving average.
Y. Oversold signal. Bear market interrupted by sideways phase.
E. Double bottom. Possibility of recovery supported by another oversold signal (Y) and confirmed by breakout above moving average (B).
F. Bond price now channelled between two rising trendlines (FF and GG).
X. Overbought warning. Bull market temporarily interrupted.
H. Breakout above trend channel (bullish).
X. Overbought warning.
J. Topping out distribution.
K. Multiple breakdown below:
    (a) extension of 1983–5 trendline (GG);
    (b) 40-week moving average:
    (c) 1986 lows.

Y.   Oversold warning.
L.   Double breakout (bullish) above:
     (a) 40-week moving average;
     (b) neckline of inverted head-and-shoulders pattern (SHS).
X.   Overbought warning.
M.   Breakdown (bearish) below moving average and below neckline of
     head-and-shoulders.

Significant points on 11-year chart (Fig. 22.15)

A.   Massive topping-out distribution 1976–9. Gradual erosion (bond
     price channelled between falling tramlines) followed by breakdown
     below tramlines (B) and 1979 selling climax.
SHS. Head-and-shoulders patterns. Bearish pattern worked in 1980.
     Inverted head-and-shoulders pattern (bullish) worked in 1981 and
     temporarily in early 1988, but failed in 1983.
B.   Start of massive saucer pattern 1979–86, culminating in end of 1945–
     81 bond bear market.
C.   Significant non-confirmation. Forty-week moving average (not
     shown on chart) kept falling through 1980 bull market.
D.   Decline between falling tramlines (bearish).
E.   Breakdown below bottom tramline. Normally very bearish but this
     is a false signal and swiftly reversed.
F.   Warnings. Prices still high but momentum evaporating.
GH. Neckline of massive three-year inverted head and shoulders.
H.   Breakout from neckline.
J.   Further breakout above 18-month old straight line joining three
     market peaks in 1984–5.
X.   Overbought momentum warning (price rise exceeding 15% in three
     months). Timely in 1981 and 1986. Too early in 1980, 1982 and 1987.
Y.   Oversold momentum warnings (price fall exceeding 12% in three
     months). All timely, but only mild rallies in late 1979 and late
     1983.

Technical analysis in practice

The main principles of technical analysis can be summarised as follows:

1.   A trend is presumed to be in force until it has been clearly broken.
2.   The longer a trend has lasted and the more frequently it has been
     confirmed (e.g. by prices reaching but failing to break through
     support or resistance lines), the more significant it becomes.

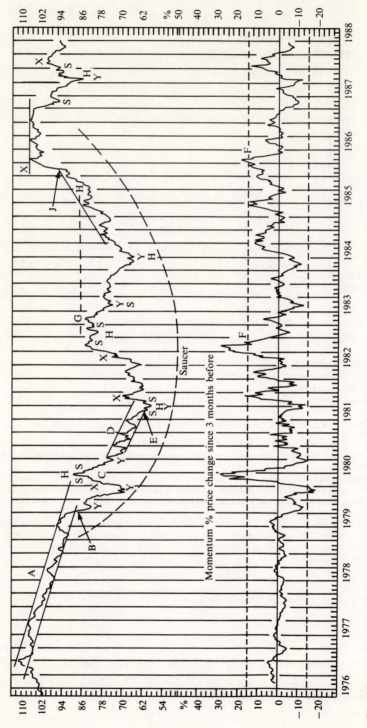

Fig. 22.15 A long-term chart pattern. Source: Bank Credit Analyst

3. Extreme momentum measures are often a warning that a direction change or at least a prolonged sideways movement lies ahead.
4. Major changes in direction are often preceded by changes in momentum.
5. Divergences (non-confirmations) between price and momentum indicators are often a warning of a possible change in the underlying trend.
6. Major changes in market direction are often preceded by an interim period of distribution.

How quickly should an investor react to an apparent trendbreak?

If the investor takes early action he risks being 'whipsawed' (a trend may appear to break several successive times in different directions involving the break-chasing investor in heavy dealing costs).

However, if the investor waits longer for a conclusive confirmation of a trendbreak he may miss a large proportion of the total price move. As an extreme example, a 40-week moving average trendbreak-chasing investor would actually have *lost* money during the 1980 bull market!

Table 22.1 illustrates possible trendbreak trading results from 1976–87.

Table 22.1. Illustration of possible trendbreak trading results, 1976–87[a]

Trendbreak signal (moving average)	No. of signals	No. of false signals	Gross profit ($000)	Possible net profit[b]
40-week	12	7	400[c]	340
13-week	28	13	490[d]	350

a Assumes each deal involves $1,000,000 nominal of Treasury 8·375% of 2000.
b Net profit assumes a transaction cost of 0·5% from dealing costs and delays, e.g. if bond rises sharply through a trendbreak point of 95, the investor may be fortunate if he can recognise the break and execute his order in time to buy before bond rises above 95·5.
c Such results can certainly not be guaranteed since they depend on a trend becoming clearly established and then lasting for some time. If trends are not long-lasting the trendbreak-chasing investor tends to accumulate a succession of small losses. For example, 110% of the gross profit on the 40-week moving average strategy depended on buying and then holding through two major moves. The other 10 signals produced an overall loss:

	Gross profit
July 1982–March 1983	160,000
Sept. 1984–March 1987	360,000
Two major signals	520,000
Other 10 signals	−120,000 (loss)
	400,000

d On the 13-week moving average strategy four major moves produced a gross profit of $590,000. The other 24 trades taken together lost $100,000.

Technical analysis or investing for value?

Technical analysis has been defined as the art (but *not* the science) of identifying a trend reversal at a relatively early stage and riding the new trend until the weight of evidence proves that the trend has again reversed. However, waiting till a trend change has been clearly signalled involves an obvious danger. The technical investor will normally buy only *after* a price has risen substantially and will not sell until *after* the price has fallen substantially. By contrast, a normal investor will usually feel that bonds offer worse value after a rise in price and better value after a fall in price. A technical enthusiast will try to resolve this paradox by claiming that a price move sufficient to trigger the technical signal will normally *reflect* a major change in the underlying fundamentals; thus buying at 90 on a strong technical picture could actually offer better value than buying at 85 on a weak technical picture.

Uses of technical analysis

The value of technical analysis is highly debatable and many fund managers will have no truck with it. Others find it a useful aid to short-term timing, but would never make a technically based investment move which ran contrary to their fundamental view.

23 Sentiment indicators

The significance of sentiment extremes

Investor sentiment extremes can be useful as contrarian indicators. A contrarian indicator works on the principle that the majority of investors are normally wrong about the market outlook. Thus, when investors are extremely bullish the market is normally near a peak and likely to fall. Conversely, when investors are extremely bearish the market is usually oversold and about to recover.

Two reasons for the contrarian effect if sentiment is extremely bullish may be identified:

1. Investors are likely to be already fully invested so that spare cash and immediate buying power are low.
2. Sentiment in the subsequent period will either be unchanged or more bearish. Thus the next move in sentiment is unlikely to produce more buying but may produce more selling.

Similarly, the contrarian effect if sentiment is bearish may occur for the following reasons:

1. Bearish investors are likely to be holding high cash reserves (implying potential buying power).
2. The next shift in sentiment is more likely to spark buying than selling.

The value of contrarian indicators

Contrarian indicators are potentially less useful for bonds than equities. Contrarian indicators are particularly useful in assessing the equity market because the flow of net new issues is generally small in relation to existing securities (average under 1% p.a. from 1971–83; negative since 1984). With a nearly fixed supply, price fluctuations are determined by fluctuations in demand which in the short term primarily reflect shifts in investor sentiment.

Contrarian indicators are still useful in the bond market, but less so than in equities. Fluctuations in investor demand are not dominant in determining prices because there are also significant changes in supply (between +8% p.a. and +20% p.a. under Reagan).

Investment advisers' optimism

Figure 23.1, based on a poll of US investment advisers, is a good example of the value of contrarian indicators.

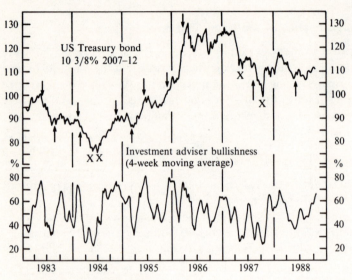

Points marked on bond price chart:
    ♦ Advisers over 75% bullish
    ♦ Advisers under 35% bullish
    X Advisers under 25% bullish

Fig. 23.1 Bond prices and market sentiment (four week moving average). Source: Hadady Corp., Pasadena, California.

When advisers were under 25% bullish, the market was normally about to rise (major bottoms in mid-1984 and autumn 1987; minor rally in spring 1987). Conversely, when these luminaries were 80% bullish, it normally paid to run like hell.

Fund managers' optimism

Figure 23.2 shows the percentage of bond mutual funds invested in liquid assets. High liquidity (indicating pessimism among bond fund managers)

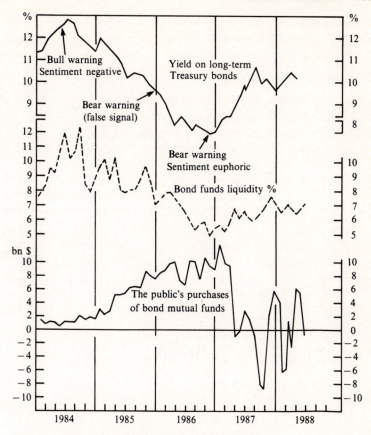

Fig. 23.2 Bond mutual funds sentiment indicators

often occurs at market bottoms (e.g. mid-1984 when long bond yields were over 12%). Low liquidity (indicating that bond fund managers are fully invested and extremely optimistic) often occurs at market peaks (e.g. late 1986 when bond yields were close to 7%). Even short-term fluctuations in liquidity show some negative correlation with future movement in bond prices.

Man-in-the-street optimism

Figure 23.2 also shows the public's purchases of bond mutual funds. Public buying often rises to extremes near market peaks (e.g. early 1987) and can go sharply negative near market troughs (e.g. autumn 1987).

However, it is a dangerous indicator because it is difficult to interpret and moves in relatively long-term cycles.

Examples of past signals

Mid-1984: Bull warning. Sentiment very negative. Investment advisers very bearish, bond fund liquidity high and public purchases low.

Late 1985: 'False' signal from investment advisers (very bullish, but for once they were right!).

Early 1987: Bear warning. Sentiment euphoric. Bond fund liquidity low and public purchases high. (Investment advisers also optimistic, though not extremely so.)

Part Six

Derivative instruments

24 Treasury futures

Description and uses

A futures contract is an obligation to buy or sell a particular commodity at a specified price on a specified future date. Treasury futures prices move closely with prices in the normal Treasury (cash) market because a futures seller is committed to eventually deliver a real Treasury bond at a specified price.

The principal US Treasury futures market is in Chicago, with significant trading in an identical contract on the London International Financial Futures Exchange (LIFFE – pronounced 'Life') (see Table 24.1).

Table 24.1. Chicago Board of Trade futures contracts

	Securities deliverable in settlement[a]
Long Treasury bond	Any bond with over 15 years to nearest call date.
Treasury note	Non-callable notes and bonds with between 6·5 and 10 years to maturity.
Short Treasury note (5 years)	Any of the four most recently auctioned 5-year Treasury notes with maturity between 4 years 3 months and 5 years 3 months.

a Quoted futures prices refer to a notional bond with 8% coupon. A conversion factor is applied if (as usual) the bond actually delivered has a different maturity or coupon.

Trading volume

Futures trading in the long Treasury bond (but not the shorts) is much higher than in the regular Treasury (cash) market. This makes futures very liquid and well suited to hedging or large position taking (see Tables 24.2 and 24.3).

Table 24.2. Daily trading volumes as % of outstanding US Treasury coupon securities, 1987

Maturity	Futures	Cash
Over 10 years	15·0	4·7
Under 10 years	0·2	2.4

Table 24.3. Trading volume in all US Treasury notes and bonds ($ bn), 1988

Cash market	14,000
Futures: Chicago Board of Trade	7,000
Chicago Mercantile Exchange	600
LIFFE	200

Uses of the futures market

The futures market is used for a number of purposes:

1. Exploitation of gearing. The initial margin on futures is typically between 2% and 5%. Thus a speculator can establish a position in Treasury bonds much greater than his immediate (or total!) cash resources.
2. Bear positions. Short selling of Treasuries in the cash market is normally impossible for an ordinary investor, and awkward for institutions or traders, since the short seller must deliver the bond to the purchaser on the next business day. A short seller can do this only if he is able to borrow the bond, which may be difficult or expensive.
3. Positioning ahead of new money arrival. If a fund manager expects the bond market to rise, he can effectively invest forthcoming new money (before it arrives!) at current prices by buying Treasury futures on margin.
4. Hedging. A holder of Treasury bonds can protect himself against a falling market by selling an equivalent volume of futures.

Possible hedgers include the following groups:

1. Marketmakers who find themselves involuntarily long or short. Rather than equalising their position by immediate forced buying or selling of a particular bond in the cash market (possibly on adverse terms), marketmakers may find it easier to take an offsetting position in futures.

2. Very large holders (e.g. pension funds) who fear that attempting to dump huge positions (especially if concentrated in a few bonds) ahead of an anticipated market fall would itself turn the market against them. The futures market can often absorb heavy selling with less price reaction since it is more liquid than the total cash market and much more liquid than any individual cash bond.

3. Market bears who do not wish to immediately sell a particular bond which appears (unsustainably) cheap relative to the general market. The holder can sell an equivalent volume of futures to offset his exposure to general market risk while postponing the sale of his particular bond till it regains its normal level relative to the general market.

4. Traders wishing to exploit anticipated changes in spreads between particular bonds and the general market. A trader can buy a particular bond which appears unsustainably cheap and short the futures to 'balance' his position. If the spread normalises as he anticipates, he will profit from the spread gain, while having protected himself from the risk of loss through a general rise in interest rates.

5. Investors wishing to postpone crystallising a capital gain tax liability. (*Caution:* this may be frustrated by tax rules on 'wash sales'.)

6. Corporate treasurers wishing to protect themselves against a possible rise in interest rates ahead of a forthcoming bond issue by their company. If interest rates rise, the immediate capital gain on a short position in Treasury futures can roughly offset the additional interest payable over the life of the planned corporate bond.

Margin requirements

Initial margin

The buyer or seller of futures must deposit an initial margin (typically at 2% to 5% of the future's nominal value) in Treasury bills or other collateral acceptable to the Exchange. This margin is held by the Clearing House as security for ultimate performance of the contract.

Variation margin

Futures positions are revalued ('marked to market') at the close of each business day. If a position has moved against the holder he must deposit additional margin to cover the move. Variation margin calls must be met in cash; collateral is *not* accepted. Daily variation margin calls force a futures investor whose position is deteriorating to quickly face the reality of his losses. This has proved a useful limit on overstretched positions.

If a position has moved in a holder's favour, the Clearing House will release margin or credit cash to his account (see Table 24.4).

Table 24.4. Illustration of margin calls

		Margin call
15 March	Buy Treasury bond futures contracts: $1,000,000 nominal at 97	Initial margin $40,000 (illustration based on 4% of nominal value of future)
16 March	Futures price drops to 96. Investor's book loss on the day = 1% of $1 m. = $10,000	Variation margin $10,000
17 March	Futures price drops to 93. Day's additional book loss = $30,000	Variation margin additional $30,000
18 March	Futures price rises to 95. Day's book gain $20,000	Variation margin $20,000 refunded
19 March	Futures price unchanged at 95. Investor sells	Variation margin no change[a] Initial margin original $40,000 released

a   Remaining net variation margin of $20,000 (representing $1m futures price fall from 97 to 95) remains deposited with the clearing house and is permanently lost when position is closed at 95.

The mechanics of delivery

Definitions

The short: A person who has sold the futures contract.
The long: A person who has bought the futures contract.

Futures contracts settled by delivery

Only 0·5% of contracts actually run to delivery. The other 99·5% of positions are closed out by reverse deals before delivery. Delivery months are March, June, September and December. Delivery days are between the first business day of the delivery month and the last-but-one business day. The short must deliver within this period on the day of his choice.

Delivery procedure (all times are US Central Standard Time)

Notification day   Two days before the first delivery day for that month's futures. Longs must declare their open positions (and notify any subsequent changes) to the Clearing House.

Day 1   Position day. (Two days before the day on which the
                     short chooses to deliver.) By 8 p.m. the short notifies
                     his clearing member that he wishes to deliver.

Day 2   Notice of intention day. By 8.30 a.m. the Clearing
                     Corporation matches the short's delivery notice with
                     the oldest long position. By 2 p.m. the short invoices
                     the matched long. Invoices are based on position-day
                     settlement price plus accrued interest to delivery day.

Day 3   Delivery day. By 10 a.m. the short deposits deliverable
                     securities at his bank for delivery to the long's bank via
                     the Fed book-entry system. By 1 p.m. the long's bank
                     accepts delivery and pays to the short's bank via the
                     Fed system.

Profit calculation on closure by delivery

The invoicing procedure is intended approximately to match the invoiced
cost and actual value of the delivered bond (though in practice the bond
delivered will normally be trading slightly below its invoiced price).

Gains and losses on the futures position itself are settled with the
Clearing House, which collects (or delivers) the variation margin
representing the difference between the original price at which a buyer or
seller acquired the futures position and the futures settlement price on
position day. Initial margin will be released after the futures positions are
liquidated on delivery day.

Conversion factors for long bonds

Futures prices are based on a notional Treasury bond with an 8% coupon.
A conversion factor is used to calculate the appropriate invoice price for
the bond actually delivered (which may have a coupon other than 8% and
a maturity anywhere between 15 and 30 years) (see Table 24.5).

Maturity date for calculation of conversion factor
The delivered bond's maturity is considered as the number of complete
calendar quarters remaining between the first day of the delivery month
and the bond's earliest call date. For example, a bond delivered against
a June 1989 futures contract with a first call date on 15 November 2006
(17 years 5 months and 14 days ahead) is treated as having 17 years and
1 quarter, i.e. 17 years 3 months, to maturity (see Table 24.6).

Table 24.5. Extract from conversion factors for Treasury futures invoicing

	Coupon Rate	
Term to maturity (years–months)	7%	7·5%
16–0	·9106	·9553
16–3	·9098	·9548
16–6	·9093	·9546
16–9	·9084	·9541
17–0	·9079	·9540

Note: The conversion factor is the price at which a bond of that coupon and maturity will have a GRY of 8%. *Source*: Financial Publishing Co., Boston, Mass.

Table 24.6. Adjusted maturity and Treasury futures invoicing factors

Bond	Adjusted maturity in June 1989 (years–months) June 1989	June 1990	Invoicing factor June 1989	June 1990
12% May 2005	15–9	14–9	1·3544	[a]
14% Nov. 2006–11	17–3	16–3	1·5588	1·5400
7·25% May 2016	26–9	25–9	0·9176[b]	0·9185

a No longer deliverable, because maturity will be below 15 years.
b Adjusted maturity was 28 years and invoicing factor 0·9166 for delivery against March 1988 futures (see Table 24.7).

Cheapest deliverable bond

Prices in the cash market may diverge from the relative prices implied by the conversion factors used in futures invoicing. The bond with the biggest discount between cash price and futures invoicing price will be the bond normally delivered.

Functions of the Chicago Board of Trade Futures Clearing Corporation

The Clearing Corporation:

(a)   records all deals;
(b)   guarantees all contracts;
(c)   determines gains and losses on all transactions;
(d)   monitors margin calls;
(e)   matches long positions with delivering sellers.

Table 24.7. Invoicing for Chicago Board of Trade futures delivery

Settlement month	March 1988
Position day	8 March 1988
Delivery day	10 March 1988
Settlement closing price on 8 March	93·01[a]
Bond delivered	7·25% of 15 May 2016
Actual maturity	28 years 2 months 7 days
Adjusted maturity	28 years 0 months
Conversion factor	0·9166
Bond price (93,031.25 × 0·9166)	85,272.44[b]
Accrued interest (116 days)	2,310.44
Total invoice price	87,582.88

a Futures prices are quoted in percentages plus thirty-seconds.
b This bond could actually be sold in the cash market on 8 March
   for about $85,875. It was therefore more valuable in the cash
   market and would not have been the bond normally delivered.

The Clearing Corporation as counterparty to every trade

Futures contracts are between buyer (or seller) and the Clearing
Corporation. This contrasts with forward contracts where buyer and
seller have claims only on each other. Thus the honouring of a futures
contract is not dependent on the creditworthiness of the original
counterparty, and positions may be closed at any time by purchase or sale
in the open market, i.e. closing a position does not depend on the
willingness of the original counterparty to also close out his position.

Futures pricing

Difference between current bond price and futures price

Futures prices will trade at a discount to current bond prices if long bonds
yield more than cash. In Table 24.8 no one will buy the future rather than
the cash bond unless he obtains a $2,000 capital gain to compensate for his
sacrifice of income, i.e. the June 1990 futures will trade at 98.

Yield differential futures pricing is enforced by arbitrageurs

For example, if the futures price in Table 24.8 was 97 and the yield
differential still 2%, arbitrageurs would buy the future (capital gain over
the next 12 months is almost guaranteed to be 3% greater than on the cash
bond but income yield is only 2% lower) and sell the cash bond. If the

Table 24.8. Alternative investments for $100,000 (June 1989 hypothetical prices)

	Yield for period to June 1990 ($)
A. Buy cash bond (price 100; yield 8%)	8,000
B. Hold cash (yield 6%) and buy June 90 futures	6,000

futures price were 99, arbitrageurs would sell the future (capital gain only 1% higher than on cash bond, and income yield 2% lower).

Normally futures prices track the cheapest deliverable bond less the following:

1. A discount (or with an inverted yield curve a premium) for the interest differential between bond yields and cash.
2. A further slight discount reflecting the fact that a long position in futures is less valuable than a long position in the current cheapest deliverable bond because:
   (a) the investor who is long of futures is not guaranteed delivery of the current cheapest deliverable bond but may receive a less attractive bond if, owing to fluctuation of market prices, another bond becomes cheaper to deliver;
   (b) the futures settlement price is fixed at 2 p.m. However the short does not have to give delivery notice till 8 p.m. If bond prices fall in cash market trading after 2 p.m., the futures short can buy a bond below futures settlement price and thus make a profit on delivery (i.e. the futures long finds himself in effect obliged to buy a cash bond at an out-of-date price).

Futures hedging

Futures hedging cannot be exact for the following reasons:

1. Interest rates on the cheapest deliverable bond (the basis of the long Treasury futures contract) will not always change in line with rates on the maturity of the bonds which the hedger actually owns.
2. The discount between a cash bond price and its futures deliverable price may vary.
3. Hedging a corporate bond position with a Treasury futures position is particularly inexact because spreads between corporate yields and Treasury bond yields are not constant.

Subject to these caveats, the simplest practical guide is that the hedger should sell futures equal to his nominal cash bond holding multiplied by the delivery conversion factor (see Table 24.9).

Table 24.9. Example of hedge ratio

Holding to be hedged:
$10,000,000 nominal of Treasury 12% of 15 May 2005.

Conversion factors for delivery:
Against March 1989 futures: 1·3575
Against March 1990 futures: 1·3458

Theoretical hedge:
Sell $13,575,000 March 1989 futures *or* $13,458,000 March 1990 futures.

Closest actual hedge:
Sell $13,600,000 March 1989 futures or $13,500,000 March 1990 futures. (Minimum futures dealing unit is one contract representing $100,000 nominal.)

---

25 Options on Treasury bonds and on Treasury bond futures

Definitions and examples

Difference between futures and options

A *futures* buyer has a binding obligation. An *options* buyer has acquired a right but no obligation. Thus his loss cannot exceed the cost of his option while his *possible* profit could be very high.

Types of option

A *call* is an option enabling the buyer to purchase a specified Treasury bond (or Treasury future) at a predetermined price through a given time period until expiration.

A *put* is an option enabling the buyer to sell a specified Treasury bond or future.

Options on bonds and options on futures are both traded. Options on Treasury futures are generally preferred, because: they are more liquid, and if an option is exercised neither holder nor writer has to produce the full cash or a specific bond immediately, but only the margin required to open a futures position.

Option price quotations

Table 25.1 gives examples of option price quotations. Prices in the table are shown in decimals for convenience. However, in the market, option premiums are conventionally quoted in percentages plus 64ths. Thus an options quote of 1·16 (1 plus ^{16}/64ths) means a decimal price of 1·25%, or $1,250 for an option on $100,000 nominal of Treasury bonds.

Table 25.1. Call options to buy $100,000 nominal of Treasury bond September futures (priced at 12 May 1988; option expires 19 August 1988[a])

	A	B	C
September futures price (on 12 May)	86·656	86·656	86·656
Option exercise price[b]	84	86	90
Option intrinsic value[c]	2·656	0·656	nil
Option time premium[d]	0·685	1·953	0·922
Option cost	3·875	2·609	0·922

a After expiry date an unexercised option becomes worthless.
b Price at which options holder can demand to buy the future.
c The excess (if any) of futures price above option exercise price. This value could be immediately realised by exercising the option, thus buying the future at exercise price, and then reselling the future at market price. For example, option holder A could buy the future at 84 and then resell at 86·656, realising 2·656. However, immediate exercise is normally unwise (unless expiration is imminent) since an option can usually be sold in the market at a price above its intrinsic value.
d Time premium reflects a market estimate of the probability that the futures price may rise above (or further above) exercise price before expiration date. Time premium will decay to zero as option expiration date approaches).

Option jargon

Premium   The price paid by the option buyer.

At-the-money   An option whose exercise price equals the bond's current market price.

In-the-money   A call option with an exercise price below the bond's market price (so that the difference could be immediately realised by exercising the option, and then reselling the acquired bond in the market) or a put option with an exercise price above the bond's market price.

Intrinsic (i.e. minimum) value   The amount, if any, by which an option is in the money. Intrinsic value cannot be negative since an option owner cannot be compelled to exercise an unprofitable option.

Out-of-the-money   A call option with an exercise price higher than the bond's current price (so that exercise produces an immediate loss) or a put option with an exercise price lower than the bond's current price.

Option writing

The option seller (or writer) receives the option price (premium), but is committed to buy or sell if the option buyer exercises. The option writer therefore accepts a high degree of market risk.

A *covered call* is a call option written by a holder of the underlying security (who can thus deliver it if called). Uncovered (or naked) option writing can be extremely dangerous.

Option strategies

Profit profiles for option investors

There are four basic actions:

1.   Buy calls.
2.   Buy puts.
3.   Write calls.
4.   Write puts.

Each action has a profit profile as shown in Figs. 25.1 to 25.4.

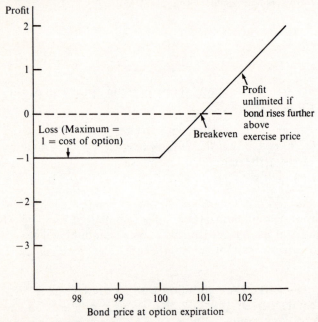

Fig. 25.1 Profit profile of call option buyer: illustrating exercise price 100, cost of call option 1. Note: Investor's maximum loss is the cost of his option 1. Investor breaks even if the bond price closes at 101 (gain on exercising option to buy at 100 exactly balances original cost of option). Investor's profit can increase without limit if bond price rises further above option exercise price.

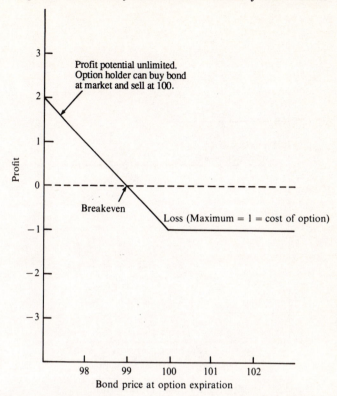

Fig. 25.2 Profit profile of put option buyer: illustrating exercise price
100, cost of put option 1

In all cases the loss is limited for a buyer (maximum loss is the cost of his
option) and possible profit is unlimited. Things are different for the
option writer. His maximum profit is the option premium he receives, but
his possible loss is unlimited.

Options strategies can reduce (or increase) portfolio risk

Paying $3,000 to buy a three-month option on $100,000 futures is less
risky than buying $100,000 futures. The maximum loss on the options is
their cost of $3,000. By contrast, the futures purchase *might* lose $12,000
in three months. (Futures crashes of this speed and magnitude occurred
four times in the five years 1983–7.)

However, investing $100,000 in options involves much greater risk than
investing $100,000 in futures, since individual options may lose 100% of
their value by expiration. Uncovered option writing can involve very high

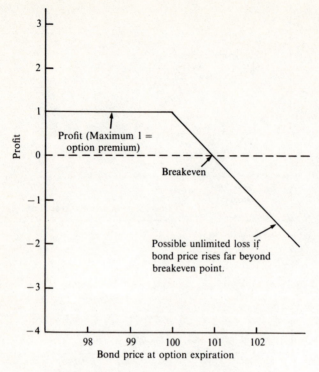

Fig. 25.3 Profit profile of call option writer

risks. However, covered option writing can be used to reduce portfolio fluctuations (see page 206).

Uses of option buying

Speculation with limited risk

The option buyer acquires control over a bond holding vastly in excess of his immediate cash resources. However, his maximum loss is the cost of his option, in contrast to the unlimited risk assumed by a futures buyer or seller. Options can therefore be an ideal speculative instrument for a risk-averse investor of limited means.

Insurance against being wrong

A bondholder who expects a sharp fall in the market can do either of the following things:

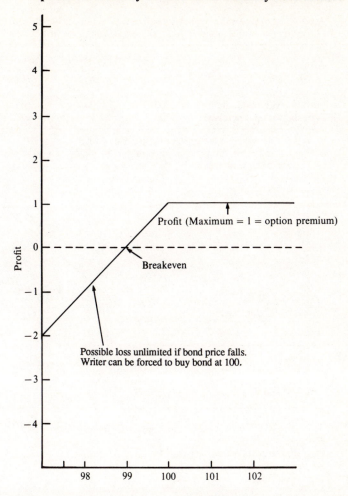

Fig. 25.4 Profit profile of put option writer

1. Sell his bond.
2. Buy put options, entitling him to sell his bond at around the current price.

If the market *does* fall sharply, the bond seller does better because he saves the price of the put options. However, if he is wrong the bond seller has cut himself off from a rising market. By contrast, the put buyer can continue to enjoy market appreciation. In effect, the put buyer has insured himself against being wrong. Table 25.2 and Fig. 25.5 compare the profit profiles from bond sale and put purchase.

Table 25.2. Future value of portfolio: bond sale and put purchase compared (illustration with present bond price 100, put option to sell at 100: cost 2)

	Bond price at option expiration		
	90	100	110
Portfolio with bond sale[a]	100	100	100
Portfolio with put purchase[b]	98	98	108

a Bond seller receives the present bond price of 100.
b Put buyer secures future bond price subject to a minimum value of 100, less the cost of his option (2).

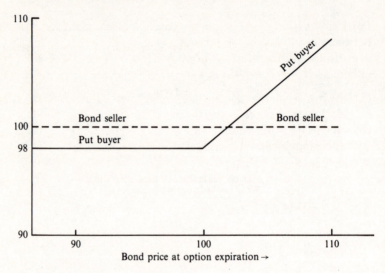

Fig. 25.5 Future value of position

Superior return in volatile market

Cash-plus-bond-call-options will produce a better return than bonds alone in the event of a violent market movement, irrespective of whether the market moves sharply up or sharply down (see Tables 25.3 and 25.4).

Table 25.3. Alternative portfolios (bond v. cash-plus-call-options)

Portfolio A: bond	100
Portfolio B: 2 call options at 102 (cost 1 each)	2
Cash	98
	100

Table 25.4. Comparison of portfolio performance (bond v. cash-plus-call-options)

	94	98	102	106	110
Price of bond at expiration date	94	98	102	106	110
Value of 1 option to buy at 102	0	0	0	4	8
Portfolio B (cash-plus-options)					
Value of 2 options	0	0	0	8	16
Less: cost of 2 options	−2	−2	−2	−2	−2
Net profit on portfolio B	−2	−2	−2	6	14
Portfolio A (bond only)					
Profit[a]	−6	−2	2	6	10

a Capital gain on bond with initial price of 100.

Portfolio A (bond only) outperforms if bond price at expiration is between 98 and 106, as illustrated in Figure 25.6.

Portfolio B (cash-plus-call-options) outperforms if bond's price is either:

(a) below 98 (in this case the capital loss on the bond is greater than the cost of the two, now worthless options), or
(b) above 106, when the profit from exercising the two options exceeds the capital gain on one bond.

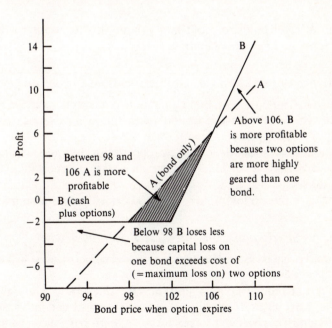

Fig. 25.6 Profit comparison (straight bond v. cash-plus-call option)

Cash-plus-options-buying

A cash-plus-options portfolio can be safer than a pure bond portfolio in circumstances where violent market moves are likely but the direction of the move is unclear, e.g.:

(a) depending on whether tomorrow's trade deficit release is good or bad;

(b) when bonds are cheap on a long-term basis, but in the short term are being pushed still lower by a strong economy (a common situation late in a bond bear market). The investor knows that the eventual bullish turning point (when the economy finally softens) is likely to be violent; however, he cannot guess the timing of the turn or the level bond prices will fall to before the turn. He therefore prefers cash plus options to a simple bond holding.

Bond-plus-put-option-strategy

A bondholder who expects a volatile market but is uncertain of its direction may buy put options to limit the downside risk on his holding, while remaining free to enjoy any price appreciation.

Note

An option buyer tends to profit in a volatile market; option writing is more profitable in a flattish market.

Equivalence of two strategies and implications for option pricing

Portfolio A: Call option on bond plus sufficient cash to exercise.
Portfolio B: Bond plus put option (with the same exercise price as portfolio A's call option).
On option expiration date the two portfolios become identical as illustrated in Table 25.5. This produces an equation important in option pricing theory:
Bond price + put option price $\approx$ Exercise price + call option price

Why the two portfolios become identical on expiration date

If the bond price is above the exercise price, both portfolios will end up with 100% cash:
Portfolio A abandons its call option (now worthless) and retains its cash.
Portfolio B exercises its put option and converts its bond into cash.
If the bond price is below the exercise price, both portfolios end up with 100% cash:

Portfolio A exercises its call and converts its cash into bond.
Portfolio B abandons its put (now worthless) and keeps its bond.

Table 25.5. Illustration of equivalence of two option strategies

		Position on option expiry	
	Now	Bond at 95	Bond at 105
A			
Cash	100	100	—
Bond	—	—	105
Call option	2	—	—
	102	100	105
B			
Cash	—	100	—
Bond	100	—	105
Put option	2	—	—
	102	100	105

———→ indicates option exercised.

Note Portfolio A (cash plus call) always has the same value as portfolio B (bond plus put).

Option writing

Rationale

Option writing is apparently a thankless pursuit since the writer's maximum profit is the premium received, while his potential loss is unlimited. However, in practice option writers can demand premiums high enough to compensate for their risks *over long periods*.

Option writing to increase income in flat markets

If a bondholder anticipates a flat or slightly down market, he can write a covered call on his bonds rather than sell outright. The call premium will offset a small price fall and be pure profit if the market remains flat. Similarly, if he anticipates a flat or slightly up market, an investor with cash might do better to write puts rather than buy bonds outright.

Option writing to reduce cost of intended purchase

An investor prepared to buy the Treasury bond slightly below its current price may write a put option. The put option premium received lowers his cost basis if the bond falls to his intended purchase limit, and is additional income if it does not. In either case, he has done better than he would have done by simply waiting for the market to weaken. (However, once he has written the option, he can no longer change his mind if the bond subsequently falls to his intended purchase level as a result of unforeseen bad news.)

Covered option writing to reduce portfolio volatility

A bondholder who writes call options on his bonds has:

(a)   reduced his loss in a down market;
(b)   improved his return in a flat or slightly up market; and
(c)   limited his profit from a sharply rising market.

In this case option writing has effectively *limited risk* by reducing the range of fluctuation in the portfolio's performance (see Fig. 25.7).

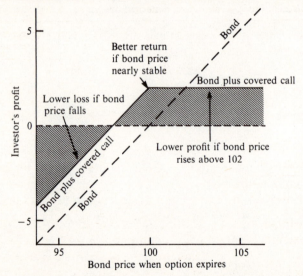

Fig. 25.7 Covered call writing to reduce portfolio fluctuations. Current bond price 100; premium of 2 received for writing call at 100. Comments on the figure indicate how covered call writing tends to stabilise the portfolio's return. For price between 95 and 105, bond plus write 1 covered call strategy yields return between −3 and +2; simple bond yields return between −5 and +5.

Exotic strategies

There are many variations, described at length in the specialist literature. We give just one example (the 'long butterfly' option strategy) by way of illustration. The strategy is illustrated in Fig. 25.8, Table 25.6 and Fig. 25.9. The objective is to profit from time premium decay (see page 306) on call options written while limiting risk.

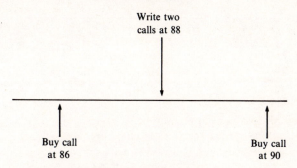

Fig. 25.8 Long butterfly option strategy

Table 25.6. Profit profile of long butterfly

	Cost of options[a]	Value of options according to bond price at expiration			
		85	88	90	92
Buy 1 call at 86	+2·8	0	2	4	6
Write 2 calls at 88	−3·1	0	0	−4	−8
Buy 1 call at 90	+0·8	0	0	0	2
Total cost/value	+0·5	0	2	0	0
Overall profit[b]		−0·5	+1·5	−0·5	−0·5

a   Prices at 8 June 1988 of options on September T-bond future.
b   Profit = value of options at expiration less their cost of 0·5.

Maximum loss: 0·5 (net cost of option position).
Maximum profit: 1·5, if option expires with bond close to 88 (exercise price of the calls written).
Breakeven points: 86·5 and 89·5 (exercise *price* of the long calls, adjusted for the net cost of the options position).

Assessment of long butterfly strategy
This is a low-risk strategy for an investor who believes bond prices will

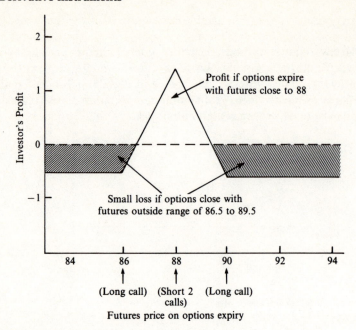

Fig. 25.9 Profit profile on long butterfly

stabilise around the mid-point of his butterfly. The time premium in the 88 call option price will decay if the futures remain close to 88 as expiration date approaches.

The option writer can normally enjoy time premium decay only by assuming high risk. However, the long butterfly's risk is limited to the original cost of his position, since if his short position in two calls moves against him, this will be offset by his long position in the two other calls moving in his favour.

Option pricing

An option price equals intrinsic value plus a time premium representing a market estimate of the probability that the underlying bond will reach a certain price before the option expires. Estimating this probability (and hence the 'correct' price for an option) is a chancy business, ultimately dependent on assuming that the degree of future bond price variability can be estimated from past bond price variability.

The usual procedure is to assume that probable future bond prices are 'normally' (or lognormally) distributed about current bond prices, with a degree of dispersion estimated from their historic standard deviation. Appendix 4 gives a simplified illustration of the principle.

An option will be more valuable if the standard deviation (a measure of bond price volatility) is high, implying a greater degree of uncertainty about future bond prices and a greater chance that a bond price will rise above (or further above) the option exercise price before the option expires.

Figure 25.10 shows theoretical prices for put and call options assuming standard deviations of either 2% or 6% of the current bond price.

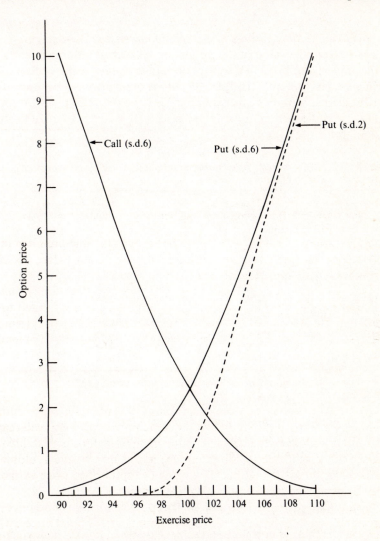

Fig. 25.10 Theoretical option values (bond price 100)

For simplicity, the illustrations assume an option with one-year life and standard deviations based on bond price *levels*. In practice, quoted options usually have lives of nine months or less and the annualised standard deviations used in option pricing models (e.g. Black–Scholes) are usually based on daily bond price *changes*.

The 'Delta'

Sensitivity of option prices to changes in underlying bond prices
The percentage value of the option always changes more violently than the underlying bond. However, the dollar value of the option always changes less violently. In Table 25.7 if the bond price rises $1 from 100 to 101, the call option's *absolute* price rise is only $0.5 (from 1·6 to 2·1). However, the option's percentage price rise is 30%, compared with the bond price rise of only 1%.

Table 25.7. Theoretical call option prices: illustrating the Delta (option exercise price 100, standard deviation of futures price 4%)

Futures price	Theoretical call option price[a]	Change in option price if futures price rises $1
95	0·20	0·13
96	0·33	0·19
97	0·52	0·27
98	0·79	0·35
99	1·14	0·45
100	1·59	0·55
101	2·14	0·64
102	2·78	0·74
103	3·52	0·80
104	4·32	0·87
105	5·19	0·92

a   Illustration assuming one-year option with exercise price of 100.

The gradient of the option price curve plotted on a chart against the underlying bond price is known as 'the Delta' (see Fig. 25.11). As can be seen, the Delta varies from nearly zero in the case of deeply out-of-the-money options to nearly one in the case of heavily in-the-money options.

Option hedging

Option hedging is normally less satisfactory than futures hedging for the following reasons:

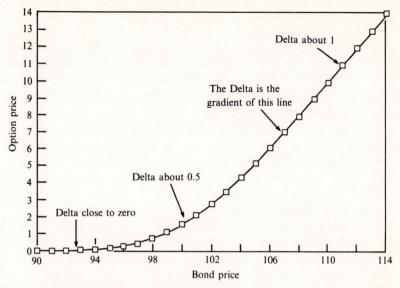

Fig. 25.11 Theoretical call option prices (option exercise price 100, standard deviation of bond price 4%)

1. The option buyer has to pay not only for his true hedge (on intrinsic value) but also for the time premium (which will decay towards zero, the longer that the hedge is kept on). Thus option hedging is normally suitable only over very short periods when time premium decay will not be significant.
2. The 'Delta' is not constant so that option hedges cannot approximate to being exact.

The following equation offers a rough guide for option hedging:

Required hedge ≈

$$\frac{\text{Nominal bond holding} \times \text{Conversion factor for futures dealing}}{\text{Option delta}}$$

Example of option hedging by bond investor (prices of 8 June 1988)
Bond holding: $10,000,000 Treasury 12% 2005
Futures delivery conversion factor: 1·3733 (for delivery in September 1988)
Futures price: 88
Option Exercise price: 88
Delta: 0·5

Theoretical required hedge ≈ ($10,000,000 × 1·3733) ÷ 0·5 = $27,466,000

Closest available hedge: Put options to sell $27,500,000 of September 1988 T-bond futures (smallest dealing unit is $100,000). The required options purchase *must exceed* the nominal value of the bond holding to be hedged because, if interest rates change, the dollar price of an option on a bond will change less than the dollar price of the underlying bond.

Example of option hedging by corporate treasurer
A company plans a bond issue in one week's time, but fears a rise in interest rates meanwhile.
Intended bond issue: $10 m.
Approximate conversion factor: 1·0 (estimated from futures conversion factor of Treasury issue with same maturity and coupon).
Treasury futures price: 100.
Option exercise price: 100.
Delta : 0·5.

Hedging guideline
Buy put options on $24 m. of Treasury bond futures ($10 m. × 1·2 ÷ 0·5). If interest rates rise, the capital gain on the bond future will roughly offset the present value of the increased coupon payments due over the life of the company's bond.

In this case option hedging is practicable for the following reasons:

1. Time premium decay will not be significant over a period as short as one week.
2. It avoids a lot of administrative hassle with futures margin calls.

Hedging 'bonus' from a big sudden move in interest rates

In the event of a big sudden change in interest rates (either up or down), the hedger's profit will *exceed* the planned hedging offset, because the Delta is not constant.

In Table 25.8 the Delta is approximately 0·5 with a futures price of 100. Thus a small change in the futures price (e.g. $1) is exactly offset by an equal and opposite change in the value of 2 put options.

However, if the futures price falls from 100 to 96, the put option's value rises not $2 but $2·7 (from 1·6 to 4·3) because the *Delta rises above 0·5* as

Table 25.8. Illustrating the Delta and hedging with put options (option exercise price 100, standard deviation of futures price 4%)

Futures price	Theoretical put option price	Approx. Delta	Combined value 1 future plus 2 put options
96	4·3	0·8	104·6
97	3·5	0·8	104·0
98	2·8	0·7	103·6
99	2·1	0·6	103·2
100	1·6	0·5	103·2
101	1·1	0·4	103·2
102	0·8	0·3	103·6
103	0·5	0·2	104·0
104	0·3	0·2	104·6

the option moves more deeply into-the-money. Thus the put option's value rises more than needed for a simple hedging offset.

Conversely, if the futures price rises from 100 to 104, the put option's value falls not by 2 but only by 1·3 because the *Delta falls below 0·5* as the option moves more deeply out-of-the money. Thus the hedger's loss on 2 puts is less than his profit on the future.

Note

This felicitous result (hedger appearing to do better than break even, whatever happens to bond prices) depends on a sharp price change occurring *over a time period so short* that the hedging profit windfall is not offset by decay of the option time premium.

Mechanics of Chicago Board of Trade option trading

General

The Chicago Board of Trade (CBOT) Clearing House guarantees each transaction, and becomes the official counter-party for both buyer and seller. Option trades are settled in cash the following business day.

Margin requirements

There are no margin requirements for option buyers. An option writer must deposit relevant bonds or other acceptable collateral. His required margin will change daily, following changes in the price of the underlying bond or future.

Option exercise time

A CBOT option holder can exercise on any day up to expiration day. The option writer has *no* control over whether or when an option is exercised.

Exercise procedure for option on futures

The option holder's broker notifies the Options Clearing House of intention to exercise in writing by 8 p.m. The Clearing House then selects a counter-party at random from the pool of outstanding writers of that particular option. The counter-party will be notified before business opens the following day.

In the case of a call option on futures, the option holder assumes a long futures position at the option exercise price, and the option writer acquires a corresponding short futures position. The Futures Clearing House will immediately collect the initial margin from both parties and also collect (or release) a variation margin representing the difference between the option exercise price and the futures closing price on the previous day (i.e. the day when the holder notified the Clearing House of his wish to exercise).

Exercise procedure for option on cash bonds

The day after notice, the matched parties conclude a bargain representing setlement of the options contract. The bargain is settled two days after notice. For example, a call option writer delivers the called bond against the option holder's payment of exercise price (plus accrued interest).

Expiration time for CBOT options on Treasury bond futures

Expiration time is at 8 p.m. Chicago time on the first Friday preceding by at least six business days the first delivery day of the relevant Treasury futures contract.

> Example:
> September 1988 Treasury futures may be delivered on Thursday 1 September (the first business day of the month). Counting back six business days brings us to Wednesday 24 August. Options on September 1988 Treasury futures therefore expire at 8 p.m. on Friday 19 August.

Closing bargains

Instead of exercising, an option buyer may realise the value of his position by selling his option in the open market. Similarly, an option writer may close his position by buying back the same option in the open market (provided he buys back *before* he receives an exercise notice). Closing bargains must be specifically designated as such so that the position is cancelled out at the Clearing House.

Part Seven

Indices and performance measurement

Introduction

An index is simply a means of providing an overall picture of market movements based on a number of representative bonds with some appropriate weighting. Clients often specify a particular index against which an investment manager's performance will be judged. There are many rival Treasury bond indices. However, the Salomon indices are probably the most widely followed.

Salomon indices

Construction

Salomon Treasury bond indices are published monthly for four separate maturity bands:

    1–3 years
    3–7 years
    7–10 years
    Over 10 years

Each index includes *all* Treasury bonds in that maturity range, weighted by market value. This avoids distortion through unrepresentative selection and automatically includes capital gains resulting from the yield curve ride.

Minor theoretical hazards of Salomon indices

The indices are not really comparing like with like since each index's average maturity (and average coupon rate) is constantly shifting as:

(a) bonds enter and then leave the index as their maturity shortens;

(b) a heavy new Treasury issue may suddenly shift an index's average maturity;
(c) in the absence of new issues or composition shifts, the passage of time alters the index's average maturity;
(d) the callable bonds included in each index may at times trade as bonds of five years' shorter maturity.

Single-bond indices

Such indices measure the performance of a hypothetical fund invested only in a single bond with the coupons immediately reinvested in the same bond. Single-bond indices are often used as a convenient internal yardstick for fund managers. Some external clients also specify a single bond (often a benchmark Treasury) against which performance is to be measured.

Advantages of single-bond index

Table 26.1 illustrates the calculation of a single-bond index. This type of index has the following advantages:

1. It is simple and easily calculated, if necessary on a daily basis (with accrued interest included).
2. Once the bond has been chosen, the index is unarguable, unlike complex indices where there is wonderful scope for choosing alternative constituents and/or weighting methods.

Table 26.1. Illustration of a single bond index[a]

Period	(1) Bonds owned (nominal value) at period start before reinvesting coupon	(2) Coupon received $(1) \times \cdot 05$	(3) Bond price	(4) New bonds purchased (nominal value) $(2) \div (3)$	(5) Total bonds owned (nominal value) at period start after reinvesting coupon $(1) + (4)$	(6) Index (= market value of bonds owned) $(5) \times (3) \div 100$
0	100·00[b]	——	90·00	——	100·00	90·00[c]
1	100·00	5·00	80·00	6·25	106·25	85·00
2	106·25	5·31	110·00	4·83	111·08	122·19
3	111·08	5·55	92·00	6·03	117·11	107·74[d]

a Bond is assumed to be a 10% Treasury, paying a 5% coupon gross half-yearly.
b Initial purchase.
c Index may be rebased to Period 0 = 100 (or to any other chosen date = 100) if desired.
d In this case the bond's index over the three half-years has risen from 90 to 107·74 (reflecting coupons of 15·86 and net capital gain of 1·88), a total gain of 17·74 points or 19·7%.

Disadvantage of single-bond index

The bond chosen may move unrepresentatively for any of the following reasons:

1. Its own particular features, e.g. unusual duration or convexity for its maturity.
2. Market changes, e.g. sharp shift in the yield curve in the bond's locality.
3. Investor preference changes, e.g. lower differential on high-coupon bonds after the 1986 US tax reform.

Any single bond chosen will tend to become less marketable (and so probably less reliable as an indicator) over time.

   If the bond is changed at intervals (e.g. as a new benchmark bond appears) a creeping distortion may be introduced because seasoned bonds usually trade on slightly higher GRYs than new benchmark bonds of the same maturity. Thus, bonds tend to underperform slightly as they cease to be benchmarks.

Ibbotson indices (since 1925)
Basis

Long-term Ibbotson indices are based on a single bond with maturity around 20 years; medium-term Ibbotson indices are based on a single bond with maturity of five to eight years. The single bond is believed to be reasonably typical (i.e. without distortionary tax or call features) and is periodically changed as shortening maturity or loss of marketability make it less representative.

Uses

The Ibbotson indices are narrowly based and not well tailored for performance measurement against specific constraints (e.g. clients specifying that average maturity may not exceed five years). However, their consistent history since December 1925 makes them extremely useful for long-term historical analysis including comparisons with other investments (see Appendix 1).

27   Performance measurement

The principal methods for measuring performance (with adjustments for new money) are money-weighted ('internal') rate of return and time-weighted rate of return.

Money-weighted (internal) return

Each sum of money is weighted by the length of time it is in the fund, and an average return calculated (see Table 27.1).

Table 27.1. Example of internal return calculation; period examined is 2 years (730 days)

	$	Day when money arrives[a]	Days in fund
Fund initial value	100	0	730
New money	5	140	590
New money	15	500	230
Fund closing value	135	730	n.a.

a   Or day when fund is valued.

Calculation method

Let x be the daily compounding factor. Each amount of money put into the fund is then weighted by x^n, where n is the number of days the money remains in the fund. The internal rate of return can then be found by solving the resultant equation, which is, for the example of Table 27.1:

$$100x^{730} + 5x^{590} + 15x^{230} = 135$$

Whence x (daily compounding factor) = 1·000177
Half-yearly compounding factor = $x^{182·5}$ = 1·0328
Half-yearly internal return = 3·28%
Conventional annual return = 6·56%

Internal return accurately measures an individual fund's return, taken in isolation. However, it is useless for performance comparisons because the internal return can vary extraordinarily, depending on the fortuitous timing of new money inflows (see Table 27.2 for an example).

Table 27.2. Internal return calculation (illustrating performance distorted by new money timing)

	Market index	Fund A	Fund B
1 January	100	100	100
1 April	100	150 (100 + 50)	100
1 July	120	180	170 (120 + 50)
1 January	100	150	142
Internal return	0	0	−6·4% p.a.

Notes
1. Bracketed figures indicate arrival of new money. Fund A receives 50 new money on 1 April. Fund B receives 50 new money on 1 July.
2. Both funds are fully invested in the market index at all times, and 'should' therefore have identical performance.
3. However, B appears to have underperformed because its new money misses the bull phase, while arriving just in time to participate fully in the bear phase. B's bear-phase performance (when B had more money) is therefore overweighted.

Time-weighted return

The whole portfolio is revalued each time new money arrives (or departs). Thus portfolio performance is measured over a number of separate mini-time segments, during each of which there is no new money distortion. The separate rates of return are then chain-multiplied together to calculate an overall return (undistorted by new money inflows) which can be converted to an annual rate of return and be compared with an index or with the performance of rival fund managers (see Table 27.3).

Table 27.3. Calculation of time-weighted return

Fund starting value   :   100
New money received :   5 on Day 140; 15 on Day 500
Fund closing value   :   135 after 2 years (730 days)

Fund value (including new money) at period-start	Fund value (before new money) at period-end
100 (at Day 0)	123 (at Day 140)
128 (Day 140)	130 (Day 500)
145 (Day 500)	135 (Day 730)

Total performance (over two years) $= \dfrac{123}{100} \times \dfrac{130}{128} \times \dfrac{135}{145} = 1 \cdot 163$

Table 27.3. Continued
Half-yearly compounding factor = $^4\sqrt{1\cdot163}$ = 1·0385

∴ Half-yearly return = 3·85%
Conventional annual return = 7·70%

Notes
1. This result does not vary with the size or timing of new money inflows, and is not affected by the mini-periods of performance comparison being of different lengths.
2. The root to be taken in calculating the annual rate of return does *not* vary with the number of separate mini-time segments. It depends solely on the total length of time over which performance is measured. For example, with a three-year performance record, half-yearly compounding factors are calculated from the sixth root of the chain-multiplied performance comparisons, irrespective of whether the number of chain-multiplied comparisons is only 1 (no new money at all) or 762 (new money injections or withdrawals on each trading day).

Use of a divisor to calculate time-weighted return

The divisor is that number which, when divided into the current value of the portfolio, removes any distortion resulting from current or past new money inflows, and produces an adjusted value which can be directly compared with the fund's base value or any other adjusted value. The return can now be calculated between any two dates.

Table 27.4. Example of time-weighted return calculation using a divisor

	(1) Fund before new money	(2) New money	(3) Fund after new money (1) + (2)	(4) Adjustment to divisor[a] (3) ÷ (1)	(5) New divisor[b]	(6) Adjusted fund value[c] (3) ÷ (5)
1 Jan. 86	100	0	100	1	1	100
21 May 86	123	5	128	1·0407[d]	1·0407	123[e]
16 May 87	130	15	145	1·1154[f]	1·1608[g]	124·9
1 Jan. 88	135	−10	125	0·9259	1·0748	116·3
1 Jan. 89	141	0	141	1	1·0748	131·2

a   Adjustment to divisor = fund value with new money ÷ fund value prior to injection of new money.
b   Divisor for each period equals divisor for previous period multiplied by adjustment factor. Divisor then remains unchanged until next arrival or departure of new money.
c   Adjusted fund value = actual value (after new money) ÷ divisor.
d   128 ÷ 123.
e   128 ÷ 1·0407.
f   145 ÷ 130.
g   1·1154 × 1·0407.

Example of return calculation (Table 27.4)
Period: From 1 Jan. 1986 to 1 Jan. 1989 (six half-years).
Performance for six half-years = $131 \cdot 2 \div 100 = 1 \cdot 312$
Performance for one half-year = $\sqrt[6]{1 \cdot 312}$
$$= (1 \cdot 312)^{0 \cdot 167}$$
$$= 1 \cdot 0463$$
Return per half-year = $4 \cdot 63\%$
Conventional annual return = $9 \cdot 26\%$

Further example
Period: 1 June 1986 to 1 Sept. 1987 (2.5 half-years).

	1 June 86	1 Sept 87
Fund value:	143	148·5
Divisor value:	1·0407	1·1608
Adjusted fund value:	137·41	127·93

Performance for 2·5 half-years = $127 \cdot 93 \div 137 \cdot 41 = 0 \cdot 931$
Performance for 1 half-year = $\sqrt[2 \cdot 5]{0 \cdot 931}$
$$= (0 \cdot 931)^{0 \cdot 4}$$
$$= 0 \cdot 972$$
Return per half-year = $-2 \cdot 8\%$
Conventional annual return = $-5 \cdot 6\%$

Hazards of time-weighted return

Theoretically the method is perfect but practically it is cumbersome since it requires a full portfolio revaluation on every separate occasion that new money arrives. In practice, rough approximation is often employed, e.g. assuming all new money to have arrived at a month-end. The resultant inaccuracy can distort comparisons.

Performance measurement criteria must be strict (and predetermined)

Suppose a fund manager sells a bond and holds the proceeds in cash pending possible reinvestment. If the bond market crashes the fund manager may want to measure the cash as still part of his bond fund (which will outperform if it is liquid during a bear market). This will distort comparisons unless similar treatment is also *consistently* applied if the bond market rises (in which case a liquid bond fund will underperform and a versatile fund manager will often be keen to measure his cash performance as part of a completely separate money market portfolio).

Part Eight

Further theory

28 Further theory on duration, convexity and returns

Duration

Bond duration decline with passage of time

Strictly speaking, modified duration declines relatively smoothly at a rate of just under one day's duration per calendar day in the intervals *between* coupon payments, and then jumps sharply when a coupon is paid. The true relationship of duration versus time is thus a sawtooth pattern about an underlying decline. However, charts usually plot duration on coupon dates only, thus showing a smooth pattern (see Fig. 28.1).

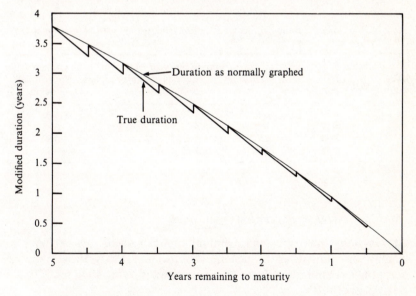

Fig. 28.1 Bond modified duration through time: bond coupon 12%, GRY 10%

Bonds, coupon retention and duration decline with time

If bond coupon payments are retained in the portfolio as cash (thus
steadily diluting the portfolio's duration) the portfolio's overall duration
will also shrink at nearly 1 per annum, even if it consists of long bonds
where quoted duration is apparently insensitive to small changes in
maturity (see Tables 28.1 and 28.2).

Table 28.1. Modified duration shrinkage with time (illustration with bond coupon 10%,
GRY 10%)

| Initial maturity | Initial duration | Duration one year later: | | Change from initial duration |
		Bond only	Bond plus year's coupons held as cash	
30	9·46	9·41	8·56	−0·90
10	6·23	5·84	5·31	−0·92
5	3·86	3·23	2·94	−0·92
3	2·54	1·77	1·61	−0·93

Table 28.2. Modified duration shrinkage with time (illustration with bond coupon 15%,
GRY 15%)

| Initial maturity | Initial duration | Duration one year later: | | Change from initial duration |
		Bond only	Bond plus year's coupons held as cash	
30	6·58	6·57	5·72	−0·86
10	5·10	4·85	4·22	−0·88
5	3·43	2·93	2·55	−0·88
3	2·35	1·67	1·45	−0·90

Duration converges at very long maturities

At very long maturities any eventual capital gain or loss becomes so
heavily discounted as to become irrelevant. Bonds then trade as
perpetuals on an income basis alone, and modified duration tends to the
reciprocal of GRY.

For example, if GRY is 12%, modified duration will be approximately
8·33 for very long maturities, whatever the bond's nominal coupon rate.
Where coupon is below GRY, duration can even shrink at very long
maturities (see Fig. 28.2).

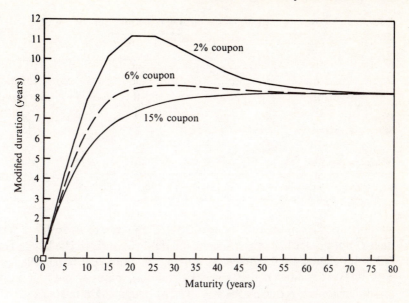

Fig. 28.2 Duration and maturity: GRY 12%, differing coupon rates.

Duration as a hedging tool

A general guideline for an efficient hedge is given by the following formula:

$$\text{Market value of long position} \times \text{duration of long position} = \text{Market value of short position} \times \text{duration of short position}$$

For example, a $10 m. market value short position in a bond with duration of 10 years could be approximately hedged by $9.1 m. market value long position in a bond with duration of 11 years. Hedging is based on *market value*, not nominal value, because modified duration measures the prospective percentage change in the *market price* of a bond.

Illustration of hedging possibilities

Table 28.3 illustrates various hedging possibilities.

An intending hedger who is long of $10 m. nominal of bond A ($8.8 m. market value) may hedge by shorting $8.8 m. market value ($10.7 m. nominal value) of bond B, which has the same duration or $8.1 m. market value of bond C (which has longer duration), or $9.5 m. market value of bond D, which has shorter duration.

Table 28.3. Illustration of hedging possibilities (all bonds priced at GRY of 10%)

	A	Possible hedges			
		B	C	D	E
Coupon %	8	7	6	12	10
Maturity (years)	10	9·5	10·5	10	7
Duration	6·5	6·5	7·1	6·0	5·0
Market value $ m.[a]	8·8	8·8	8·1	9·5	11·4
Bond price	88	82	74	112	100
Nominal value $ m.	10	10·7	10·9	10·7	11·4

a   Hedge's market value multiplied by hedge's duration must equal 57·2 (A's duration of
    6·5 years multiplied by A's market value of $8·8 m.).

Shorting $11.4 m. market value of bond E apparently also offers a good hedge, but in fact involves a significant yield curve risk. The hedge may fail if the yield spread between seven-year and ten-year bonds changes.

Bond B is the safest hedge, since B's duration, maturity and coupon are all similar to A's, reducing the risk that the hedge might fail because of a reshaping of the yield curve or a shift in investors' preferences between high and low coupon bonds.

Convexity

The following factors produce high convexity:

1. Convexity increases *disproportionately* as duration increases.
2. With two bonds of equal *maturity,* the lower coupon (higher duration) bond has more convexity.
3. With two bonds of equal *duration,* the higher coupon bond has more convexity.
4. Convexity is greatest in bonds where duration is most sensitive to a change in GRY (see Fig. 28.3).

Portfolio convexity can be increased by the following strategies:

1. Buy options (exposure to interest rate *shifts* greatly increased, but option cost in effect represents a significant sacrifice of yield).
2. Replace a single bond with a 'barbell' (portfolio of two bonds: one long and one short). Table 28.4 compares the investment characteristics of a simple bond and a barbell. With a normal yield curve, the barbell has higher convexity but lower yield. Thus the simple bond outperforms *unless* interest rates change substantially (in this example by at least 160 basis points) (see Fig. 28.4).

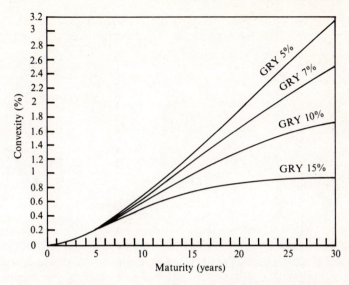

Fig. 28.3 Convexity and maturity: bond coupon 7%, varying maturity.
Source: Salomon Brothers.

Table 28.4. Comparison of portfolio alternatives (15 May 1988)

	Maturity (years)	Price	GRY	Yield with one-year yield-curve ride (%)	Duration	Convexity
Single bond						
7·25%, 1996	8·5	89·92	8·97	9·50	6·09	0·47
Barbell						
8·125%, 1991	3	100·07	8·10	8·51	2·62	0·09
7·25%, 2016	28	80·68	9·18	9·18	10·36	1·83
Comparison						
Barbell[a]	14·2		8·58	8·81	6·07	0·86
Single bond	8·5		8·97	9·50	6·09	0·47

a   Average of the two bonds, weighted by market value.

Performance allows for:

(a)   income from bond coupons;
(b)   capital gain or loss from interest rate change; and
(c)   capital gain from yield curve ride.

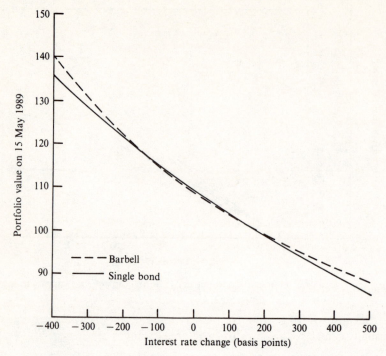

Fig. 28.4 Performance comparison one year ahead: barbell v. single bond (15 May 1988 = 100).

If interest rates are unchanged the single bond's portfolio value rises from 100 to 109·5 in the year (reflecting income plus yield-curve ride) while the barbell portfolio rises to only 108·8. However, if interest rates show a major change (either up or down) the barbell does better than the single bond. For example, if rates rise 300 basis points the barbell falls to 95, while the single bond falls further to 94·2 (see Fig. 28.5).

Formal definition of convexity

Convexity is related to the rate of change of volatility (modified duration) with respect to yield, or the second differential of the bond price with respect to yield. Formally,

$$\text{Convexity} = \frac{1}{P} \cdot \frac{d^2 P}{d Y^2}$$

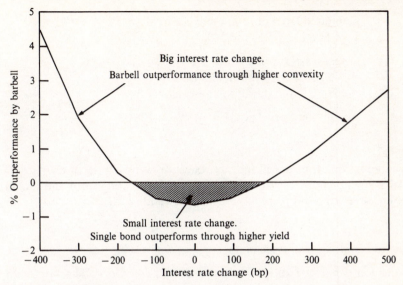

Fig. 28.5 Relative performance comparison: barbell minus single bond.

Because the algebraic formula is unduly complicated, convexity is usually calculated backwards from price changes:

$$\text{Convexity} = \frac{1,000,000}{\text{Bond price}} \times (dP_1 - dP_2)$$

Where dP_1 = bond price change from 1 bp fall in GRY.
dP_2 = bond price change from 1 bp rise in GRY.

Bond price forecasting with duration and convexity

Bond price % change $\approx$ $-$(Modified duration $\times$ GRY change)
(approximate)
$$+ \text{ convexity} \times \frac{(\text{GRY change})^2}{2}$$

Example

Bond maturity	12 years
Coupon	8%
GRY	9%
Price	92·75
Modified duration	7·42
Convexity	0·75

Approx. bond price % change if GRY falls 200 basis points:

Estimated from duration alone $\approx$ $(-7\cdot42) \times (-2) = 14\cdot84\%$

Estimated from duration and convexity $\approx 14\cdot84 + (0\cdot75 \times 2^2 \div 2) = 14\cdot84 + 1\cdot50 = 16\cdot34\%$

Forecast bond price at GRY of 7%
$= 106\cdot51$ (with duration alone)
$= 107\cdot91$ (from duration and convexity)

Actual bond price at GRY of 7% $= 108\cdot03$

Note
The approximation is still inexact, because convexity itself changes as GRY rises or falls. Purists can progress to calculating third and fourth differentials of bond price with respect to yield!

Comparison of bond-price impact of duration and convexity

Duration cannot be directly compared with convexity. The impact of duration relates to the change in interest rates. Convexity relates to half the square of the change in interest rates. The two measures are therefore directly comparable only when assessing an interest rate change of precisely 2% (since $2 = \frac{1}{2} \times 2^2$).

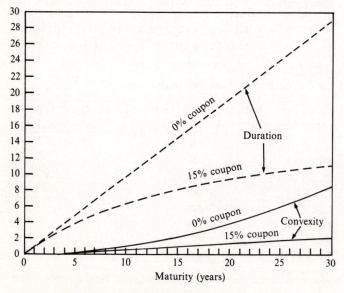

Fig. 28.6 Duration and convexity: GRY 7%.

Thus in Fig. 28.6 at maturity of 16 years on the 15% bond, modified duration (eight years) will have eight times as much bond-price-impact as convexity (1%) only if interest rates change by precisely 2%.

Figure 28.7 relates duration to (convexity ÷ 2). The two influences can then be directly compared for an interest rate change of 1%. With a smaller interest rate change the impact of convexity will be relatively less important. With a higher interest rate change convexity will be relatively more important as shown in Table 28.5. However, although convexity gains in *relative* importance with a big change in interest rates, duration always remains the predominant influence.

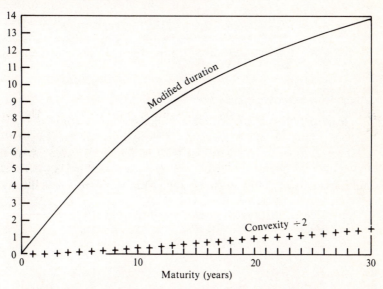

Fig. 28.7 Duration and convexity: bond GRY 6%, coupon 6%.

Table 28.5. Bond price impact (%) of duration and convexity (bond coupon 6%, maturity 21 years, GRY 6%, price 100, modified duration 12 years, convexity 2%, convexity ÷ 2 = 1%)

GRY change	Modified duration	Calculated convexity	Total	New bond price
−3%	+36	+9	+45	146[a]
−2%	+24	+4	+28	128
−1%	+12	+1	+13	113
0			0	100
+1%	−12	+1	−11	89
+2%	−24	+4	−20	80

a Does not add because second-order convexity effects (page 236) become significant with a big change in interest rates.

Even at this long maturity, duration has six times as much impact as convexity on bond performance even if GRY changes by 200 basis points from 6% to 4% (or 8%).

General rule
Duration has q times as much bond-price impact as convexity, where:

$$q = \frac{\text{Modified duration} \times 2}{\text{Convexity} \times \text{Change in interest rates}}$$

Example
Modified duration   9
Convexity   1·5
Interest rate change 3%

$$q = \frac{9 \times 2}{1·5 \times 3} = 4$$

Bonds with negative convexity

For a normal bond (non-callable bullet maturity) convexity is always positive. However, if a bond is priced close to par with an early call date, upside performance is constrained by the call feature (price cannot rise far above 100) and convexity can become negative (see Fig. 28.8). Such bonds must normally trade on unusually high yields to compensate the investor.

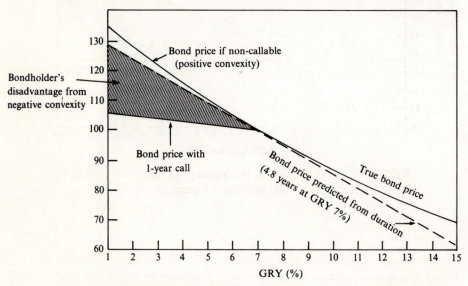

Fig. 28.8 Callable bond and negative convexity: maturity six years (callable at 100 in one year), coupon 7%.

Accumulated returns and breakeven time

Illustration

If interest rates rise, the bond price falls, reducing the return to date. However the roll-up rate for reinvesting coupons rises, raising the future accumulated return (defined on page 114).

For example, suppose a 10-year bond with 10% coupon is bought at par. Interest rates then immediately rise to 14% and the bond price drops to 79. However, future coupons can now be reinvested in the same bond to yield 14% and the investor's benefit from the increased roll-up rate will eventually offset his initial capital loss. In this case the investor catches up after 6.5 years, and thereafter enjoys increasing benefit from the higher interest rate (see Fig. 28.9).

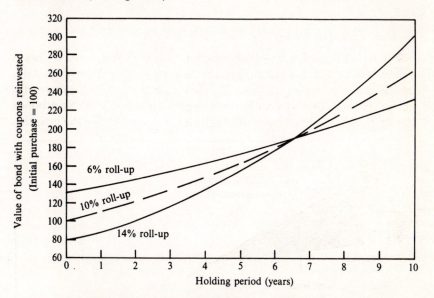

Fig. 28.9 Accumulated returns breakeven point: initial GRY 10%, maturity 10 years, Macaulay duration 6·5 years.

General rule

The breakeven point where higher roll-up offsets initial capital loss (or lower roll-up income offsets initial capital gain) equals a bond's initial Macaulay duration.

Part Nine

Introduction to investment strategies

29 Analysing Treasury bonds against the attraction of alternative investments

Alternatives and investment cycles

Investments competing with Treasury bonds include the following:

1. Treasury bills and bank deposits.
2. Corporate bonds.
3. Equities.
4. Inflation hedges (e.g. real estate, commodities, gold).
5. Foreign bonds.

The relative attraction of bonds depends on their intrinsic value (real yield), their comparative value and the state of the economic cycle.

Relative attraction varies with the economic cycle

The following list indicates the preferred investment according to the state of the economy.

Economy	*Preferred investment*
Recession	Bonds
Early boom	Bonds and equities
Mid-boom	Equities and commodities
Late boom	Commodities
End boom	Cash

Investors should be wary of chasing securities outside the normally favourable point of the economic cycle unless valuation indicators are extremely attractive (see Fig. 29.1).

Relative attraction also varies with the US political cycle

Table 29.1 compares the performance of investments at different stages of the political cycle in the US.

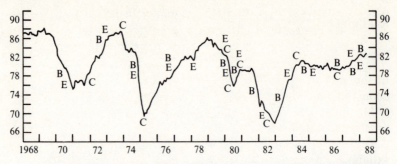

Fig. 29.1 Investments and the economic cycle. The line shows the rate of capacity utilisation. An upturn indicates an economic upswing; a downturn indicates economic deceleration. Letters above the line indicate major peaks in bonds (B), equities (E) and commodities (C); letters below the line indicate major bottoms. Interruptions in the sequence are relatively rare, instances occurring in late 1987 and in the out-of-phase equity bear market in 1977.

Table 29.1. Presidential election cycle and investment returns, 1952–87

Year in election cycle	Real GNP	CPI	Average total return (% p.a.)	
			T-bonds	SP500 stocks
Pre-election year	3·8	4	1	21
Presidential election year	3·3	4	5	15
Post-election year	1·6	5	4	3
Mid-term	3·2	4	10	11
Average	3	4	5	12

Notes

1. Bonds do best in mid-term, which often coincides with relative economic weakness and inflation slowdown.
2. Stocks do best in the two years leading up to a presidential election.
3. Over the whole period 1952–88 stocks outperformed bonds by 7% p.a., reflecting:
   (a) the normal risk premium of about 3% p.a. for holding stocks rather than (supposedly safer) bonds;
   (b) upturn in inflationary expectations which depressed the performance of bonds relative to equities; and
   (c) investors developing greater faith in equities' long-term growth potential.

Real yields

Intrinsic value

In the case of Treasury bonds 'intrinsic value' means real yield after deducting *future* inflation (*not* past inflation). Unfortunately, the level of future inflation is unknown so published 'real yield' comparisons are usually estimated from the inflation rate in the recent past.

Real yields so calculated have historically fluctuated (with big variations) about a long-term average of 2%. In early-1989 they were over 4%, a level exceeded only twice in the past 60 years, both in freak periods:

1. The 1929–33 depression, when nominal yields were only 3% but inflation fell to minus 10%.
2. The 1981–8 period of Reaganomics.

The current abnormally high real yield level of 4% suggests that the historical odds still favour the investor who hopes for a future capital gain when (if) the real long-term yield eventually drops back to normal (see Fig. 29.2).

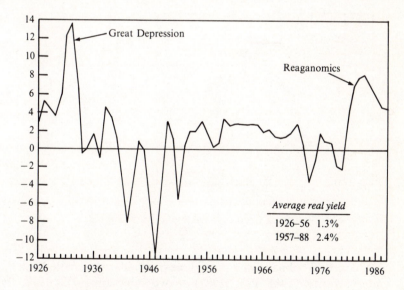

Fig. 29.2 Treasury bond real yields, 1926–88. Real yield = long Treasury bond yield minus same year's increase in consumer prices. Data source: Ibbotson.

Risks in using real yields as investment criteria

Problems related to the use of real yields include the following:

1. Real yields can change as well as nominal yields.
2. Real yields can remain outside their historically normal range for long periods.
3. Knowing the true real yield depends on an accurate forecast of future inflation.

Real yields appeared high in 1983, but rose further in 1984 as the economy boomed, while the budget deficit remained out of control. Real yields were 6% in spring 1986 (long-bond yield 7%; inflation 1%). However, an investor who correctly guessed that real yields would fall to 5% within two years would not have enjoyed a capital gain, because inflation rebounded to 4% and nominal bond yields rose to 9%.

Bank Credit Analyst model

Figure 29.3 shows a real-yield-based estimate of bond value.

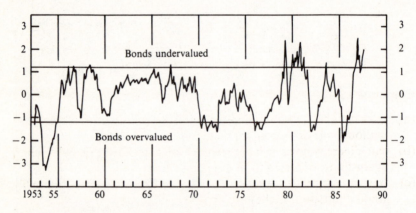

Fig. 29.3 Bank Credit Analyst bond valuation index.

Confidence is enhanced by past success in indicating periods of bond undervaluation (1981, 1984, 1987) or overvaluation (1972, 1977, 1983, 1986). However, the model's early-1989 indication that bonds are cheap depends on an estimate that the underlying long-term inflation rate is only 4%.

Corporate bonds

Corporate bond minus Treasury bond yield spread

The higher yield on corporate bonds reflects the risk of default, poorer marketability and the smaller pool of potential buyers than for Treasuries. The spread between corporate yields and Treasury yields normally *overcompensates* for the risk of default, making corporates attractive to long-term investors.

However, the spread can fluctuate considerably (see Fig. 29.4) and one should be particularly wary of buying corporates ahead of a recession which will raise investor fears of corporate default.

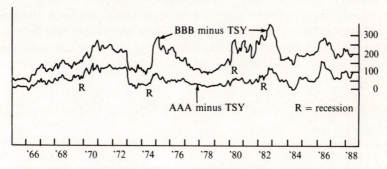

Fig. 29.4 Yield spread: AAA or BBB corporate bond minus long Treasury: 1965–88. Source: Bank Credit Analyst.

Corporate bonds are relatively attractive to long-term investors who:

(a) intend to hold to final maturity and so can enjoy the higher yield without worrying about marketability;
(b) can diversify over a large number of corporate bonds to guard against portfolio ruin from a single default;
(c) buy when spreads are relatively high and likely to narrow (normally when a recession is about to end).

Equities

We consider four possible methods of comparing equities and bonds:

1. The Kerschner–Pradilla model.
2. The yield ratio.
3. Historic scattergram.
4. The yield spread.

These models all suggested extreme overvaluation of equities against bonds in autumn 1987. Most suggested that the big valuation discrepancy had almost vanished in early 1988, but partly reappeared by mid-summer.

The Kerschner–Pradilla model

The anticipated total return on equities is defined as the projected normalised dividend yield plus the expected long-term dividend growth rate (both estimated from a proprietary poll of institutional investors). The current spread between Treasury bond yields and anticipated equity total return is then compared with spreads over the previous 20 years to estimate the probability that bonds will outperform equities (an average spread implying a 50% probability of bonds outperforming).

On average over the past 20 years, bonds have tended to outperform equities *unless* the anticipated total return on equities has been 2·75% higher (this figure representing the average risk-premium demanded by investors for holding equities rather than bonds). See Figure 29.5.

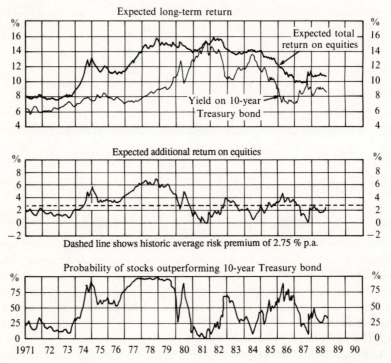

Fig. 29.5 Kerschner–Pradilla model. Source: PaineWebber.

The main hazards of the Kerschner–Pradilla model are as follows:

1. Investor preferences can diverge from 'value' for long periods of time.
2. The 'normal' risk premium may shift.

The possible reasons for shift in risk premium are as follows:

1. Potential equity investors *might* be pushed into accepting a lower risk premium by a developing supply shortage of equities relative to bonds. Corporate share-buybacks, leveraged buyouts and cash takeovers have removed over $350 bn of US equities (over 10% of the total) from the market since 1984. By contrast, no one expects a supply shortage in Treasury bonds.
2. Investors' perceptions of the gap between equity riskiness and bond riskiness *might* be changed by experience, e.g. Black Monday, or the sharp increase in bond price volatility after 1979 illustrated in Figure 1.5 on page 10. However the Kerschner–Pradilla model has actually performed well in the face of such theoretical hazards. Indeed both of the experiences cited actually pushed relative performance dramatically in the direction suggested by the model: bond underperformance in late-1979 and spectacular equity underperformance in October 1987.

Equity yield and bond yield comparisons

The ratio comparison between equity yields and bond yields since 1880 in Fig. 29.6 indicates the historically abnormal extreme reached by October 1987.

The scattergram in Fig. 29.7 illustrates the two 'tramlines' between which the equity: bond yield relationship has consistently fallen since 1959, and the extreme position in October 1987.

Figure 29.8 is less clearcut. The yield differential was high in autumn 1987 (even by post-1980 standards) but less so than in 1981 and 1984.

An historically abnormal relationship is cause for grave suspicion. However it does not guarantee an offsetting future movement since 'normality' itself alters over time. For example, equities normally yielded more than bonds from 1930 to 1955 because depression-remembering investors were more worried by equities' riskiness than impressed by their growth potential; the post-1955 change to bonds yielding more than equities reflected a *permanent* shift in investor perception.

Kerschner–Pradilla type models can help to check whether abnormal yield relationships are simply fluctuations or whether they may reflect an underlying change in investors' perceptions of the sustainable rate of long-term dividend growth.

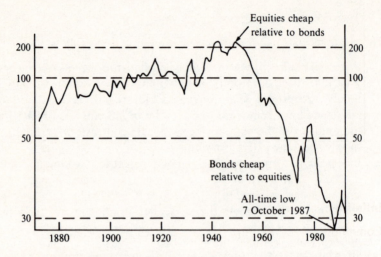

Fig. 29.6 SP400 dividend yield as percentage of AAA bond yield, 1871–1987. Source: Bank Credit Analyst.

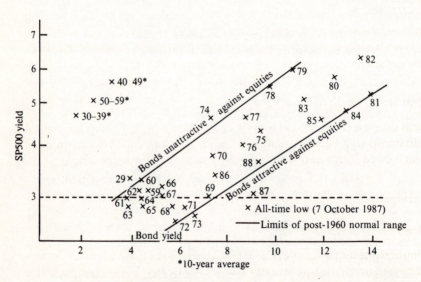

Fig. 29.7 SP500 dividend yield and long-term Treasury bond yield.

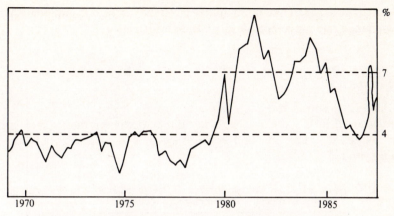

Fig. 29.8 10-year Treasury yield minus SP500 dividend yield.

Inflation hedges

Commodities tend to outperform bonds when:

(a)   it is late in the economic cycle, inflationary pressures are rising and businesses are scrambling to rebuild inventories; and

(b)   real interest rates are low (as in 1970–9).

Commodity prices are extremely volatile because demand can fluctuate quite violently while in the short term supply is relatively fixed. Thus commodity prices can rise extremely sharply in late-boom and then collapse suddenly at the first whiff of recession.

  Gold usually moves earlier in the cycle than most commodities. It has less industrial demand and is a purer inflation hedge.

Real estate

Real estate is often a good long-term inflation hedge, but a poor cyclical inflation hedge because real estate prices are affected by interest rates which often start rising relatively early in an economic upswing.

Foreign currency bonds

Bond bet or currency bet?

Unusual international interest rate differentials are often useful indicators of buying or selling opportunities in US bonds (see Fig. 4.5 on page 28). However, over short periods the performance of a currency-unhedged switch into a foreign bond market can be as heavily influenced by exchange rate movements as by bond performance.

Correlation of exchange rate changes and dollar value of foreign investments

Table 29.2 shows the *correlation* of foreign investment performance (measured in US dollars) with the dollar exchange rate. Correlation measures the direction and consistency of a relationship but not its magnitude.

Table 29.2. US dollar performance of foreign markets: 1973–87 (% correlation of annual performance with strong dollar)

Bonds	−75
Cash	−60
Equities	−25

Figures in this table and in Table 29.3 are unweighted geometric averages of data for Japan, UK, Germany, France and Canada.

All foreign investments in Table 29.2 show a negative correlation, i.e. their US dollar value tends to fall if the dollar is strong.

The negative correlation is particularly marked for bond prices because a falling foreign exchange rate against the US dollar tends to produce not only exchange rate losses but also a falling foreign bond price. This occurs because a falling exchange rate often implies:

(a)   higher inflation;
(b)   excess money creation which will have to be countered by higher interest rates, and
(c)   a deterrent to bond buying by non-residents.

The correlation is less negative for equities because:

(a)   currency devaluation helps corporate profits, and
(b)   excess money creation tends to produce both a weak exchange rate and a strong stock market (see page 60).

Relative importance of exchange rate changes and foreign bond market performance

Table 29.3 compares the *magnitude* of currency impact and foreign market impact on the US dollar performance of foreign investments. From 1973 to 1987 foreign bond performance (measured in local

Table 29.3. Contribution to US dollar total return from foreign investments: 1972–87

	Exchange rate impact	Foreign market performance (in local currency)		
		Cash	Bonds	Equities
Magnitude of impact[a]				
Monthly performance	2	0·7	2	4
Annual performance	10	8	12	22
5-year performance	26	49	68	160
15-year performance	33	230	334	439
Relative importance of exchange rate impact[b]				
Monthly performance		73[c]	50	33
Annual performance		55	46[d]	32
5-year performance		35	30	14
15-year performance		13	9	7

a   Average fluctuation in value (regardless of sign) for each month, each year, each 5-years or for full 15-years. For example, exchange rates showed an average monthly fluctuation of 2%; equity prices showed an average monthly fluctuation of 4% (sometimes in the same direction as the exchange rate fluctuation, sometimes in the opposite direction). Thus exchange rate is considered to have accounted for 33% and local market performance for 67% of total impact on monthly US dollar performance of investments in foreign equities.
b   Magnitude of exchange rate impact as percentage of exchange rate impact plus foreign market impact.
c   For monthly dollar performance of investment in foreign cash deposits exchange rate impact $= 2 \div (2 + 0·7) = 2 \div 2·7 = 73\%$.
d   N.B. Over 1 to 5-year periods bond performance was almost as dependent on currency fluctuations as was cash performance.

currency) had an impact of 12% (either plus or minus) on *each year's* total return measured in dollars. Exchange rate changes had an average impact of 10%. Thus over one-year periods the US dollar return was nearly as dependent on currency performance as on bond market performance. Indeed the figures in Table 29.3 understate the importance of currency impact because there was also a tendency for weak foreign bond prices to coincide. with weak foreign exchange-rates. Thus, exchange rates had an indirect as well as a direct impact in depressing the total return measured in US dollars.

Exchange rate impact relatively less important over long periods

Over shorter time periods, e.g. one-month, currency impact tends to be even more dominant. However, over longer periods currency impact becomes relatively less important. Currency impact contributed only 30% to total return over five-year periods and only 9% to total return measured over the full 15 years.

This dilution of currency impact occurs because in the longer-term exchange rate fluctuations are limited (real exchange rates cannot diverge indefinitely) whereas there is no such constraint on long-term bond market performance. Thus, over one-year periods, 8% bond market returns and 8% exchange rate fluctuations are both quite common. Over 15 years 200% local currency total return from bonds (7·6% p.a.) is still quite common; however, a 200% change in a respectable foreign currency exchange rate is extremely rare.

International nominal yield spreads: uses and hazards

An investor can use charts to assess the historically normal spread and switch from US into foreign bonds and back if the spread moves outside the normal range (hedging the currency if desired). For example, the US–Japan spread history in Fig. 29.9 might encourage an investor to:

(a) switch US bonds into Japanese bonds if the yield spread falls below 3%; and
(b) switch Japanese bonds into US bonds if the yield spread rises above 4%.

The hazards of following this procedure automatically are illustrated by the following factors:

1. The wide historical variations in spread.
2. The possibility of spreads moving (permanently?) into a new range, e.g. US–UK after 1976, US–Canada after 1985.

Unusual yield spreads can be useful for shortlisting *potential* switches between bond markets in different countries. However, contemplated switches should always be checked against economic analysis of the countries concerned.

International real yield spreads

Real yields are likely to converge in a world where information flows are improving and exchange controls diminishing. Moreover, real yield comparisons reduce the danger of a mistaken switch being triggered by a nominal yield discrepancy which simply reflects a deterioration in relative inflation differentials.

Problems with real yield spreads include the following:

1. A comparison of true real yields depends on correctly estimating *relative* future inflation rates. Correctly guessing future inflation is hard enough for one country, let alone two!

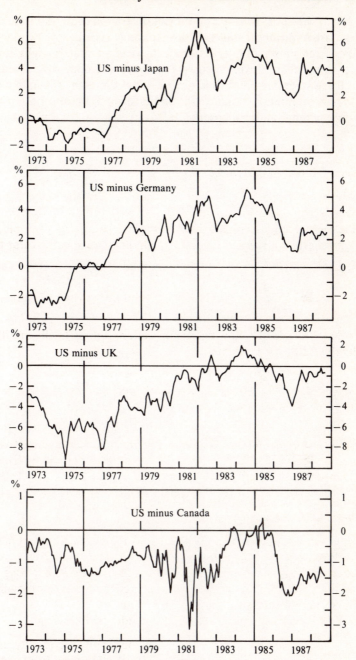

Fig. 29.9 International nominal yield spreads (10-year government bonds). Source: Bank Credit Analyst.

2. In the short run real yields can diverge because different countries are at different stages of the economic cycle.
3. Exploitation of international real-yield anomalies might be thwarted by exchange-rate changes, unless the currency risk is hedged, e.g. US–Germany real yield differential dropped by 1% in late 1985, but Deutschmark bonds still outperformed because the US dollar exchange rate collapsed.

Overall strategy

The keys to investment success are correctly anticipating major changes in the level of interest rates (primarily related to the economic cycle), and bond selection (primarily related to critical anomaly analysis, e.g. can a yield spread between two similar bonds be justified?).

Anomaly exploitation offers a pleasant supplement to income and the success ratio is assisted by mathematical constraints which reduce the chances of catastrophic error. However, *significant outperformance depends on getting the overall interest rate picture right.*

Client objectives and portfolio constraints

Limits on discretion

A fund manager is rarely told simply to invest in Treasuries for the best long-term performance. There is usually some more detailed constraint, e.g. not exceeding a given degree of capital risk.

Client's baseline position and scope for risk tolerance

The client's objective may range from a need to meet a single liability due in six months to a need to fund a stream of pension payments for 30 years. Is the portfolio constrained to tightly matching a particular liability schedule? Or will an 'immunised' portfolio (assets with the same average duration as the liabilities) suffice? Is the client able (well-capitalised) and willing to accept a limited risk from mismatching?

The risk from mismatching

There are two types of risk associated with mismatching:

1. There is a *capital risk* if the investor is too long. Bonds may have to be sold at a loss when liabilities fall due.
2. There is an *income risk* if the investor is too short. When bonds mature, the available reinvestment rate may have fallen too low to produce a future sum sufficient to meet liabilites.

Table 30.1 illustrates these risks.

Table 30.1. Illustrating the risk of mismatching

Example: $10m. liability due in 1 year.

Alternative	Risk
1. Manager can purchase $10m. Treasury bill maturing in 1 year.	1. None.
2. Manager expects interest rates to rise, so buys 3-month T-bill, hoping on maturity to reinvest in a higher yielding 9-month bill, thus producing more than $10m. by year end.	2. If rates fall, the 9-month bill may no longer have a yield sufficient to produce $10m.
3. Manager expects interest rates to fall, so buys 3-year bond (instead of 1-year bill) hoping to realise a capital gain when liabilities fall due at year end.	3. If rates rise, the 3-year bond may produce a capital loss when sold after 1 year, thus leaving investor with less than $10m.

A possible approach to portfolio structuring

Underlying theme

What is the best risk–reward trade-off consistent with the client's objectives? or: What is the optimum method of achieving the client's desired duration?

Principal factors to consider

The following factors should be taken into consideration:

1. The client's objectives, risk tolerance and tax position.
2. The interest rate macro-outlook: up, down or neutral? (And the probability of being wrong.)
3. The most appropriate areas of the yield curve.
4. The most attractive bonds within the chosen sector.
5. Anomaly and arbitrage possibilities.

The ideal buying area of the yield curve would combine the following attributes:

1. An historically attractive spread against neighbouring maturities.
2. A strong yield curve ride.
3. A duration appropriate to both the client's objectives and the fund manager's own interest rate view.

Such perfect combinations seldom arise in practice, so the investor must usually compromise.

Sources of Treasury bond portfolio performance

Summary
A bond portfolio's total return comes from three main sources:

(a) yield;
(b) capital gains from correctly anticipating interest rate changes, and
(c) exotic techniques.

Yield includes the following:

1. The gross redemption yield.
2. Additional return from the yield curve ride.
3. Supplementing income by bond lending.

Capital gains can result from positioning a portfolio to benefit from the following:

1. Changes in the overall level of interest rates.
2. Changes in the shape of the yield curve.
3. The overall interest rate environment being stable or volatile.

Exotic techniques include the following:

1. The use of futures and options.
2. The exploitation of anomaly and arbitrage opportunities.

Bond lending opportunities

Bondholders can supplement income by lending bonds to dealers who have gone short and must borrow the bond to meet their delivery commitment. Lending fees typically range between 1% p.a. and 9% p.a., varying according to the scarcity of the particular bond that a dealer needs to borrow. In early August 1988 the 10-year bond was being lent at 4% p.a. and the 30-year bond (which was scarcer owing to a dearth of new issues) at 7% p.a.

Bond borrowing demand is normally highest in actively traded recent issues ('on-the-run' bonds), i.e. the issues where dealers' positions are most likely to become heavily unbalanced. Because of these bond-lending income-supplementing possibilities, on-the-run bonds often yield 5–10 basis points less than other comparable bonds (which may offer better value for non-lending investors).

Most bond borrowing is for very short periods (often overnight) so lending is an erratic though useful supplement to income.

Exploiting interest rate change or stability

The investor can do the following:

1. Hold high-volatility bonds when rates are likely to fall; switch to lower volatilities when rates are likely to rise.
2. Hold options (or high-convexity bonds) if rates are likely to be volatile; write options if rates are likely to be stable.

Anomaly and arbitrage opportunities

In a perfect market, arbitrage opportunities would not exist. However, in the actual market investors differ in a number of aspects:

1. Tax rates.
2. Volatility assumptions.
3. Time horizons.
4. Risk constraints.
5. Ability to borrow money (or bonds).

These variations may lead to price imperfections.

Exploitable price imperfections

The following examples illustrate how price imperfections may be exploited:

1. Foreign investors may have tax or exchange-control incentives to sell US Treasury bonds immediately before a coupon payment. Relatively cheap bonds may then become available to investors who have no disincentive to buying bonds immediately before a coupon payment.
2. High-coupon bonds have shorter duration than low-coupon bonds of the same maturity, but usually trade on higher GRYs. Therefore investors without aversion to high-coupon bonds can achieve a superior GRY v. duration trade-off.

3. The yield curve may be distorted at times of heavy official intervention in the foreign exchange market (normally reflected in major buying or selling of US Treasury bills by foreign central banks).
4. Institutional risk constraints or an imbalance between the maturity distribution of US Treasuries and the maturity distribution of insurance company and pension fund liabilities may create cheap or expensive sectors of the yield curve which unconstrained investors can exploit.

Riskless arbitrage

Explicit riskless arbitrage opportunities (identical bonds quoted at slightly different prices in different markets) are very rare. However, mispricing occasionally allows a synthetic asset to be created at a price differing from the real asset. Examples of such situations include:

1. A combination of Treasury bills plus Treasury futures may be briefly priced out of line with the underlying cash bond.
2. Stripped Treasuries may be slightly mispriced against Treasury coupon securities so that it is possible either to split a normal bond into stripped principal and separate coupons which can be sold at a profit, or to buy up strips and reassemble a conventional bond at a cost below its market value.
3. Forward foreign exchange rates may briefly diverge from the level which equalises the yield on US short Treasuries and the dollar yield obtainable from short-maturity German government DM bonds (with Deutschmark proceeds sold forward into dollars).

Riskless arbitrage opportunities appear only rarely and briefly. They are swiftly eliminated through exploitation by professional arbitrageurs.

Implied arbitrage

An investor can also seek implied arbitrage opportunities, where profit is not riskless but is probable on a projected scenario. The simplest example is buying one bond and shorting another which has similar coupon and maturity but a lower GRY. Profit is not guaranteed, but is probable since such anomalies seldom last indefinitely. (*Caution:* it may be expensive to borrow the bond which an arbitrageur wants to sell short. This borrowing cost might make the projected arbitrage unattractive.)

More subtle (oversubtle?) example of implied arbitrage

An investor is bullish on the stock market but thinks that stocks are slightly expensive against bonds. If he is right, he can effectively buy stock-call options cheaply by buying options on Treasury bonds. The bond options will cost less than stock options (because of bonds' historically lower price volatility) but, if the investor is right about the equity v. bond valuation discrepancy, bond prices are likely to match or surpass any rise in the equity market.

Risks in implied arbitrage

Such subtleties can involve significant risk, because the implied arbitrage depends on a market or economic judgement which is much more likely to be wrong than a simple mathematical assessment of 'correct' yield spreads.

Aspects of risk analysis

Capital security versus the search for yield

Suppose an investor seeks maximum yield (implying with a normal yield curve, maximum maturity extension) subject to an overall risk limitation that he must have a guaranteed minimum return of zero over a one-year time horizon. For absolute security he could buy (at a discount) a 12-month Treasury bill with face value equal to his original capital, and then invest his 'surplus' funds to seek maximum return. Alternatively, he can:

(a)   ascertain how far interest rates must rise for his capital loss on any bond purchase to exceed the year's income and reduce his total return to below zero; and

(b)   decide whether an interest rate rise of this magnitude is a serious risk or negligible.

The breakeven calculation

Suppose an investor buys a four-year 10% coupon bond at 98 (four-year GRY 10·62%). Over one year, he receives coupons of 10 and breaks even if the bond price falls 10 points, i.e. to 88 (three-year GRY 15·12%). Table 30.2 shows the future interest rate scenario necessary for a bond purchase on 15 August 1988 to produce a minimum total return of zero over the following year.

Table 30.2. Treasury yields and one-year breakeven calculation

Current maturity on bond (years)	Current GRY 15 Aug. 1988	Breakeven GRY on same bond (with 1-year shorter maturity) 15 Aug. 1989[a]	GRY change on same bond (basis points)
2	8·69	18·61	992
3	8·84	14·07	523
4	8·92	12·58	366
5	9·03	11·92	289[b]
7	9·23	11·40	217
10	9·37	11·04	167
30	9·43	10·47	104

a GRY which produces a capital loss exactly equal to 1 year's income. If future GRY is above the indicated level, capital loss will exceed income and total return will fall below zero. See Appendix 14 for generalised formula to derive future GRY consistent with any given target return.

b 289 b.p. yield rise from 9·03% to 11·92% (while maturity shortens from five years to four years) implies a 300 b.p. shift in the yield curve (from 8·92% to 11·92%) at a constant maturity of four years.

Assessment of breakeven probabilities

The two-year bond yields 8·69%. In August 1989 (one year ahead) an offsetting capital loss of 8·69% on the bond (by now a one-year bond) results only if one-year interest rates rise to 18·61% (from their present 8·23%). This risk is so remote that the investor might well decide he could extend his maturity to two years without imperilling his minimum guaranteed zero return objective.

The five-year bond yields 9·03%. An offsetting capital loss of 9·03% on the bond (by now a four-year bond) will result if four-year yields rise 300 basis points, from 8·92% now to 11·92% in one year's time. Is this risk still negligible or does it rule out maturity extension?

The risk increases further at long maturities where small interest rate rises can produce big capital losses. The ten-year bond's total return over one year falls to zero if nine-year yields rise 171 basis points, from 9·33% to 11·04%. Total return becomes an overall loss of 5% if yields rise to 12·04%.

The thirty-year bond's return is reduced to zero by an interest rate rise of only 104 basis points, from 9·43% to 10·47%, and turns into a 5% capital loss if rates rise to 11·10%.

Interest rate scenario consistent with other total return objectives

A similar methodology can be applied to calculate the future interest rate consistent with other total return objectives.

For example, suppose a 9% coupon eight-year bond is priced at 90, with flat yield of 10% p.a. and GRY of 10·9%. Flat yield over six months is 5%. Total return over six months will rise to 7% if the investor also makes a capital gain of 2%. This will occur if the bond's GRY falls to 10·6% (raising the bond price to 91·8).

Figure 30.1 shows the August 1989 yield curves consistent with various one-year total return objectives.

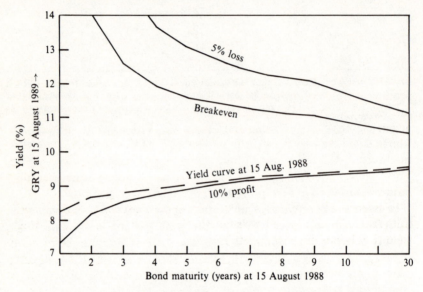

Fig. 30.1 Yield curve shape one year ahead: future GRY and one-year total return on bond purchase.

For example, an investor buying a seven-year bond in August 1988 will, over the following year, achieve:

(a) a 10% total return if six-year GRY in August 1989 falls to 9·06% (from current 9·12%);
(b) breakeven if six-year GRY rises to 11·4%, and
(c) a 5% loss if six-year GRY rises to 12·7%.

Alternative methods of pursuing a minimum return objective

The investor may choose between the following possibilities:

1. Accept low yield (Treasury bill) and absolute security of meeting a minimum return objective.

2. Risk extending maturity if a sufficiently adverse interest-rate scenario is extremely unlikely (e.g. interest rate rise of 523 basis points needed to prevent breakeven on buying the three-year bond).
3. Extend maturity, but hedge against an extreme interest-rate rise by purchase of (cheap) deeply out-of-the-money put options. Buying options *may* be cheaper than distorting the whole portfolio simply to guard against the remote possibility of an extremely adverse interest rate move. However, this depends on the cost of the options.

Generalised illustration of interest rate rise threat to total return

Figure 30.2 shows how the interest rate rise needed to reduce one-year total return to zero varies with initial GRY. High yielding bonds will not produce a total return below zero unless already high yields rise much further. By contrast, only a small interest rate rise is needed to produce a negative total return on low yielding bonds. For example, an investor who buys the 30-year bond on an initial GRY of 7% will find his one-year total return reduced to zero if interest rates rise only 60 basis points to 7·6%. However, an initial GRY of 15% will not produce a one-year total return below zero unless interest rates rise 270 basis points to 17·7%.

In essence, Fig. 30.2 gives an alternative demonstration of the general truth that an investor's capital is safer in bonds with low maturity and high yield (i.e. bonds of short duration).

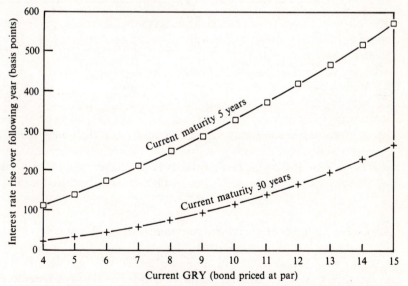

Fig. 30.2 Rise in interest rates which would reduce 1-year total return to 0%.

Profit opportunities in wider portfolios

Wider portfolios

If the portfolio is not restricted to Treasury bonds, potential profit sources extend to correctly anticipating changes in:

(a)   quality spreads, e.g. Treasuries v. corporates;
(b)   relative attractions of Treasuries against equities, inflation hedges and other investments;
(c)   foreign bond markets, and
(d)   exchange rates.

Portfolio return and risk tolerance

More risky assets tend to produce higher returns *in the very long term.* Thus long-term portfolios with risk tolerance often find high Treasury holdings inappropriate. Treasury bonds are most attractive to investors with short or medium time horizons who place a premium on risk reduction or high marketability.

Efficient frontiers

Optimum risk versus return trade-off

The 'efficient frontier' represents the concept that there is some optimum investment combination which will maximise probable return for any given acceptance of risk.

An illustration: maximum yield for given duration
Consider a portfolio limited to Treasuries, but permitted to raise duration to a maximum of five years. The investor could choose between a series of possible combinations, all of which would have the same modified duration, e.g. a single seven-year bond, or a mixed portfolio with a two-year and 30-year bond. However, only one of the possible portfolios would have the maximum GRY achievable with the desired duration.

Duration (price risk) versus yield trade-off

In the normal (positively sloped) yield curve (see Fig. 30.3) there is usually a single bond which will offer a higher GRY for any duration than a mixed portfolio of longer and shorter bonds (or cash and bond), and offer shorter duration for any GRY than a mixed portfolio.

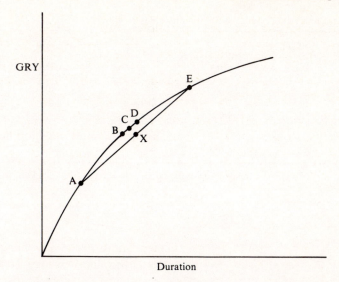

Fig. 30.3 Normal trade-off between yield and duration. Single bond gives better trade-off than mixing two bonds (see text for explanation).

The curve A,B,C,D,E shows the normal relationship with GRY increasing more slowly than duration.

A mixed portfolio (containing bonds A and E) produces a yield–duration combination somewhere on the straight line AE which is always below the curve ACE and offers a worse trade-off. For example, X has the same yield as B but longer duration; X has the same duration as D but lower yield; X has both lower yield *and* longer duration than C.

A practical example

In Table 30.3 adding 50% cash to a single-bond portfolio halves the duration and reduces the yield. However, the same reduction in duration (with less sacrifice of yield) could be achieved by simply moving to another single bond with shorter maturity. For example, the four-year bond offers the same modified duration (3.3 years) as a portfolio mixing a 10-year bond and cash. However, the four-year bond yields 8·2%, the mixed portfolio only 7·4%.

Alternatively the two-year bond offers a slightly higher yield than the mixed portfolio (7·7% v. 7·4%) and also shorter duration (1·8 v. 3·3). These trade-offs are also exhibited graphically in Fig. 30.4.

The improved trade-off from switching to a single bond is not costless since it involves some loss of convexity. The ultra-sophisticated can

Table 30.3. Bond yield v. duration trade-off at 3 May 1988

Bond maturity	Single bond only		Single bond mixed with 50% cash	
	Duration	GRY	Duration	GRY[a]
0 (cash)	0	5·9	0	5·9
2	1·8	7·7	0·9	6·8
3	2·5	7·9	1·3	6·9
4	3·3	8·2	1·7	7·1
5	4·1	8·3	2·1	7·1
10	6·6	8·9	3·3	7·4

a   Mixed portfolio GRY is the average of the bond yield and the 5·9% yield on cash.

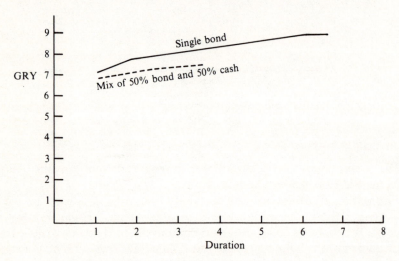

Fig. 30.4 The efficient frontier: yield–duration trade-off (3 May 1988). Note: For any given duration a single bond portfolio gives a higher yield than a mixture of bonds and cash. For any given yield a single bond portfolio has lower duration than a mixed portfolio.

explore three-dimensional efficient frontiers which attempt to optimise the choice between competing trade-off possibilities!

Impact of yield curve kink on yield duration trade-off

The opposite situation to that in Fig. 30.3 can occasionally arise if there is a downward kink in the yield curve. In Fig. 30.5 bond B gives a better yield and shorter duration than a mixed portfolio containing bonds A and C. However, a mix of bonds B and D gives both higher yield and shorter duration than the single bond C.

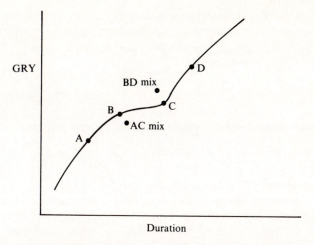

Fig. 30.5 Yield–duration trade-off with kinked yield curve.

Yield versus convexity trade-off

An investor anticipating violent interest rate fluctuations can add convexity to his portfolio in three ways, all of which imply some sacrifice of yield:

1. Switch between bonds, e.g. with market yields of 10%, equal duration (8.57 years) is offered by a 6% coupon 15-year bond (convexity 1.04) and by a 10% coupon 20-year bond (convexity 1.17); the higher-convexity bond will normally trade on a slightly lower GRY.
2. Replace a single bond with a barbell (mixed portfolio of long bond plus short bond).
3. Buy options; the options' cost is effectively a deduction from yield.

One of these alternatives may be more efficient, i.e. involve less sacrifice of yield to achieve the desired increase in convexity.

Treasuries versus other instruments: long-term return versus risk trade-off

Common stocks tend to have a much higher *long-term* return than Treasury bonds. Therefore the more long-term an investor's perspective and the higher his ability to tolerate risk, the less he will be inclined to buy Treasuries (except for temporary liquidity or trading).

At one extreme, an investor with a known large liability due in three months' time might be 100% invested in Treasury bills. At another, a portfolio with a 50-year time horizon and the ability to tolerate 80% capital loss might be optimally invested 100% in common stocks (holding Treasuries only occasionally for trading or temporary liquidity during anticipated equity bear markets).

Diversification

There are two ways of reducing fluctuations in portfolio value:

1. Increasing the number of securities in a portfolio reduces issue-specific risks, e.g. a particular bond might suffer disproportionately from tax changes or a reshaping of the yield curve.
2. Mixing securities whose prices are weakly correlated means that extreme price movements in some holdings may sometimes be diluted by opposite price movements in other holdings. At a theoretical extreme, a portfolio's value would never change if it were equally divided between two violently volatile securities whose price movements' correlation was minus 100%.

Reducing correlation between a portfolio's Treasury bond holdings

In a pure Treasury bond portfolio, correlations of price movements between issues of similar maturity are extremely high. Even spreading holdings over widely differing maturities (three-year and 30-year bond prices will show lower correlation than nine-year and ten-year bond prices) can seldom reduce correlation much below 90%.

Moreover, maturity spreading is often an inefficient way of reducing portfolio risk since a portfolio diversified between different (less correlated) maturities will for any given GRY usually have longer duration (higher risk of price loss in the event of a general rise in interest rates) than a single bond as illustrated in Fig. 30.3 on page 267.

Reducing correlation by mixing other securities with Treasury bonds

If the portfolio is not restricted to Treasuries, then moderate diversification into corporate bonds, equities and foreign currency bonds may reduce portfolio fluctuations. This can occur *even though* each of these investment classes individually has greater price volatility than a Treasury bond. For *small* additions of other investments, the low correlation with Treasury bond prices (tending to stabilise price movements in the overall portfolio) outweighs the higher volatility in the additional instrument's own pricing record.

Table 30.4 illustrates the past correlation between price movements in Treasury bonds and some other investments.

Table 30.4. Examples of correlation with long Treasury bond prices (correlations based on monthly price changes). Sources: Salomon (foreign securities), PaineWebber (gold: 1974–87), Ibbotson (other securities: mid-1978 to mid-1988)

	(%)
High-grade long corporate bonds	95
Medium-term Treasury bonds	90
Eurodollar bonds	85
Foreign currency bonds (currency hedged)	60
(unhedged)	45
US equities: SP500	35
: Small company stocks	25
Foreign equities: (unhedged)	25
(currency hedged)	10
Gold	0

Paradoxically, if the investor's criterion for risk reduction is reducing monthly fluctuations in a Treasury bond portfolio's dollar value, he may do better to buy foreign bonds unhedged. The added risk from currency fluctuation may be more than offset by the portfolio-stabilising influence of a lower correlation with US Treasury bond price movements.

Historical risk and return impact of adding foreign currency bonds to a US Treasury portfolio

A fund manager with a favourable view of foreign bond fundamentals need not be deterred from *moderate* diversification through fear of increasing portfolio risk. Figure 30.6 illustrates the past impact on portfolio value fluctuations of adding foreign-currency bonds to a US Treasury portfolio. Due to the low correlation between US and foreign bond price movements, adding up to 30% of foreign bonds actually *reduced* the portfolio's dollar value fluctuation, *despite* the introduction of an exchange rate risk. In such circumstances, moderate diversification may be more efficient (involve less yield sacrifice) than maturity shortening as a means of reducing portfolio fluctuations. Indeed, in 1971–84 the addition of foreign bonds not only reduced portfolio value fluctuations but (owing to the relative outperformance of foreign bonds in that particular period) actually increased returns.

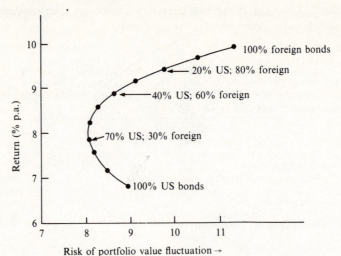

Risk of portfolio value fluctuation →
(Annualised % standard deviation of monthly changes in portfolio value)

Fig. 30.6 Risk–return trade-off for international bond portfolio, 1971–84. Source: Cholerton, Pieraerts and Solnick, 'Why invest in foreign currency bonds?', *Journal of Portfolio Management* (Summer 1986).

Introduction to super-subtleties

An illustration

Suppose an investor anticipates an equal worldwide fall in interest rates at a time when US Treasuries yield 10% and German government bonds yield 7%. If all interest rates now fall 1%, German bonds will outperform because their lower GRY gives them longer duration (see Table 30.5).

Table 30.5. Projected 10-year bond price change (assuming worldwide interest rate fall of 1%)

	Initial GRY	Initial bond price	Bond price after 1% fall in interest rates
US	10	100	106·5
Germany	7	100	107·4

On this projected scenario a US investor can switch US bonds into German bonds, hedging the exchange risk by forward sale of Deutschmarks back into dollars. He has then created a synthetic US Treasury bond which will outperform if interest rates fall.

Depending on relative prices, forward foreign exchange rates (and the accuracy of the investor's judgement!) such ingenuity *may* offer a superior risk : reward trade-off than extending maturity or buying options.

Deeper exploration of such subtleties must be left to specialist works.

31 Index matching

Methods

An index constructed from a single bond or small number of bonds can be matched simply by buying the bonds concerned. However, where the index has a large number of bonds, e.g. Salomon indices, buying all the component bonds may be impractical. The investor must then seek to approximate the characteristics of the index, for example by constructing a bond portfolio with the same average duration.

Simply matching duration still leaves a risk that portfolio performance will diverge from the index, if the yield curve changes shape. However, this risk can be reduced by matching for convexity as well as duration. The convexity constraint will normally force the manager to spread his bond portfolio along the yield curve in roughly the same proportion as the index components.

In general the problems of devising a portfolio to match an index are similar to the problems encountered in immunising any set of liabilities (see Chapter 32). However, there is also the general problem that a real portfolio has trading costs whereas indices do not.

Designing a portfolio to outperform an index

A manager who can select from the whole universe of Treasury bonds can usually find a few individual bonds with a better yield v. risk trade-off or better convexity v. duration trade-off than the index-average. If the manager can then construct a portfolio with equal duration and yield but higher convexity than the index, he has virtually-guaranteed outperformance. Sometimes this may be possible simply by underweighting on-the-run bonds (which usually have GRYs slightly below average for their maturity).

Furthermore an index may have one of the following quirks which makes it likely to underperform a real portfolio:

1. An index based on a notional constant maturity bond can be beaten by a real bond which enjoys the additional return from the yield curve ride.
2. An index calculated as a geometric average will be outperformed by the same bonds in a real portfolio valued as an arithmetic average.
3. An index cannot enjoy the additional income from bond lending (page 259), whereas a real portfolio can.

Disadvantages of Treasury bond index matching

As interest rates fluctuate an unconstrained fund manager will ideally aim to lengthen duration when rates are high and bonds attractive, and to shorten duration when rates are low. Passive index matching actually does the reverse of this, because a portfolio of unchanged maturity will shorten in duration as GRY rises (see page 126), and vice versa.

Thus index-matching is unlikely to be an optimum strategy unless the investor is specifically seeking to match a liability schedule for which a particular index is a convenient proxy.

Contrast with potential advantages from equity indexing

There are two ways in which bond indexing contrasts with equity indexing, as follows:

1. Over the long term equities are likely to outperform Treasury bonds by about 3% per annum and corporate bonds are likely to outperform Treasuries by about 1% per annum. Equity index matching thus tends to lock in long-term performance, whereas Treasury index matching tends to lock it out.
2. Index-matching an equity portfolio provides automatic diversification which reduces risk. However, index-matching a Treasury bond portfolio does relatively little to reduce risk because the price performance of different Treasury bonds is very highly correlated.

32   Dedication

Concept

'Dedication' refers to the construction of a portfolio to provide a stream of payments (from coupons, reinvested income and principal redemption) that match the timing of the investor's anticipated liabilities (e.g. an insurance company's or pension fund's estimated future payout obligations).

Dedication offers the following advantages:

1. It reduces the uncertainty of the investor's future net financial position.
2. It frees the investor to use the most appropriate strategy for 'surplus' (non-dedicated) funds.
3. In some cases it stabilises the balance-sheet treatment of liabilities which are matched by dedicated assets.

Techniques

There are four main dedication techniques:

1. Exact matching. This minimises uncertainty but provides no scope to benefit from active management.
2. Immunisation. Assets do not specifically match liabilities, but have the same average duration (sensitivity to interest-rate changes). This element of flexibility provides some scope for investment expertise and enhanced returns but involves a small risk: if the shape of the yield curve changes, asset prices may move slightly differently from the change in value of the immunised liabilities.
3. Mixture of matching and immunisation. Yield curve reshapings tend to be most severe at shorter maturities. Thus risk can often be limited if shorter-term liabilities are strictly matched, while only longer-term liabilities are immunised.

4. Contingent immunisation. If market yields are sufficiently high, the portfolio may be able to dedicate sufficient assets to immunise liabilities and still have 'surplus' funds free for active management.

The risks of immunisation are shown in Table 32.1.

Table 32.1. Illustration of immunisation risks (based on Treasury yield curve at 5 July 1988)

	Maturity (years)	Duration	Available GRY if strictly matched	Convexity if strictly matched
Liabilities				
Liabilities:	3	2·6	8·2	0·08
	7	5·2	8·8	0·34
	30	10·4	9·0	1·86
Average liability	13·3	6·1	8·7	0·76
Assets				
Matching liabilities	13·3	6·1	8·7	0·76
Immunising liabilities	9	6·1	8·9	0·50

Notes
1. As an alternative to strict matching, the investor could immunise by buying a 9-year bond with the same duration as the average liabilities but 20 basis points higher yield.
2. However, suppose the yield curve steepens so that 9-year GRYs rise relative to 3-year GRYs. In this case 9-year bonds might have to be sold at a loss to meet the 3-year liabilities when they fall due, leaving the remaining assets with a value below that of the remaining liabilities.
3. The immunised portfolio also has lower convexity than the matched portfolio, so might underperform with a major change in the level of interest rates even if there is no reshaping of the yield curve.
4. Technically speaking, immunisation should be based on Macaulay duration rather than modified duration. However, in practice, results will be very similar whichever duration measure is used and will be identical if the same interest rate is used to calculate the duration of both assets and liabilities.

Abbreviations

a.r.	annual rate
BCA	Bank Credit Analyst
bp	basis points
CBO	Congressional Budget Office
CBOT	Chicago Board of Trade
CD	Certificate of deposit
CRB	Commodities Research Bureau
FOMC	Federal Open Market Committee
FV	future value
GAO	General Accounting Office
GNP	Gross National Product
GRY	Gross Redemption Yield
H1	first half of year
OMB	Office of Management and Budget
PV	present value
Q1	first quarter of the year
s.a.	seasonally adjusted
TB	Treasury bill
v	discounting factor (see Appendix 7)

Glossary

Accrued interest

Interest which has become notionally due to the bondholder since the last coupon payment date but which will not actually be paid until the next coupon date.

Suppose a coupon is paid on 15 May. By 28 June the bondowner will have notionally acquired the right to a further 44 days' interest, but this interest will be paid only as part of the next coupon (representing 184 days' interest) paid on 15 November. Buyers of US Treasury bonds have to pay the seller gross accrued interest in addition to the agreed ('clean') price.

Accumulated returns

Anticipated future value of all receipts from a bond, including capital repayment, coupons and interest from reinvesting coupons for the time remaining to the bond's maturity.

Add

Intervention by the Fed to add liquidity to the money markets thus making it easier for banks to meet their reserve requirements.

Agency

A security issued by a sponsored arm of the US federal government, e.g. Farm Credit Bank, Federal National Mortgage Association ('Fannie Mae'). Such securities are not normally guaranteed by the US government, although it would be extremely reluctant to see an agency default. Agency securities usually trade at a yield slightly higher than Treasury securities.

Arbitrage

Attempt to profit from pricing discrepancy between identical (or similar) securities in two different markets.

Balance-of-term breakeven yield

The future interest rate required to equalise the total yields from:

(a)   holding a long bond to maturity;
(b)   buying a short bond now and switching the proceeds into the long bond when the short bond matures

Barbell

Two-bond portfolio mixing a long bond and a short bond.

Basis point

A measure of yield equal to one-hundreth of a percentage point. For example, if yields move from 7% to 7·5% they have risen by 50 basis points.

Bear

Pessimistic investor or falling market.

Benchmark bond

A heavily traded issue (usually the on-the-run bond) quoted as a guide to the general level of interest rates.

In fact on-the-run bonds normally have GRYs slightly below average, because their price usually includes a slight premium for superior marketability and their yield can sometimes be supplemented by bond lending.

Bid price

The price at which a dealer will buy a bond.

Bond

Treasury security with an initial maturity of more than 10 years.

Borrowed reserves

Bank reserves obtained by borrowing from the Fed's discount window.

Black Monday

19 October 1987. US stock market fell 22·6% (from 2247 to 1739 on the Dow-Jones index) surpassing previous one-day record fall of 12·8% (from 299 to 261) on 28 October 1929. Causes included:

(a)   gross overvaluation of equities, both absolutely and relative to bonds;
(b)   worldwide tightening of monetary policy;
(c)   market loss of confidence in US politicians.

Long Treasury bond yields were 10·4% at the start of Black Monday, rose to 10·5% at midday, then fell to 10·2% as the stock market collapse provoked a 'flight to quality'.

Bracket creep

See Fiscal drag.

Bull

Optimistic investor or rising market.

Bullet maturity

A single fixed maturity date undistorted by sinking fund provisions (which usually involve partial redemptions before final maturity either by the issuer buying back bonds in the market or by the bonds being drawn for early redemption at par).

Call

1.   Right of bond issuer to redeem prior to maturity. Some older Treasury bonds may be called at par within five years of maturity.
2.   Option giving holder the right (but not the obligation) to buy at a predetermined exercise price.

CD

Certificate of deposit, issued by a bank or thrift and evidencing the holder's right to repayment of a deposit (plus interest) on maturity. Large CDs are usually negotiable, i.e. they may be sold to third parties in the open market.

Central Bank

Government-sector bank normally responsible for managing most or all of the following:

(a)   supervision of the financial markets and banking system;
(b)   banknote issue and circulation;
(c)   interest-rate policy;
(d)   foreign exchange market intervention;
(e)   foreign exchange controls.

Examples include the Federal Reserve System, The Bank of England, The Bank of Japan and the German Bundesbank.

Chicago Board of Trade

The Clearing House, guarantor and principal regulatory organisation for Chicago futures trading.

Clean price

A bond price quoted without accrued interest. (The standard method of quoting price in the US Treasury market.)

Congressional Budget Office

Bipartisan body which produces budget analysis and forecasts.

Contrarianism

Investment philosophy based on the principle that the majority of investors are usually wrong. Thus, extreme investor euphoria is a possible warning of a forthcoming fall in the bond market.

Correlation

Tendency for changes in one variable to be associated with changes in another variable. Correlation is measured on a scale ranging from +100% (perfect correlation) through 0 (no association) to −100% (perfect negative association). (See Table 30.4 and Appendix 13.)

Dealing spread

The difference between a dealer's bid (buying) price and his offer (selling) price.

Dedication

A set of possible techniques to construct a portfolio to match the interest sensitivity of an investor's liabilities (see Chapter 31).

Delta

Rate at which an option's value changes with respect to the price of the underlying security.

Discounted present value (PV)

The current value of a future payment, discounted to allow for the interest rate, since a future payment is less valuable than immediate cash-in-hand. For example, if the interest rate is 10% p.a. a payment of $110 due in a year's time has a present value of $100.

Discount rate

1. Interest rate at which the Fed lends at the discount window.
2. Conventional method of quoting interest rate on Treasury bills. (See Appendix 6.)
3. Interest rate used in estimating the present value of a future payment.

Discount securities

Treasury bills and stripped Treasuries pay no coupon, but sell at a discount from par, thus providing a guaranteed capital gain to maturity in lieu of interest.

Discount window

Fed last-resort lending facility for banks facing a temporary shortage of liquidity. The level of discount-window borrowing is often a Fed operating target.

Drain

Intervention by the Fed to remove surplus liquidity from the money markets and reduce the availability of bank reserves.

Duration (Macaulay)

A measure of a bond's effective life. Formally defined as the weighted average length of time to receipt of a bond's coupons and capital repayment, the weights being the present values of the sums involved.

Duration (modified)

A measure of the sensitivity of a bond price to a change in interest rates, so called because it may be easily calculated from Macaulay duration:

$$\text{Modified duration} = v(\text{Macaulay duration})$$
$$= \text{Macaulay duration} \div (1 + i)$$

Usually referred to as 'volatility' in the UK gilts market.

Econometrics

Mathematical technique for deriving the best-fit equation to describe the past relationship between economic variables.

Efficient frontier

Optimum trade-off point between two desirable investment criteria, e.g. low risk and high return.

Fed

Abbreviation for Federal Reserve Board or Federal Open Market Committee or the New York Federal Reserve Bank (which acts as the Federal Open Market Committee's operating agent in the money market and foreign exchange markets).

Fed funds

Deposits held by a commercial bank at a Federal reserve bank. Such deposits may be lent to other banks who need funds to meet their reserve requirements at the Fed. Fed funds interest rate is effectively a rate for overnight unsecured interbank lending. Federal Reseve open-market operations are often heavily influenced by a desire to keep the Fed funds interest rate within a particular target range.

Federal Open Market Committee

Twelve-member committee which meets about eight times a year to determine the broad outlines of US monetary policy (page 31).

Federal Reserve Board

Seven-member organisation which acts as the US Central Bank. Supervises day-to-day monetary policy.

Fiscal drag ('bracket creep')

The tendency for tax receipts to rise faster than inflation if income tax brackets are not raised. The same real income is then represented by higher nominal income and is taxed at a higher marginal rate.

Prior to the inflation-indexing of the income tax systems, 1% inflation produced a rise in income tax yield of about 1·6% in both the UK and the US. Now 1% inflation produces an automatic rise in tax receipts of only about 0·98% in the US because income tax brackets have been inflation-indexed but many US excise taxes, e.g. on gasoline, are fixed in money terms so their yield lags behind inflation.

Fiscal policy

Budget policy, especially using a budget deficit (or surplus) as an economic regulator.

Flat yield (or 'running yield')

Bond coupon rate divided by the price.

Flower bonds

Irreverent term for some old low-coupon bonds which may be tendered at par in payment of Federal estate duties if owned by the deceased at the time of death. Urgent deals should be clearly time-stamped.

Foreign Targeted Notes

Special issues of Treasury securities between July 1984 and February 1986 designed to appeal to international investors keen to preserve their anonymity. Foreign Targeted Notes are free of withholding tax if a custodian bank simply declares that the beneficial owner is not a US citizen or a US resident.

Fundamental analysis

Attempting to predict bond market developments from the analysis of underlying factors, e.g. inflation outlook, strength of the economy, monetary and fiscal policy. Contrasts with technical analysis: attempting to predict future bond market developments from past bond price and activity patterns.

Futures contract

An immediately firm and binding contract to buy or sell a Treasury security (or other specified commodity) at a fixed price at a fixed future date arranged through a recognised exchange which guarantees the contract. (This contrasts with a forward contract, which is a purely bilateral deal between the contracting parties.)

General Accounting Office

Government department responsible to Congress (*not* the administration) for the investigation of government accounts.

Gilts

UK government securities.

Gramm–Rudman

Desperation law, designed to impose automatic spending cuts if the OMB forecasts a budget deficit above the target laid down in the Gramm–Rudman laws. Described by Senator Rudman as 'a bad idea whose time has come'. Now much watered down.

Gross National Product

The total value of all goods and services produced in an economy.

Gross redemption yield (GRY)

A yield measure allowing for both interest receipts and the capital gain or loss obtained through holding the bond to maturity (see Chapter 17). Formally defined as the interest rate at which the current bond price equals the discounted present value of its future payments (coupons plus capital repayment on maturity).

Hedging

Attempt to reduce fluctuations in a portfolio's value by offsetting the price risk in one position by holding another position whose value is likely to move in the opposite position, e.g. a bondholder might hedge by shorting futures or buying put options; a foreign buyer of US Treasury securities might hedge the exchange-rate risk by a forward sale of US dollars back into his own currency.

Immunisation

Construction of a portfolio which matches the average duration of an investor's liabilities but not the specific maturity schedule.

Indexing

1. System by which income tax brackets (and sometimes excise duty rates) are automatically raised in line with inflation. (US income tax brackets have been indexed since 1985.) Indexing also applies to US social security benefits, but not to most excise taxes.
2. Index-linked bonds (where coupon payments and capital redemption automatically rise in line with inflation) are available in the UK gilts market but not in the US Treasury market.

Inventories

American terminology equivalent to 'business stocks' in the UK.

LIFFE (pronounced 'Life')

London International Financial Futures Exchange.

M-1

Narrow measure of US money supply available for instant spending. Includes currency in circulation, demand and other checkable deposits and travellers' cheques.

M-2

Broader measure of US money supply. Includes M-1 plus:

(a)   retail (under $100,000) time deposits;
(b)   money market funds available to the public;
(c)   overnight repos with US banks, and
(d)   overnight eurodollar deposits at Caribbean branches of US banks.

M-3

M-2 plus:

(a)   large (over $100,000) time deposits, and
(b)   negotiable certificates of deposit and deposits in institution-only money market funds.

Margin

Cash or other collateral required to be deposited as security for the ultimate performance of a contract.

Matched sale (reverse repo)

Agreement to sell a security combined with simultaneous agreement to repurchase it at a fixed price at a slightly later date. The normal method by which the Fed drains liquidity from the money market. Also a common method by which dealers finance their positions.

Maturity (redemption)

Date when bond's capital value is repaid.

Moving average

An average of prices over a particular past period (e.g. last 30 trading days or last six months). The average will change slightly every day. For example, a three-month moving average for 15 August will average prices from 16 May to 15 August; for 16 August it will average prices from 17 May to 16 August.

Municipal bond

Bond issued by a state or local government.

Net yield

Yield after tax. Contrasts with gross yield (yield before tax).

Nominal value

Value at which a bond will ultimately be redeemed and on which the value of coupons is calculated. Nominal value differs from market value unless the market price happens to be 100.

Non-borrowed reserves

Bank reserves obtained from any source other than discount window borrowing.

Normal distribution

A common pattern of dispersion of points in a series about their average, often represented by a bell-shaped graph (see Appendix 4).

Note

Treasury coupon security with an initial maturity of 10 years or below.

Offer price

The price at which a dealer will sell a bond.

Office of Management and Budget

Government department in charge of budget planning and forecasting.

On-the-run bond

Most recent and most actively traded issue in each maturity group.

Option

A contract giving the right (but *not* the obligation) to buy or sell a Treasury bond (or other commodity) at a fixed price up to a fixed future date.

Par

A bond price of 100%, i.e. market price equal to nominal value.

Peg (1941–51)

US Treasury attempt to peg (hold down) long-bond yields by pressurising the Fed to buy long Treasury bonds in the open market (page 6).

Ponzi finance

Carlos Ponzi ran a pioneering pyramid swindle in 1919–20. His Massachusetts savings bank expanded rapidly by offering depositors extremely high real rates of interest, which were paid exclusively out of the capital subscribed by the next generation of depositors. Such financing methods are still illegal in the private sector.

Premium

1. A bond price above par.
2. Price paid for an option.

Primary dealer

Principal marketmaker recognised by the Fed.

Put

Option giving the holder the right (but *not* the obligation) to sell a security at a predetermined price.

Redemption

Repayment of the bond's nominal capital value on maturity.

Repo (sale and repurchase agreement)

An agreement to buy a security, combined with a simultaneous agreement that the seller will repurchase at an agreed price at a later date. Thus repos are effectively a form of security short-term lending.
Repos are:

(a) the normal method by which the Fed supplies liquidity to the money markets;
(b) a principal means by which dealers in Treasury securities finance their positions (repoing either with the Fed or investing institutions).

Reserves

Funds held by commercial banks in cash or (non-interest bearing) deposits at the Fed.

Reserve requirement

Obligation on deposit-taking institutions to maintain reserves (in cash or in deposits at the Fed) equal to specified percentages of demand deposits and other liabilities.

Roll-up rate

Estimated future interest rate at which bond coupons can be reinvested.

Running yield

See Flat yield.

Seasonal adjustment

Process of smoothing economic data to damp down seasonal influences which distort the underlying trend. For example, even in a booming economy industrial production falls sharply in December and July, reflecting holiday closures. Seasonal adjustment removes the normal seasonal distortion (estimated from the average distortion in prior years) thus helping the investor to gauge the true underlying trend.

Short position

An investor has sold a security he does not own. The investor loses if the security price rises, but profits if it falls.

SP500

A broad-based index of US stock market prices compiled by Standard and Poor's Corporation and including approximately 500 companies weighted by market capitalisation. The companies included account for about 75% of the total market value of equities quoted on the New York Stock Exchange.

Spread

1. The yield difference between two bonds (usually quoted in basis points).
2. Difference between a dealer's bid and asked price for the same bond.

Standard deviation

A measure of the degree of dispersion of numbers in a series about their average (see Appendix 12).

Stripped Treasury

Bond where the principal and coupons have been separated. Each coupon and the final principal payment then trade separately as independent zero coupon bonds.

Strips may have tax advantages for some investors. Strips also offer *precise* matching for future liabilities (and are thus useful in some dedication programmes). By contrast, a conventional bond's total return is always slightly uncertain because the investor does not know the interest rate at which the bond's future coupons will be reinvested.

Thrift

Generalised term for US non-bank savings institutions, including savings and loan institutions (roughly equivalent to UK building societies), credit unions and mutual savings banks.

Tick

Fractional unit in which prices are quoted. In the US Treasury market a Tick is one thirty-second, e.g. a quoted price of 95·16 means $95^{16}/_{32}$ or $95\frac{1}{2}$.

Treasury

The US government department primarily responsible for government economic policy.

Volatility

1. The *general* tendency of bond prices to fluctuate over time. Usually measured as the annualised standard deviation of bond price changes (see Appendix 12). Historic volatility is calculated from past price changes. Implied (expected future) volatility is estimated from options prices.
2. The *specific* sensitivity of a bond price to a change in interest rates. (Usually referred to as 'modified duration' in American markets, since the formula can be directly deduced from 'Macaulay duration').

Withholding tax

Income tax deducted at source from income.

Yield curve

Curve on a graph illustrating the general relationship between bond yield and maturity (see Fig. G.1).

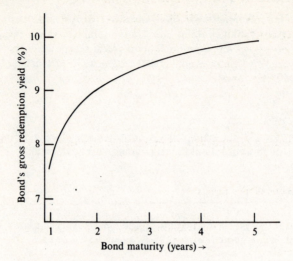

Fig. G.1 Illustrative yield curve.

Appendix 1. Long-term returns on US Treasury bonds and some alternative investments

Table A1.1 provides a comparison of investment performance for 1925–87.

Table A1.1. Comparison of investments

	Compound return (% p.a.) Dec. 1925–Dec. 1987[a]	Annual return (Normal range)[b]
Treasury bill (1 month)	3·5	0 to 7
Medium-term Treasury (8 years)	4·8	−1 to 11
Long Treasury bond (20 years)	4·3	−4 to 13
Corporate bond	4·9	−3 to 14
SP500 equities	9·9	−9 to 33
Small company equities	12·1	−18 to 53

Source: Ibbotson, Roger G. and Rex A. *Stocks, bonds, bills and inflation* (SBBI), 1982. Updated in *SBBI 1988 Yearbook*, published by Ibbotson Associates Inc., Chicago.
a   Compares with consumer price inflation of 3·0% p.a. over same period.
b   Arithmetic average plus or minus one standard deviation, i.e. range normally covering about 40 out of the 62 annual observations.

Over long periods of time more risky investments tend to yield a higher return. However, the relationship is not guaranteed. Long government bonds underperformed medium-term government bonds over this 62-year period because long bonds suffered disproportionate capital losses as yields rose from the range of 2% to 4% (typical over 1925–60) to 9% at end 1987 (see Fig. A1.1 and Table A1.2).

A comparison of rates of return for government bonds, government bills and equities in the US and the UK is given in Table A1.3.

Table A1.2. Rates of return on long Treasury bonds

	Average yield	Nominal total return[a]	Real total return[a]	CPI inflation
1926–56				
UK	3·6	3·4	0·5	2·9
US	2·9	3·1	1·5	1·6
1956–86				
UK	9·3	7·2	0·0	7·4
US	7·3	5·5	0·8	4·6

a   Income plus capital gain or loss.

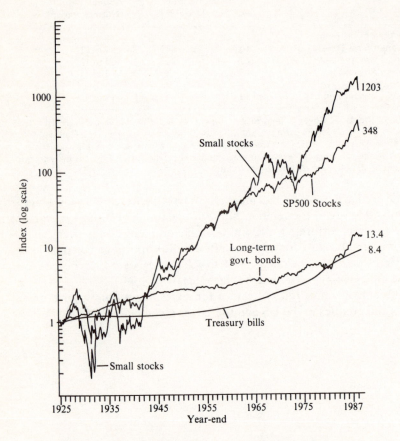

Fig. A1.1 Compounded value of US investment, 1925–87 (index: end-1925 = 100). Source: Ibbotson.

Table A1.3. Comparative real rates of return

| | 1926–56 | | 1956–86 | |
	UK	US	UK	US
Treasury bonds	0·5	1·5	0·0	0·8
Treasury bills	−1·3	−0·5	0·8	1·1
Equities	4·8	8·3	7·2	4·8

Source for rates of return:
USA: Ibbotson.
UK: BZW.

Appendix 2. US budget, economy and debt 1952–88

Table A2.1 summarises federal budget revenue and expenditure growth, GNP growth, the inflation rate and bond yields for various periods between 1952 and 1988.

Table A2.2 gives further detail on budget trends and the US national debt for the same period.

Table A2.1. Federal finance, GNP and inflation (average increase % p.a. for each period)

	1952–64	1964–74	1974–80	1980–4	1984–8
Constant prices (1982 $)					
Budget revenue	1·0	3·0	2·7	0·2	5·0
Expenditure	1·2	2·8	4·6	3·0	2·7
Real GNP	3·0	3·3	2·6	2·4	3·4
Current $					
Budget revenue	4·5	8·9	11·4	6·5	8·1
Expenditure	4·8	8·6	13·4	9·6	5·5
Nominal GNP	5·3	8·5	10·9	8·4	6·4
Federal debt outstanding	1·7	4·4	10·6	14·6	13·1
Inflation (GNP deflator)	2·1	5·1	8·0	5·9	3·0
Nominal yield on long Treasury bonds	3·5	5·5	7·8	11·7	9·7
Real yield	1·4	0·4	−0·2	5·8	6·7

Table A2.2. US budget and debt (averages for each period as % GNP)

	1952–64	1964–74	1974–80	1980–8
President	Eisenhower Kennedy	Johnson Nixon	Ford Carter	Reagan
Budget as % GNP				
Revenue	18·1	18·3	18·5	19·0
Expenditure	18·7	19·4	21·1	23·2
Deficit	–0·6	–1·1	–2·6	–4·2
Debt interest as % GNP	1·3	1·2	1·3	2·1
Federal debt outstanding (held by public) as % GNP	51·2	31·9	26·9	35·4

Appendix 3. US government finances 1789–1988

Tables A3.1 and A3.2 summarise federal government finances for 1789–1916 and 1917–1988.

Table A3.1. Summary of federal government finances ($m.), 1789–1916

Fiscal year	Receipts	Expenditures	Surplus or deficit	Outstanding debt
1789–91	4·4	4·3	0·2	77·2
1792	3·7	5·1	−1·4	80·4
1793	4·7	4·5	0·2	78·4
1794	5·4	7·0	−1·6	80·8
1795	6·1	7·5	−1·4	83·8
1796	8·4	5·7	2·7	82·1
1797	8·7	6·1	2·6	79·2
1798	7·9	7·7	0·2	78·4
1799	7·6	9·7	−2·1	83·0
1800	10·4	10·8	0·0	88·0
1801	12·9	9·4	3·5	80·7
1802	15·0	7·9	7·1	77·1
1803	11·1	7·9	3·2	86·4
1804	11·8	8·7	3·1	82·3
1805	13·6	10·5	3·1	75·7
1806	15·6	9·8	5·8	69·2
1807	16·4	8·4	8·0	65·2
1808	17·1	9·9	7·1	57·0
1809	7·8	10·3	−2·5	53·2
1810	9·4	8·2	1·2	48·0
1811	14·4	8·1	6·4	45·2
1812	9·8	20·3	−10·5	56·0
1813	14·3	31·7	−17·3	81·5
1814	11·2	34·7	−23·5	99·8
1815	15·7	32·7	−17·0	127·3
1816	47·7	30·6	17·1	123·5
1817	33·1	21·8	11·3	103·5
1818	21·6	19·8	1·8	95·5
1819	24·6	21·5	3·1	91·0
1820	17·9	18·3	−0·4	90·0
1821	14·6	15·8	−1·2	93·6

Table A3.1. Continued

Fiscal year	Receipts	Expenditures	Surplus or deficit	Outstanding debt
1822	20·2	15·0	5·2	90·9
1823	20·5	14·7	5·8	90·3
1824	19·4	20·3	−1·0	83·8
1825	21·8	15·9	6·0	81·1
1826	25·3	17·0	8·2	74·0
1827	23·0	16·1	6·8	67·5
1828	24·8	16·4	8·4	58·4
1829	24·8	15·2	9·6	48·6
1830	24·9	15·1	9·7	39·1
1831	28·5	15·3	13·3	24·3
1832	31·9	17·3	14·6	7·0
1833	34·0	23·0	10·9	4·8
1834	21·8	18·6	3·2	0·0
1835	35·4	17·6	17·6	0·0
1836	50·8	30·9	20·0	0·3
1837	25·0	37·2	−12·3	3·3
1838	26·3	33·9	−7·6	10·4
1839	31·5	26·9	4·6	8·6
1840	19·5	24·3	−4·8	5·3
1841	16·9	26·6	−9·7	13·6
1842	20·0	25·2	−5·2	20·2
1843	8·3	11·9	−3·6	32·7
1844	29·3	22·3	7·0	23·5
1845	29·9	22·9	7·0	15·9
1846	29·7	27·8	1·9	15·6
1847	26·5	57·3	−30·8	38·8
1848	35·7	45·4	−9·6	47·1
1849	31·2	45·1	−13·8	63·1
1850	43·6	39·5	4·1	63·5
1851	52·6	47·7	4·9	68·3
1852	49·8	44·2	5·7	66·2
1853	61·6	48·2	13·4	59·8
1854	73·8	58·1	15·8	42·2
1855	65·4	59·7	5·6	35·6
1856	74·1	69·6	4·5	32·0
1857	69·0	67·8	1·2	28·7
1858	46·7	74·2	−27·6	44·9
1859	53·5	69·1	−15·6	58·5
1860	56·1	63·1	−7·1	64·8
1861	41·5	66·6	−25·0	90·6
1862	52·0	474·8	−422·8	524·2
1863	112·7	714·7	−602·0	1119·8
1864	264·6	865·3	−600·7	1815·8
1865	333·7	1297·6	−963·8	2677·9
1866	558·0	520·8	37·2	2755·8
1867	490·6	357·5	133·1	2650·2
1868	405·6	377·3	28·3	2583·5
1869	371·0	322·9	48·1	2545·1
1870	411·3	309·7	101·6	2436·5
1871	383·3	292·2	91·2	2322·1
1872	374·1	277·3	96·6	2210·0

Table A3.1. Continued

Fiscal year	Receipts	Expenditures	Surplus or deficit	Outstanding debt
1873	333·7	290·4	43·4	2151·2
1874	305·0	302·6	2·4	2159·9
1875	288·0	274·6	13·4	2156·3
1876	294·1	265·1	29·0	2130·9
1877	281·4	241·3	40·1	2107·8
1878	257·8	237·0	20·8	2159·4
1879	273·8	267·0	6·9	2299·0
1880	333·5	267·6	65·9	2091·0
1881	360·8	260·7	100·0	2019·3
1882	403·5	258·0	145·5	1857·0
1883	398·3	265·4	132·9	1722·0
1884	308·5	244·1	104·4	1625·3
1885	323·7	260·2	63·5	1578·6
1886	336·4	242·5	94·0	1555·7
1887	371·4	267·9	103·5	1465·5
1888	379·3	267·9	111·3	1384·6
1889	387·0	299·3	87·8	1249·5
1890	403·1	318·0	85·0	1122·4
1891	392·6	365·8	26·8	1005·8
1892	354·9	345·0	9·9	968·2
1893	385·8	383·5	2·3	961·4
1894	306·4	367·5	−61·2	1016·9
1895	324·7	356·2	−31·5	1096·9
1896	338·1	352·2	−14·0	1222·7
1897	347·7	365·8	−18·1	1226·8
1898	405·3	443·4	−38·1	1232·7
1899	515·7	605·1	−89·1	1436·7
1900	567·2	520·9	46·4	1263·4
1901	587·7	524·6	63·1	1221·6
1902	562·5	485·2	77·2	1178·0
1903	561·9	517·0	44·9	1159·4
1904	541·1	583·7	−42·6	1136·3
1905	544·3	567·3	−23·0	1132·4
1906	594·9	570·2	24·8	1142·5
1907	665·9	579·1	86·7	1147·2
1908	601·9	659·2	−57·3	1177·7
1909	604·3	693·7	−89·4	1148·3
1910	675·5	693·6	−18·1	1146·9
1911	701·8	691·2	10·6	1154·0
1912	692·6	689·9	2·7	1193·8
1913	714·5	714·9	−0·4	1193·0
1914	725·1	725·5	−0·4	1188·2
1915	683·4	746·1	−62·7	1191·3
1916	761·4	713·0	48·5	1225·1

Table A3.2. Summary of federal government finances ($ bn) 1917–88

Fiscal year	Budget receipts	Budget expenditures	Surplus or deficit	Outstanding debt
1917	1·1	2·0	−0·9	3·0
1918	3·7	12·7	−9·0	12·5
1919	5·1	18·5	−13·4	25·5
1920	6·7	6·4	0·3	24·3
1921	5·6	5·1	0·5	24·0
1922	4·0	3·3	0·7	23·0
1923	3·9	3·1	0·7	22·4
1924	3·9	2·9	1·0	21·3
1925	3·6	2·9	0·7	20·5
1926	3·8	2·9	0·9	19·6
1927	4·0	2·9	1·2	18·5
1928	3·9	3·0	0·9	17·6
1929	3·9	3·1	0·7	16·9
1930	4·1	3·3	0·7	16·2
1931	3·1	3·6	−0·5	16·8
1932	2·0	4·7	−2·7	19·5
1933	2·0	4·6	−2·6	22·5
1934	3·0	6·5	−3·6	27·1
1935	3·6	6·4	−2·8	28·7
1936	3·9	8·2	−4·3	33·8
1937	5·4	7·6	−2·2	36·4
1938	6·8	6·8	−0·9	37·2
1939	6·3	9·1	−2·9	40·4
1940	6·6	9·5	−2·9	50·7
1941	8·7	13·7	−4·9	57·5
1942	14·6	35·1	−20·5	79·2
1943	24·0	78·6	−54·6	142·6
1944	43·7	91·3	−47·6	204·1
1945	45·2	92·7	−47·6	260·1
1946	39·3	55·2	−15·9	271·0
1947	38·5	34·5	4·0	257·1
1948	41·6	29·8	11·8	252·0
1949	39·4	38·8	0·6	252·6
1950	39·4	42·6	−3·1	256·9
1951	51·6	45·5	6·1	255·3
1952	66·2	67·7	−1·5	259·1
1953	69·6	76·1	−6·5	266·0
1954	69·7	70·9	−1·2	270·8
1955	65·5	68·4	−3·0	274·4
1956	74·6	70·6	3·9	272·8
1957	80·0	76·6	3·4	272·4
1958	79·6	82·4	−2·8	279·7
1959	79·3	92·1	−12·9	287·8
1960	92·5	92·2	0·3	290·9
1961	94·4	97·7	−3·3	292·9
1962	99·7	106·8	−7·2	303·3
1963	106·6	111·3	−4·8	310·8
1964	12·6	118·5	−5·9	316·8
1965	116·8	118·2	−1·4	322·2
1966	130·8	134·5	−3·7	329·5
1967	148·8	157·5	−8·6	341·3

Table A3.2. Continued

Fiscal year	Budget receipts	Budget expenditures	Surplus or deficit	Outstanding debt
1968	153·0	178·1	−25·2	369·8
1969	186·9	183·6	3·2	367·1
1970	192·8	195·6	−2·8	382·6
1971	187·1	210·2	−23·0	409·5
1972	207·3	230·7	−23·4	437·3
1973	230·8	245·7	−14·9	468·4
1974	263·2	269·4	−6·1	486·2
1975	279·1	332·3	−53·2	544·1
1976	298·1	371·8	−73·7	631·9
1977	355·6	409·2	−53·6	709·1
1978	399·6	458·7	−59·2	780·4
1979	463·3	503·5	−40·2	833·8
1980	517·1	590·9	−73·8	914·3
1981	599·3	678·2	−78·9	1003·9
1982	617·8	745·7	−127·9	1147·0
1983	600·6	808·3	−207·8	1381·9
1984	666·5	851·8	−185·3	1576·7
1985	734·1	946·3	−212·3	1817·0
1986	769·1	990·3	−221·2	2120·1
1987	854·1	1003·8	−149·7	2345·6
1988	909·0	1064·1	−155·1	2600·8

Data Sources
1789–1933 *Historical statistics of the USA: colonial times to 1970* (US Census Bureau).
1934–87 *Historical tables on budget of the US Government* (Office of Management and Budget).

Note
Change in public debt does not always tally with budget surplus or deficit owing to:

(a) fluctuations in the Treasury cash balance;
(b) other financial transactions;
(c) omission or inconsistent treatment of some off-budget items, e.g. buildup of cash in social security trust funds (net inflow of $20 bn in 1987 and $39 bn in 1988) is treated as reducing the overall budget deficit, but is still included in the total public debt figure as representing debt owed by the federal government to itself as a trustee;
(d) omission of transitional quarter (with a deficit of $15 bn) in 1976 when fiscal year end changed from 30 June to 30 September;
(e) erratic accounting in earlier years, especially pre-1870 when Treasury accounts lagged behind actual tax collections and spending payments, and omitted some items, e.g. distribution of $28 m. surplus revenue to the individual states in 1837.

Appendix 4. Estimating theoretical option values: a simplified illustration

Estimated distribution of future bond prices

A frequency distribution of past bond prices (or daily price changes) will usually look something like Fig. A4.1.

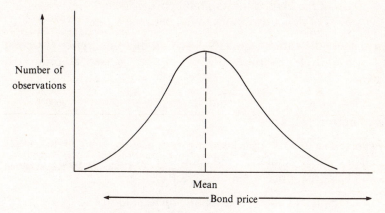

Fig. A4.1 The normal distribution.

This bell-shaped pattern approximates to the theoretical 'normal distribution' which is uniquely defined by:

(a) the average of all prices in the distribution; and
(b) their standard deviation (a measure of the dispersion of prices about their average).

Thus we can calculate a mathematically precise probability of any particular future bond price (and hence deduce the 'correct' value for an option) if we assume that:

(a) the probable future price of a Treasury bond is normally distributed about its current price; and

(b)   its future standard deviation can be estimated from its past price fluctuations.

Normal distribution and standard deviation

The standard deviation is a measure of dispersion about the mean (for method of calculation see Appendix 12). In a normal distribution about 68% of observations will be within one standard deviation of the mean, 95% within two standard deviations and 99·7% within three standard deviations. For example, if the mean is 90 and the standard deviation is 3, one would expect:

> 68% of the observations to fall between 87 and 93
> 95% of the observations to fall between 84 and 96
> 99·7% of the observations to fall between 81 and 99

Unfortunately the future standard deviation of a bond price (or bond price change) is not known. It can only be guessed at from past experience.

Basis of option valuation

The expected value of an option on expiry equals the value of the option for each possible price of the bond multiplied by the probability that the bond will be at that price when the option expires.

> *Example of option value estimation as at March 1987*
> (Quoted figures are illustrative only)
>
> | | |
> |---|---|
> | March 1988 call option exercise price | : 100 |
> | Time to expiry | : 1 year |
>
> | | |
> |---|---|
> | March 1988 futures price (in March 1987) | : 100 |
> | Standard deviation (over past year) | : 6% |

We can now estimate theoretical option values *if* (a big *if*) we assume:
(a)   the standard deviation remains at 6% for the next year; and
(b)   the possible prices of the March 1988 future when the option expires are normally distributed about the current price of the March 1988 future (100).

> For example, we know from the standard tables of the normal distribution that 68% of observations will be within one standard deviation either side of the mean. In this case

therefore, we estimate 34% probability of a future bond price between 100 and 106 (mean plus one standard deviation) and 34% probability of a future bond price between 94 and 100 (mean minus one standard deviation).

The concept is illustrated graphically in Fig. A4.2 and detailed numerically in Table A4.1.

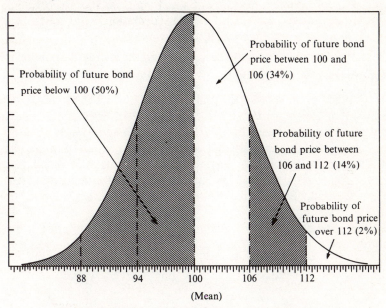

Fig. A4.2 Probability distribution of future bond prices: normal distribution with mean 100, standard deviation 6. Note: Area under curve measures probability of indicated range of bond prices.

Table A4.1. Estimating an approximate option value

Possible bond price range on option expiry	Value of option in this price range	Average value of option	Probability of this price range[a]	Contribution to overall future value of option
Under 100	0	0	0·50	0
100–106	0 to 6	3	0·34	1·02
106–112	6 to 12	9	0·14	1·26
112–118	12 to 18	15	0·02	0·30
Over 118	Over 18	Over 18	Negligible	0
			1·00	2·58[b]

a Probability taken from standard tables of the probability distribution within the normal distribution, assuming a mean of 100 and standard deviation of 6.
b The option's current price (= discounted future value) should be slightly lower.

Results

The theoretical value of a call option to purchase the bond at 100 in 12 months' time is approximately 2·58, assuming future bond prices are normally distributed about 100 with a standard deviation of 6. The accuracy can be improved by examining smaller subdivisions of the possible future bond price range. Estimating from subdivisions of 0·05 standard deviations (instead of 1 standard deviation as illustrated above) gives a more accurate theoretical future value of 2·38.

More precise valuation methods

Theoretical option values are usually calculated from the Black–Scholes formula, measuring bond prices' propensity to fluctuation from the annualised standard deviation of daily *price changes* (rather than price levels). The Black–Scholes formula assumes that expected future prices are distributed *lognormally*, e.g. that if the current price is 100, future prices of 50 or 200 are equally likely (equivalent to assuming that interest rates are equally likely to move either up or down by a given number of basis points).

This asymmetry has some advantages (if current bond price is 100, a future bond price above 200 is possible while a future price below zero is not) and enables the Black–Scholes method to project values for options with way-out exercise prices and very long times to expiration.

Theoretical hazards

1. The theoretical propensity of bond prices to fluctuate alters as a bond's duration is altered by GRY change or maturity shortening. Some analysts therefore prefer option valuation models based on yield fluctuations rather than price fluctuations.
2. The assumption of lognormal distribution may be true for probable prices of Treasury bond futures, but cannot be strictly true in the case of an actual Treasury bond whose probable prices must converge towards par as maturity approaches.

Note on time premium decay

If futures bond price equals option exercise price, the time premium will decay towards zero in proportion to the square root of the time remaining to expiration.

Appendix 5. Quoted and true annual Treasury bond yields

Table A5.1 compares conventionally quoted annual Treasury yields and true annual yields.

Table A5.1. Quoted and true annual US Treasury bond yields

Quoted yield[a]	True annual yield[b]
5	5·06
6	6·09
7	7·12
8	8·16
9	9·20
10	10·25
11	11·30
12	12·36
13	13·42
14	14·49
15	15·56
16	16·64

a The conventionally quoted annual yield in both US and UK Treasury markets is actually
twice the semi-annual yield.
b Comparable with quoted Eurobond yields, which are true annual yields.

Formula for converting semi-annual bond yields to true annual bond yields

$$\text{True annual yield} = \text{Quoted yield} \times \left(1 + \frac{\text{quoted yield}}{400}\right)$$

Example
Conventionally quoted US Treasury bond yield = 12%

$$\text{True annual yield} = 12 \times \left(1 + \frac{12}{400}\right) = 12 \times 1·03 = 12·36\%$$

Appendix 6. Treasury bill discount rate and bond equivalent yield

Table A6.1 shows the bond equivalent yield of 3-month and 12-month bills for varying Treasury bill discount rates.

Table A6.1. Treasury bill discount rate and bond equivalent yield

Treasury bill discount rate	Bond equivalent yield	
	3-month bill	12-month bill
4	4·10	4·18
5	5·13	5·27
6	6·18	6·37
7	7·23	7·50
8	8·28	8·64
9	9·34	9·80
10	10·40	10·98
11	11·47	12·18
12	12·55	13·40
13	13·63	14·64
14	14·72	15·90
15	15·81	17·19
16	16·91	18·50

Explanation

Treasury bill interest rates are normally quoted on a 360-day discount basis. For example, a 52-week (364-day) bill with a quoted discount of 10% for 360 days, will sell at a true discount of 10·111 (10 × 364 ÷ 360), and be priced at 89·889. Its true annual yield is:

$$\frac{10 \cdot 111}{89 \cdot 889} \times \frac{365}{364} = 11 \cdot 28\%$$

This true annual yield of 11·28% is conventionally quoted as a yield of only 10·97% on the bond-equivalent (six-monthly yield) basis. This accords with the formula in Appendix 5, since:

$$10 \cdot 97 \times \left(1 + \frac{10 \cdot 97}{400}\right) = 11 \cdot 28$$

For bills maturing within six months, bond equivalent yield is simply the discount rate (converted from 360-day rate to 365-day rate) divided by the bill's price. For example, a 90-day bill with a 12% discount rate (360-day basis) will be priced at 97. Its bond equivalent yield will be:

$$\frac{12}{97} \times \frac{365}{360} = 12 \cdot 55\%$$

Appendix 7. Mathematical glossary

Conventional notation

P = bond price

g = coupon rate

y = yield

i = $y \div 200$ (half-yearly interest factor)

v = $1 \div (1 + i)$ (half-yearly discounting factor)

x = $(1 + i)$ (half-yearly compounding factor)

n = number of time periods (normally half-year periods in US Treasury analysis)

PV = present value

FV = future value

$a_{\overline{n}|}$ = discounted present value of a regular stream of n equal future payments.

S_n = accumulated future value of a regular stream of n equal future payments (with these payments reinvested as received and accumulating at compound interest).

Appendix 8. Mathematical formulae

Annuity certain

$$a_{\overline{n}|} = \frac{1 - v^n}{i}$$

Accumulated future value

$$S_n = \frac{(1 + i)^n - 1}{i}$$

Bond price

$$P = 100v^n + \frac{g}{2} \cdot a_{\overline{n}|}$$

Balance-of-term breakeven yield

$$\text{Breakeven yield} = \frac{Y_B \cdot a_{\overline{n}|(B)} - Y_A \cdot a_{\overline{n}|(A)}}{a_{\overline{n}|(B)} - a_{\overline{n}|(A)}}$$

Modified duration

$$\text{Modified duration} = \frac{v^2}{2P}\left[\frac{g}{2}\left\{\frac{(1 - v^n)}{(1 - v)^2} - \frac{nv^n}{(1-v)}\right\} + 100nv^{n-1}\right]$$

Macaulay duration

$$\text{Macaulay duration} = \text{Modified duration} \div v$$

Appendix 9. Proof of formula for modified duration (volatility)

Definition

Modified duration is a measure of the proportionate percentage change in bond price associated with an infinitesimally small opposite change in gross redemption yield.

Mathematical definition

$$\text{Modified duration} = -\frac{dP}{dy} \cdot \frac{100}{P}$$

$$= \frac{dP}{dv} \cdot \frac{dv}{dy} \cdot \frac{-100}{P}$$

First term $\left(\dfrac{dP}{dv}\right)$

Assuming bond has a remaining life of exactly n half-years to maturity,

$$P = \frac{g}{2}(v + v^2 + v^3 + \ldots + v^n) + 100v^n$$

$$\therefore \frac{dP}{dv} = \frac{g}{2}(1 + 2v + 3v^2 + \ldots + nv^{n-1}) + 100nv^{n-1}$$

$$= \frac{g}{2} \cdot S + 100nv^{n-1}$$

where $S = 1 + 2v + 3v^2 + \ldots + nv^{n-1}$

Second term $\left(\dfrac{dv}{dy}\right)$

$$v = 1 \div (1 + y/200)$$
$$= (1 + y/200)^{-1}$$

$$\therefore \frac{dv}{dy} = \frac{d\,(1 + y/200)^{-1}}{d\,(1 + y/200)} \cdot \frac{d\,(1 + y/200)}{dy}$$

$$= -\,(1 + y/200)^{-2} \cdot \frac{1}{200}$$

$$\therefore \frac{dv}{dy} = \frac{-v^2}{200}$$

since $(1 + y/200)^{-1} = v$

Value of S

$$S = 1 + 2v + 3v^2 + \ldots + (n-1)\,v^{n-2} + nv^{n-1}$$

$$\therefore vS = 0 + v + 2v^2 + \ldots + (n-2)v^{n-2} + (n-1)v^{n-1} + nv^n$$

$$\therefore S - vS = 1 + v + v^2 + \ldots + v^{n-2} + v^{n-1} - nv^n$$

$$\therefore S\,(1 - v) = \frac{(1 - v^n)}{(1 - v)} - nv^n$$

$$\therefore S = \frac{(1 - v^n)}{(1 - v)^2} - \frac{nv^n}{(1 - v)}$$

Derivation of formula

$$\text{Modified duration} = \frac{dP}{dv} \cdot \frac{dv}{dy} \cdot \frac{-100}{P}$$

$$= \left[\frac{g}{2}\!\left(S + 100nv^{n-1}\right) \right] \left(\frac{-v^2}{200}\right) \left(\frac{-100}{P}\right)$$

$$= \frac{v^2}{2P} \left[\frac{g}{2} \left\{ \frac{(1 - v^n)}{(1 - v)^2} - \frac{nv^n}{(1-v)} \right\} + 100nv^{n-1} \right]$$

$$= v(\text{Macaulay duration}) \text{ (see Appendix 10)}$$

Appendix 10. Relationship between Macaulay duration and modified duration (volatility)

Definition

Macaulay duration is the weighted average length of time between purchase of a bond and receipt of its benefits (interest payments and capital repayment) where the weights are the present values of the benefits involved. Table A10.1 gives an example of this.

Table A10.1. Factors for derivation of Macaulay duration

Time to receipt	Benefit	Discounting factor to present value (= v^n)	Weight (= benefit × v^n)
1	$g/2$	v	$\frac{gv}{2}$
2	$g/2$	v^2	$\frac{gv^2}{2}$
3	$g/2$	v^3	$\frac{gv^3}{2}$
n	$g/2$	v^n	$\frac{gv^n}{2}$
n	100	v^n	$100v^n$

Note

The half-yearly bond coupon ($g/2$) is received each half-year. Capital repayment on maturity (100) is received at time n. v is the factor which discounts to present value for one period. v^n is the discounting factor for n periods.

Macaulay duration = Weighted average time =
$$\frac{\Sigma\,(\text{Time period} \times \text{weight})}{(\text{Sum of weights})}$$

$\therefore$ Macaulay duration =

$$\frac{\dfrac{g}{2} \cdot v + 2\dfrac{g}{2} \cdot v^2 + 3 \cdot \dfrac{g}{2} \cdot v^3 + \ldots + n\dfrac{g}{2} \cdot v^n + n \cdot 100v^n}{\text{(half-years) } \dfrac{g}{2}(v + v^2 + v^3 + \ldots + v^n) + 100v^n}$$

The denominator of this equation is the formula for the price of a bond.

$\therefore$ Macaulay duration =

$$\frac{\dfrac{g}{2}(v + 2v^2 + 3v^3 + \ldots + nv^n) + 100nv^n}{P}$$

The numerator of this equation is $\dfrac{v \cdot dP}{dv}$

since $\dfrac{dP}{dv} = \dfrac{g}{2}(1 + 2v + 3v^2 + \ldots + nv^{n-1}) + 100nv^{n-1}$

$\therefore$ Macaulay duration = $\dfrac{v \cdot dP}{P \cdot dv}$
(half-years)

$\therefore$ Macaulay duration = $\dfrac{v}{2P} \cdot \dfrac{dP}{dv}$
(whole years)

$$= \frac{v}{2P} \cdot \frac{dP}{dy} \cdot \frac{dy}{dv}$$

$$= \frac{v}{2P} \cdot \frac{dP}{dy} \cdot \left(-\frac{200}{v^2}\right) \quad \text{since } v = \left(1 + \frac{y}{200}\right)^{-1}$$

$$\text{and } \frac{dv}{dy} = \frac{-v^2}{200}$$

$$= \frac{dP}{dy} \cdot \left(\frac{-200v}{2Pv^2}\right)$$

$$= \left(\frac{dP}{dy} \cdot \frac{-100}{P}\right)\frac{1}{v}$$

$$= \text{Modified duration} \div v$$

Thus,

Modified duration = v(Macaulay duration)

= Macaulay duration $\div (1 + i)$

See example on page 125.

Appendix 11. Formal proof of formula for balance-of-term breakeven yield

We consider two alternative investments:

(a) buy long bond B and hold to maturity;
(b) buy short bond A, hold to maturity, then switch redemption value into bond B and hold to maturity.

Since all bonds are held to maturity, their relative values may be assessed in terms of the present values of their discounted GRYs without reference to prices.

PV of (a) $= Y_B \cdot a_B$ where $a_B = a_n$ for bond B $Y_B = $ GRY for bond B

PV of (b) $= Y_A \cdot a_A + Y_{Bal.term} (a_B - a_A)$

At breakeven balance-of-term, these two present values will be equal.

Hence:

$$Y_B \cdot a_B = Y_A \cdot a_A + Y_{Bal.term} (a_B - a_A)$$

$$\therefore Y_{Bal.term} = \frac{Y_B \cdot a_B - Y_A \cdot a_A}{a_B - a_A}$$

$$= \frac{Y_B \cdot a_{n(B)} - Y_A \cdot a_{n(A)}}{a_{n(B)} - a_{n(A)}}$$

Appendix 12. Standard deviation and bond price volatility

Formula for standard deviation

$$\text{S.D. of } X = \sqrt{\frac{\text{Sum of (each observed value of } X - \text{mean of } X)^2}{(N - 1)}}$$

where N = number of observations

Table A12.1 illustrates the calculation of bond price volatility.

Table A12.1. Calculation of bond price volatility (defined as the annualised standard deviation of the natural logarithm of returns)

Month end	Bond price	Quarter's performance factor	X natural log of performance	Difference from average (X−mean of X)	Difference squared
Dec.	100				
Mar.	103	1·0300	0·0296	0·0346	0·0012
Jun.	101	0·9806	−0·0196	−0·0146	0·0002
Sept.	96	0·9505	−0·0508	−0·0457	0·0021
Dec.	98	1·0208	0·0206	0·0257	0·0007
Sum			−0·0202	0·0000	0·0042
Average			−0·0051		

In this case,

S.D. of quarterly performance =

$$\sqrt{\frac{0·0042}{(4-1)}} = \sqrt{0·0014} = 0·0374 \text{ or } 3·74\%$$

Annualised volatility = 3·74% × $\sqrt{4}$ = 7·48%

Warning
This example is for illustration only. Standard deviations calculated from a small number of observations should be treated with extreme caution.

Factors for annualised volatility

To convert to annualised volatility multiply by:

$\sqrt{4}$ in the case of quarterly volatility
$\sqrt{12}$ for monthly volatility
$\sqrt{52}$ for weekly volatility
$\sqrt{253}$ for daily volatility (assuming 253 trading days per year)

Conversions may also be made backwards.

Example
Annualised volatility = 16%
Daily volatility (standard deviation of daily price changes)
$$= 16\% \div \sqrt{253}$$
$$= 16\% \div 15{\cdot}91$$
$$\approx 1\%$$

Illustration of interpretation (with annualised volatility 16%; daily volatility 1%).

Assume annualised volatility is 16% and daily volatility 1%. If the bond price is close to par and the average price change for period is zero, then one would expect the following results:

1. About 68% of daily price changes will fall within the range minus 1% to plus 1%, since in a normal distribution 68% of observations fall within 1 standard deviation either side of the mean (which is zero in this case).
2. The average size of the daily price movement, *considered regardless of sign*, also will be about 1% (i.e. negative price movements would average about -1% and positive price movements would average about $+1\%$, while overall price change for the whole period averaged zero).

Annualised bond price volatility for 1926–88 is shown in Fig. A12.1 and for 1986–8 in Fig. A12.2.

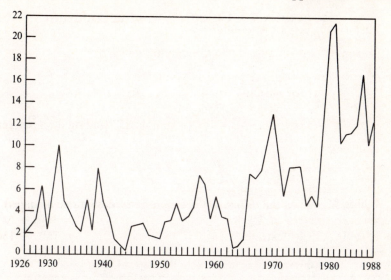

Fig. A12.1 Annualised bond price volatility (%), 1926–88.

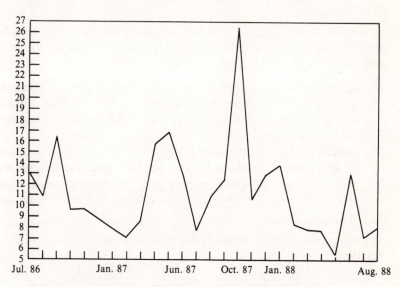

Fig. A12.2 Annualised bond price volatility (%), 1986–8.

Appendix 13. Calculation of correlation coefficient

$$\text{Correlation} = \frac{\Sigma\,(X_d \cdot Y_d)}{\sqrt{\Sigma X^2_d} \cdot \sqrt{\Sigma Y_d^2}}$$

Where X_d means the difference between each individual value of *X and the average value of X*.

Table A13.1 illustrates this.

Table A13.1. Correlation of bond and equity prices in early 1988

	X (bond price % change)	Y (SP500 % change)
Jan.	3	4
Feb.	3	3
Mar.	−2	3
Apr.	−3	−1
Sum	1	9
Average	0·25	2·25

	X_d (difference from average)	X_d squared	Y_d (difference from average)	Y_d squared	X_d multiplied by Y_d
Jan.	2·75	7·56	1·75	3·06	4·81
Feb.	2·75	7·56	0·75	0·56	2·06
Mar.	−2·25	5·06	0·75	0·56	−1·69
Apr.	−3·25	10·56	−3·25	10·56	10·56
Sum	0	30·75	0	14·75	15·75

Correlation =
$$\frac{15\cdot75}{\sqrt{30\cdot75} \cdot \sqrt{14\cdot75}} = \frac{15\cdot75}{5\cdot55 \times 3\cdot84} = \frac{15\cdot75}{21\cdot31} = 0\cdot74 \text{ or } 74\%.$$

Conclusion: There was a strong relationship between bond and equity prices in this period, as might be guessed from the graph in Fig. A13.1.

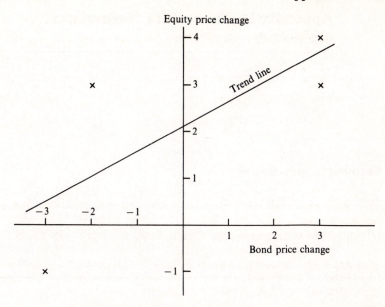

Fig. A13.1 Relationship between equity and bond prices in early 1988.

Warnings
1. This example is given simply to illustrate the mathematical method. In practice correlations based on very small samples or calculated over unduly short time periods should be treated with great caution.
2. Correlation indicates some relationship, but not necessarily cause and effect.
3. High correlation indicates a strong and consistent relationship, but not necessarily an influence of great magnitude. Correlation could be 100% if equity prices always rose only 0·1% when bond prices rose 10% and always fell only 0·2% when bond prices fell 20%.

Appendix 14. Future GRY consistent with one-year target return

Formula (approximate)

$$\text{Future GRY} \approx \text{Current GRY} + \frac{D - \sqrt{V^2 + 2C\,(\text{Target} - \text{GRY})}}{C}$$

Where C, D = convexity, duration of bond with same GRY and 1-year shorter maturity.

GRY and target yield must both be expressed either on a semi-annual basis (the normal US Treasury yield convention) or on a true annual basis.

Example

Bond coupon 8%.   Maturity 10 years.   Price 82.   GRY 11%.

Duration (10 years)	= 6·37
(9 years)	= 6·0
Convexity (9 years)	= 0·47
GRY	= 11% (semi-annual basis)
	= 11·30% (true annual basis)
Target return	= 15% (semi-annual basis)
	= 15·56% (true annual basis)

$$
\begin{aligned}
\text{Future GRY} &\approx 11 + \frac{6 - \sqrt{36 + 0\!\cdot\!94\,(15 - 11)}}{0\!\cdot\!47} \\[2mm]
&= 11 + \frac{6 - \sqrt{36 + 3\!\cdot\!76}}{0\!\cdot\!47} \\[2mm]
&= 11 + \frac{6 - 6\!\cdot\!31}{0\!\cdot\!47} \\[2mm]
&= 11 - \frac{0\!\cdot\!31}{0\!\cdot\!47} \\[2mm]
&= 11 - 0\!\cdot\!65 \\[2mm]
&= 10\!\cdot\!35\% \text{ (semi-annual basis)}
\end{aligned}
$$

Conclusion

Bond will produce total return of 15% (income plus capital gain) on a semi-annual basis over one year if bonds GRY falls from 11% now to 10·35% in one year's time.

Appendix 15. Present value of a regular stream of future payments (A_n)

Table A15.1 shows the value of A_n for discount rates of 2%, 4% and 6% according to the number of periods.

Table 15.1. Discounted present values

Number of periods	Discount rate (%)		
	2	4	6
1	0·980	0·962	0·943
2	1·942	1·886	1·833
3	2·884	2·775	2·673
4	3·808	3·630	3·465
5	4·713	4·452	4·212
6	5·601	5·242	4·917
7	6·472	6·002	5·582
8	7·325	6·733	6·210
9	8·162	7·435	6·802
10	8·983	8·111	7·360
11	9·787	8·760	7·887
12	10·575	9·385	8·384
13	11·348	9·986	8·853
14	12·106	10·563	9·295
15	12·849	11·118	9·712
16	13·578	11·652	10·106
17	14·292	12·166	10·477
18	14·992	12·659	10·828
19	15·678	13·134	11·158
20	16·351	13·590	11·470
22	17·658	14·451	12·042
24	18·914	15·247	12·550
26	20·121	15·983	13·003
28	21·281	16·663	13·406
30	22·396	17·292	13·765
32	23·468	17·874	14·084
34	24·499	18·411	14·368
36	25·489	18·908	14·621
38	26·441	19·368	14·846
40	27·355	19·793	15·046
42	28·235	20·186	15·225

Table 15.1. Continued

Number of periods	Discount rate (%)		
	2	4	6
44	29·080	20·549	15·383
46	29·892	20·885	15·524
48	30·673	21·195	15·650
50	31·424	21·482	15·762
52	32·145	21·748	15·861
54	32·838	21·993	15·950
56	33·505	22·220	16·029
58	34·145	22·430	16·099
60	34·761	22·623	16·161
70	37·499	23·395	16·385
80	39·745	23·915	16·509
90	41·587	24·267	16·579
100	43·098	24·505	16·618
200	49·047	24·990	16·667
∞	50·000	25·000	16·667

Example of interpretation
The present value of a stream of 30 future payments of $1 per half-year at a discount rate of 4% per half-year is $17.292.

Appendix 16. Compounded future value of a regular stream of payments commencing one period from now (S_n)

Table A16.1 shows the value of S_n for interest rates of 2%, 4% and 6% according to the number of periods.

Table 16.1. Accumulated future values

Number of periods	Interest rate (%)		
	2	4	6
1	1·000	1·000	1·000
2	2·020	2·040	2·060
3	3·060	3·122	3·184
4	4·122	4·246	4·375
5	5·204	5·416	5·637
6	6·308	6·633	6·975
7	7·434	7·898	8·394
8	8·583	9·214	9·897
9	9·755	10·583	11·491
10	10·950	12·006	13·181
11	12·169	13·486	14·972
12	13·412	15·026	16·870
13	14·680	16·627	18·882
14	15·974	18·292	21·015
15	17·293	20·024	23·276
16	18·639	21·825	25·673
17	20·012	23·698	28·213
18	21·412	25·645	30·645
19	22·841	27·671	30·906
20	24·297	29·778	33·760
22	27·299	34·248	36·786
24	30·422	39·083	43·392
26	33·671	44·312	50·816
28	37·051	49·968	59·156
30	40·568	56·085	68·528
32	44·227	62·701	79·058
34	48·034	69·858	90·890
36	51·994	77·598	104·184
38	56·115	85·970	119·121
40	60·402	95·026	135·904
42	64·862	104·820	154·762

Table 16.1. Continued

Number of periods	Interest rate (%)		
	2	4	6
44	69·503	115·413	199·758
46	74·331	126·871	226·508
48	79·354	139·263	256·565
50	84·579	152·667	290·336
52	90·016	167·165	328·281
54	95·673	182·845	370·917
56	101·558	199·806	418·822
58	107·681	218·150	472·649
60	114·052	237·991	533·128
70	149·978	364·290	967·932
80	193·772	551·245	1,746·600
90	247·157	827·983	3,141·075
100	312·232	1,237·624	5,638·368

Example of interpretation
A stream of 30 future payments of $1 per half-year will compound to
$56.085 if reinvested at an interest rate of 4% per half-year (8% p.a.).
(Although not shown in the table, S_{200} at 6% per period compounds to
$1,918,748!)

Appendix 17. Gross redemption yields

Tables A17.1 to A17.3 show bond prices at different GRYs for 30-year, 10-year and 5-year maturity.

Table A17.1. Thirty-year maturity

GRY	Coupon			
	0	4	8	12
15	1·30	27·62	53·94	80·26
14	1·73	29·80	57·88	85·96
13	2·29	32·35	62.42	92.48
12	3·03	35·35	67·68	100·00
11	4·03	38·93	73·83	108·72
10	5·35	43·21	81·07	118·93
9	7·13	48·40	89·68	130·96
8	9·51	54·75	100·00	145·25
7	12·69	62·58	112·47	162·36
6	16·97	72·32	127·68	183·03
5	22·73	84·55	146·36	208·18

Table A17.2. Ten-year maturity

GRY	Coupon			
	0	4	8	12
15	23·54	43·93	64·32	84·71
14	25·84	47·03	68·22	89·41
13	28·38	50·42	72.45	94.49
12	31·18	54·12	77·06	100·00
11	34·27	58·17	82·07	105·98
10	37·69	62·61	87·54	112·46
9	41·46	67·48	93·50	119·51
8	45·64	72·82	100·00	127·18
7	50·26	78·68	107·11	135·53
6	55·37	85·12	114·88	144·63
5	61·03	92·21	123·38	154·56

Table A17.3. Five-year maturity

GRY	Coupon			
	0	4	8	12
15	48·52	62·25	75·98	89·70
14	50·83	64·88	78·93	92·98
13	53·27	67·65	82.03	96.41
12	55·84	70·56	85·28	100·00
11	58·54	73·62	88·69	103·77
10	61·39	76·83	92·28	107·72
9	64·39	80·22	96·04	111·87
8	67·56	83·78	100·00	116·22
7	70·89	87·53	104·16	120·79
6	74·41	91·47	108·53	125·59
5	78·12	95·62	113·13	130·63

Example of interpretation
For an 8% bond with 10 years to maturity, priced at 93.5, the GRY is 9% p.a.

Index

home
  mortgages 22
  sales 71
housing starts 56, 70, 87

Ibbotson indices 221, 293–5
immunisation 257, 276–7, 286
implied future yields 145–6
index matching 274–5
indexing
  portfolio strategy 275
  tax brackets 286
index-linked bonds 286
indices (bond market) 219–21
industrial production 24, 70
inflation 22, 26–7, 62–6, 89, 296, *see also*
      real yields
insurance companies 21, 39
interest rate
  cycle and economic cycle 53–4
  determinants of 9, 11, 24–9, 53–7, 73, 90
interest rates *see* bond yields, discount
      rate, economic cycle, Federal funds,
      Federal Reserve, fundamental
      analysis, international comparisons,
      real yields, yield curve, yield spread
inter-dealer brokers 33
internal purchases 80
international comparisons 14, 18–23, 27–8,
      92–4, 251–6
inventories 24, 71, 286
inverted yield curve 61, 134, 194
investment adviser bullishness 182
investment techniques 257–77 *see also*
      bond selection methods, breakeven
      yields
investor sentiment 11, 181–4, 248–50
investors 15–16, 21, 35–41
Italy 14, 29

Japan 11, 14, 29, 92–3, 252, 254–5
Johnson, Lyndon 6, 296
Johnson, Manuel 87

Kennedy, John F. 4, 296
Kerschner, Edward 248
Kerschner–Pradilla model 248–9
Kettl, Donald 6

leading indicators 55, 71
liability
  matching 257, 276–7
  structure of institutions 39, 257
LIFFE 20, 187–8, 286
loan guarantees 95
long butterfly strategy 207

Macaulay duration *see under* duration
Macaulay, Frederick 124
margin requirements 188–90, 213, 287
Martin, Preston 11
matched sale 287
mathematical tables 324–9
mathematics 105–8
maturity 4–6, 14–15, 18, 21, 38, 136
mismatching risks 257–8
modified duration *see under* duration
momentum 174
M-1 73, 286
money market funds 40
money supply 7, 58–61, 63, 68, 89, 286–7
money-weighted return 222–3
mortgages 22
moving average 174, 287
municipal bonds 22, 38, 287
mutual funds 40

national debt 3–4, 13–14, 19, 21, 296–303
national debt to GNP ratio 3, 4, 14, 19,
      296–7
net cashflow yield 121
net yield 119–21, 287
new issues 42–5
Nixon, Richard 6, 53, 296
nominal value 288
non-borrowed reserves 74, 85, 288
non-marketable securities 13
normal distribution 288, 303–6
note (treasury security) 6, 13–14, 82, 288

offer price 288
Office of Management and Budget 98–100,
      288
official reserve assets 41
off-budget deficit 100
on-the-run bonds 274, 288
open market operations 16, 32, 73–86
option
  exercise 214
  pricing 208–11, 303–6
  writing 204–6
options 196–215, 288, 303–6
orders 70–1
outright purchases 79–80, 82

PaineWebber ix, 63, 248
par value 288
par yield curves 138
passes 79–80
peg 6, 288
pension funds 21, 39
performance
  measurement 222–5